D0154295

SENTIMENTAL BODIES

SENTIMENTAL BODIES

SEX, GENDER, AND CITIZENSHIP IN THE EARLY REPUBLIC

Bruce Burgett

PRINCETON UNIVERSITY PRESS   PRINCETON, NEW JERSEY

Copyright © 1998 by Princeton University Press
Published by Princeton University Press, 41 William Street,
Princeton, New Jersey 08540
In the United Kingdom: Princeton University Press,
Chichester, West Sussex

Library of Congress Cataloging-in-Publication Data

Burgett, Bruce, 1963–
Sentimental bodies : sex, gender, and citizenship in the early
republic / Bruce Burgett.
   p. cm.
Includes bibliographical references and index.
ISBN 0-691-01559-7 (cl : alk. paper)
1. American literature—1783–1850—History and criticism. 2. Politics
and literature—United States—History—19th century. 3. Politics
and literature—United States—History—18th century. 4. United
States—Intellectual life—1783–1865. 5. Gender identity in literature.
6. Sentimentalism in literature. 7. Body, Human, in literature.
8. Citizenship in literature. 9. Sex role in literature.   I. Title.
PS217.P64B87 1998
810.9′358—dc21   98-6479   CIP

This book has been composed in Caledonia

Princeton University Press books are printed
on acid-free paper and meet the guidelines
for permanence and durability of the Committee
on Production Guidelines for Book Longevity
of the Council on Library Resources

http://pup.princeton.edu

Printed in the United States of America

10 9 8 7 6 5 4 3 2 1

Contents

Acknowledgments   vii

1. Introduction: Body Politics   3

PART ONE: SENTIMENT AND CITIZENSHIP   25

2. United States Liberalism and the Public Sphere   27

3. The Patriot's Two Bodies: Nationality and Corporeality in
George Washington's "Farewell Address"   55

PART TWO: SENTIMENT AND SEX   79

4. Corresponding Sentiments and Republican Letters:
Hannah Foster's *The Coquette*   81

5. Masochism and Male Sentimentalism: Charles Brockden Brown's
Clara Howard   112

PART THREE: SENTIMENT AND SEXUALITY   135

6. Obscene Publics: Jesse Sharpless and Harriet Jacobs   137

7. Afterword: Closeted Sentiments   155

Notes   161

Index   205

Acknowledgments

MANY PEOPLE and a few institutions helped me to complete this book. I would like to thank the Andrew W. Mellon Foundation for a dissertation fellowship that allowed me to begin the project. I would also like to thank the Graduate School at the University of Wisconsin for two summers of research support, and the National Endowment for the Humanities for a timely summer stipend that allowed me to complete the final writing and revision.

Sentimental Bodies began as a dissertation at U.C. Berkeley, and my first acknowledgments must go to my advisors and friends there: Judy Berman, Mitch Breitweiser, Jonathan Elmer, Carol Hamilton, Joe Harrington, Celeste Langan, Curtis Marez, Lori Merish, Jacqueline Shea Murphy, Carolyn Porter, Mary Ryan, Cindy Schrager, and Shelley Streeby. Many in that list have continued to provide me with intellectual prodding and encouragement, while other colleagues—new and old—have read and usefully criticized all or part of this book: Kate Adams, Dale Bauer, Lauren Berlant, Sarge Bush, Bob Fanuzzi, Glenn Hendler, Gordon Hutner, Tom Schaub, Maurice Wallace, Michael Warner, and Sarah Zimmerman. Jay Fliegelman and Linda Zerilli—my two readers at Princeton University Press—provided crucial support and helpful suggestions, as did my editor, Deborah Malmud. Special thanks also to four of my favorite nonacademics, all of whom responded (and continue to respond) to my ideas with various degrees of skepticism, insight, and suspicion: Donald Burgett, Paul Jahn, Brenda Majercin, and Mark Ward.

Permission to reprint revised versions of previously published articles were generously granted by *Arizona Quarterly* and *Genders*. Chapter 5 is reprinted from *Arizona Quarterly* 52 (1996): 1–25, by permission of the Regents of the University of Arizona. Chapter 6 is reprinted from *Genders* 27 (1998).

Finally, and most importantly, I would like to thank (too weak a word) both Brenda Majercin, who has contributed more to this book than she knows, and Judy Berman, who knows exactly how much she has contributed since she has read every line with care. Without her, this book would not have been possible.

SENTIMENTAL BODIES

1

Introduction: Body Politics

X-RAY Does the body still exist at all, in any but the most
mundane sense? Its role has been steadily diminished,
so that it seems little more than a ghostly shadow seen
on the x-ray plate of our moral disapproval. We are
now entering a colonialist phase in our attitudes to
the body, full of paternalistic notions that conceal a
ruthless exploitation carried out for its own good. This
brutish creature must be housed, sparingly nourished,
restricted to the minimum of sexual activity needed
to reproduce itself and submitted to every manner of
enlightenment and improving patronage. Will the
body at last rebel, tip those vitamins, douches and
aerobic schedules into Boston Harbor and throw off
the colonialist oppressor?
  (*J. G. Ballard*, "Project for a Glossary of the
  Twentieth Century," *1992*)[1]

Reading the Revolutions

Much recent cultural criticism has identified the public sphere as a crucial
category for rethinking the oppositions that have haunted political discourse
at least since the democratic revolutions of the late eighteenth century: literature and politics, theory and practice, ideology and everyday life, civil society and the state, the body and the body politic. *Sentimental Bodies* enters
into these critical debates by exploring the relations among sentiment, embodiment, and citizenship in the post-revolutionary United States. Drawing
on the materialist and sensationalist psychology of the early Enlightenment,
the sentimental literary culture of the period relied upon readers' affective,
passionate, and embodied responses to fictive characters and situations in
order to produce political effects. As such, sentimentalism located readers'
bodies as both pre-political sources of personal authenticity *and* as public
sites of political contestation. The body thus served two contradictory functions within sentimentalism: it provided a surface upon which sensations
were expressed for a public that could imagine itself as respecting the autonomy of every body, and it provided a literary site for the management of those

sensations through collective and potentially heteronomous means. Previous
studies of sentimentalism have tended to emphasize one side of this contradiction. Jane Tompkins, for example, stresses sentimentalism's democratic
potential, while Ann Douglas highlights its normalizing effects. *Sentimental
Bodies*, in contrast, focuses on the literary and political public spheres—the
spaces that make the *res publica*—as the sites in and through which these
contradictory understandings of the body and its sensations are deployed and
contested. By highlighting the structural basis of this contradiction, *Sentimental Bodies* situates literary critical debates concerning the political history
of sentimentalism within political theoretical debates concerning the location
of the body within a body politic that claims to be both republican and democratic. A focus on sentiment, I will argue, raises questions central to any
republican or democratic political culture by exploring the boundaries that
divide private from public life, civil from state authority, subjection from
citizenship, in post-revolutionary political theory and cultural practice.

The questions this study addresses are not new. Mary Wollstonecraft, for
one, concludes her 1794 history of the "origin and progress" of the French
Revolution with a political critique that similarly interweaves the themes of
the body and the body politic. Drawing a scatological analogy between these
two bodies, Wollstonecraft argues that France had "grown up and sickened
on the corruption of a state diseased." "But," she continues,

> as in medicine there is a species of complaint in bowels which works its own cure
> and, leaving the body healthy, gives an invigorated tone to the system, so there is
> in politics: and whilst the agitations of its regeneration continues, the excremen-
> tious humors exuding from the contaminated body will excite a general dislike and
> contempt for the nation; and it is only the philosophic eye, which looks into the
> nature and weighs the consequences of human actions, that will be able to discern
> the cause, which has produced so many dreadful effects.[2]

In response to anti-Jacobin writings published in England and the United
States early in the 1790s, Wollstonecraft's reading of the Revolution replaces any reactionary "dislike and contempt" for its "progress" with her
own sympathetic articulation of the democratic and republican principles
that lay at its "origin." France's "disease" results not from the excesses of
either democracy or republicanism, but from the lingering effects of the
ancien régime's unenlightened despotism: "The deprivation of natural,
equal, civil and political rights, reduced the most cunning of the lower orders to practice fraud, and the rest to habits of stealing, audacious robberies,
and murders."[3] The "antidote" to this "poison" requires not a reactionary
move back toward that despotism (a misdiagnosis Wollstonecraft credits to
counter-revolutionary writers like Edmund Burke), but a more vigilant application of democratic and republican principles.[4] By focusing on the "excrementious humors" of the Revolution, Wollstonecraft's "philosophical

eye" penetrates the body politic, assuring her reader that "reason beaming on the theater of political changes, can prove the only sure guide to direct us to a favorable or just conclusion." "It is," she adds, "the uncontaminated mass of the French nation, whose minds begin to grasp the sentiments of freedom, that has secured the equilibrium of the state."[5]

There are limits to Wollstonecraft's philosophical vision, however. By framing those "cunning" members of the "lower orders" as "excrementious humors exuded from the contaminated body," Wollstonecraft differentiates between the disorderly agents of corrupt social practices and the enlightened citizens they could become through the clarification and expansion of normative political principles. This need to abstract "regenerative" principles from "contaminating" practices leads Wollstonecraft to an ambivalent assessment of the Revolution. On the one hand, she paints a portrait of the lower classes that even Burke could admire: "The concourse, at first, consisted mostly of market women, and the lowest refuse of the streets, women who had thrown off the virtues of one sex without having power to assume more than the vices of the other. A number of men followed them, armed with pikes, bludgeons, and hatchets: but they were strictly speaking a mob, affixing all the odium to the appellation it can possibly import." On the other hand, she warns against the Burkean reading of this portrait. The "mob" that attacked the *hôtel de ville* in October 1789 ought "not to be confounded with the honest multitude, who took the Bastille" three months earlier: "such a rabble has seldom been gathered together; and they quickly showed, that their movement was not the effect of public spirit."[6] Where the "odiousness" of the "mob" stems from its tendency to act on the "emotions of the moment," the "honesty" of the "multitude" attests to its "public spirit": the "natural feelings of man . . . that on sudden occasions manifest themselves with all their pristine purity and vigour."[7] That Wollstonecraft is able to distinguish between these two apparently spontaneous forms of public affect—"momentary" and "natural" feelings—evinces a progressive alternative to those "empirics" and "despots" who have killed "thousands": "the improvements made both in medicine and moral philosophy have kept a sure, though gradual pace." An enlightened "public spirit" grounded in the "natural feelings of man" promises to substitute "taste" for "*ennui,*" "philosophy" for "imagination," "sentiments of freedom" for "gothic tournaments."[8]

For Wollstonecraft, then, the problem with both the French Revolution and the anti-Jacobinism it provoked lies in their common failure to differentiate between "philosophic" cause and "dreadful" effect, between the political principles of a regenerated body politic and the social practices of as yet contaminated bodies. The solution to that problem lies in the rational application of enlightened political principles to unenlightened social practices. Juxtaposing the French and the American Revolutions in a move that would soon become a commonplace of democratic political theory, Wollstonecraft accordingly faults the French revolutionaries, in contrast to the Americans, for rashly attempting to realize a "state of perfection for which the minds of the people were not sufficiently prepared."[9] The result, Wollstonecraft argues, is the revolutionary terrorists' failure to constitute and maintain a republican body politic adapted to the demands of as yet unenlightened forms of democratic sociality. Wollstonecraft shares this stylized contrast between the two revolutions with contemporaries (and political antagonists) like this anonymous writer in the Federalist *Gazette of the United States*: "There is a difference between the French and American Revolution. In America no barbarities were perpetrated—no men's heads were struck upon poles—no ladies' bodies mangled . . . . The Americans . . . set limits to their vices, at which their pursuits rested."[10] She also shares it with later political theorists, ranging from Alexis de Tocqueville to Hannah Arendt. Tocqueville's *Democracy in America* famously differentiates between the French and American Revolutions by suggesting that, unlike the former, the latter was driven on by "[n]o disorderly passions . . .; on the contrary, it proceeded hand and hand with a love of order and legality."[11] Arendt's *On Revolution* repeats this argument by contrasting the French revolutionaries who allowed their "ocean-like sentiments" to "drown the foundations of freedom" with the American revolutionaries who allowed "no pity to lead them astray from reason."[12] "The shift from the republic to the people," Arendt concludes from this contrast, "meant that the enduring unity of the future political body was guaranteed not in the worldly institutions which this people had in common, but in the will of the people themselves."[13]

Leaving aside for the moment questions concerning the accuracy of this historiography, what interests me in it is the consistency with which each of these defenses of republican principles leads its author to abstract political from social issues, and then to allegorize that distinction through reference to the American and French Revolutions. Again, this tendency is most marked in Arendt, but each of these aspiring heirs to—and readers of—the American Revolution represent, applaud, and eventually other that revolution as passionless and purely political; their polemics are concerned more specifically with the French Revolution and the problematic expansion of democratic demands to social rather than political concerns. The "will of the people," for each of these writers, threatens to collapse the distinction between political and social life upon which the stability and durability of the republican body politic depends. Conversely, the socialist heirs to the French Revolution contend that this type of historiography is necessarily ideological since the very ability to abstract political principles from social practice masks the real economic and, more generally, sociological determinants of those principles. Within this narrative, the American Revolution predictably becomes not exemplary, but merely one example—or even an exception—in a teleological history that equates human liberation with the socialist realization of democracy. Karl Marx's critique of liberalism in "On the Jewish Question," for instance, refers to "the North American states only as an example" while, less than ten years later and after the failed European revolutions of 1848, Friedrich Engels alludes to "the special American conditions."[14] In *The Eighteenth Brumaire of Louis Napoleon*, Marx's interpretive struggle to account for this failure forces him to construct an historical counter-agent in the form of a "lumpenproletariat" every bit as "odious" as Wollstonecraft's "mob": "this scum, offal, refuse of all classes" is "the only class upon which [Bonaparte] can base himself unconditionally."[15] In 1851, the same "failure" leads Engels to represent the United States not only as an *exception* within an otherwise universal narrative, but also as a *displaced example* of European false consciousness, a sort of *lumpenfrance*.

The political effects of this socialist narrative are as well known as those of its liberal counterpart. Where the heirs to the American Revolution tend to ignore the sociological conditions that enabled and betrayed the political forms of modern republicanism, the heirs to the French Revolution tend to reduce those forms to the sociological reality of what Marx calls "human sensuous activity."[16] "Only when real, individual man resumes the abstract citizen into himself," Marx concludes in "On the Jewish Question," ". . . only when man has recognized and organized his *forces propres* as *social forces* so that social force is no longer separated from him in the form of political force, only then will human emancipation be completed."[17] Between these two antithetical narratives, these two contradictory determinations of the essence of a truly democratic republic, then, a consensus prevails. The divergence between these two inheritances produces a series of oppositions that include such familiar pairings as political and social, public and private, idealism and materialism, rationality and sentimentality. Yet both analyses depend essentially on the stability of these oppositions. More precisely, they depend on them until, for Wollstonecraft, a "medical and moral philosophy" irreducible to its social determinants can prepare the "minds of the people" for a "state of perfection" or, for Marx, a universal proletarian class consciousness, freed from ideological struggle, provides the human realization of political emancipation. On the one hand, the liberal and socialist narratives split in their assessments of the relative merits of the French and American Revolutions; on the other hand, they concur in their common, if unspoken agreement on two central points: that their interpretive struggles over the meaning of modern republicanism will focus on the heterogeneous remains of those revolutions; that their political struggles to achieve a democratic republic will concern the status and location of the body within the body politic. In each case, the political and cultural project of rendering republicanism modern requires a reimagining of the relation between the structural conditions of a republican body politic and the politics of the democratic bodies that inhabit those structures.

Sentimental Bodies intervenes into this battle over and between these two revolutions by taking seriously the corporeal metaphors that structure it. Marx's reference to "human sensuous activity" as the ground of his dialectical materialism echoes Wollstonecraft's analogy between "medical" and "moral" philosophy because both writers share a typically modern understanding of the body as both a ground and a site of political debate. In different ways, the focus on the body common to Wollstonecraft and Marx results from the political and cultural pressures placed upon a republican body politic in the process of becoming democratic. Briefly stated, this crisis reflects a tension between two meanings of the term "politics." Understood in the broad sense as a name for the ideological struggle over public opinion formation (what Antonio Gramsci refers to as the "war of position"), "politics" expands to include virtually all forms of sociality, including intimate and corporeal relations. In doing so, it threatens to collapse the structural boundary between political and social life without which the term "politics" itself would be meaningless. Understood in the narrow sense as a name for the public space of that ideological struggle, "politics" shores up the boundary between political and social life, but only at the expense of depoliticizing those forms of sociality, intimacy, and corporeality that fall outside of the public realm. If Wollstonecraft's failure to resolve this tension lies in her inattention to the broad sense of the term, then Marx's complementary failure lies in his inattention to its narrower significance. His prescription for "human emancipation" assumes, but never adequately theorizes, the institutions within which "man" will "recognize" and "organize" "his *forces propres* as *social forces.*" Where Wollstonecraft reifies the opposition between the momentary "emotions" of democratic bodies and the natural "feelings" of republican citizens, Marx collapses that opposition. What Wollstonecraft and Marx both undertheorize are the public sphere institutions that link the political forms of republicanism to their corresponding forms of embodiment. For reasons that the remainder of this introduction will address, the cultural discourse of sentimentalism bridges this gap by manifesting both the forms of mediation that promise to make social relations republican and the forms of embodiment that promise to make political relations democratic.

The Body Politic

In a series of articles published in the early 1980s, political theorist Claude Lefort provides a useful starting point for this investigation of the political and cultural history of sentimentalism in the United States. Lefort argues that the liberal attempt to purify the political sphere of its social contaminants and the socialist attempt to reduce that sphere to its social determinants *both* betray the novelty of the modern "democratic adventure." For Lefort, both misapprehend the significance of the paradoxical installation and isolation of a "political stage" *within* society: "The disappearance of natural determination, which was once linked to the person of the prince or to the existence of a nobility, leads to the emergence of a purely social society in which the people, the nation and the state take on the status of universal entities, and in which any individual or group can be accorded the same status."[18] No longer identifiable with either the individual body of the sovereign or the collective body of the populace, the abstractions "people," "nation," and "state" function as political symbols that are simultaneously foundational *and* unrepresentable. But, Lefort adds, this denaturalization of political authority does not necessarily imply a rigid distinction between politics and society: "Neither the state, the people nor the nation represent substantial entities. Their representation is itself, in its dependence upon a political discourse and upon a sociological and historical elaboration, always bound up with ideological debate."[19] The specificity of modern democracy thus lies in its establishment of an *immanent* and *nonteleological*, rather than *reconciliatory* or *oppositional* relation between the political and the social.[20] Lefort's understanding of democracy consequently differs from socialist theories, which tend toward totalitarianism when they attempt to close the gap between political and social relations. It also contrasts with liberal theories, which tend toward formalism when they attempt to stabilize that gap. The "revolutionary and unprecedented feature of democracy," Lefort insists, lies in its institutionalization of the "locus of power" as an *"empty place."*

This "empty place" triangulates the antithesis between political and social relations, but it does not mark an historical synthesis that transcends either politics or society. Rather, it names the space of an ongoing debate that includes the terms of the antithesis itself. Implicit in this argument are two interrelated distinctions. Lefort consistently draws an opposition between structure and ideology or, in his own (quasi-Lacanian) terms, between "symbolic" and "imaginary" forms of power. An essay on Tocqueville, for example, applauds *Democracy in America* for suggesting that the "symbolic" significance of terms like "'fellow,' 'society' and 'humanity' can only be reconciled with freedom if the representation of their realization is held in check": "The desire to realize it would result in a flight into the imaginary, and that in turn would have the effect of introducing a scission between, on the one hand, the realms of opinion, power and science and, on the other, the people who are subject to them."[21] For symbolic terms to remain nonideological, in other words, they must provide a regulative horizon for ideological practice *and* ensure that that horizon never becomes identifiable with any historically specifiable set of actions or actors. In accordance with this distinction, Lefort separates "modern" from "classical" democracy by pointing to the symbolic basis of the former and its corresponding lack of an ontologically stable distinction between political and social realms.[22] The crisis of interpretation common to Wollstonecraft and Marx results from this disincorporation of both political and social authority. Prior to any attempt by a social movement to dominate by inhabiting the symbolic space of modern democratic sovereignty, the very institution of such a space acts to preclude its inhabitation by introducing an element of negativity into society itself. The resulting gap between society and any of its various representations (or representatives) leads Lefort to conclude by literalizing the metaphor of "institutionalization": "The survival and extension of the public space is a political question . . . that lies at the heart of democracy."[23]

This rethinking of democracy has implications that are political in both the broad and the narrow senses outlined above.[24] The first of these implications is ideological and has been usefully explored in the writings of Ernesto Laclau and Chantal Mouffe, most notably in *Hegemony and Socialist Strategy*. Accepting Lefort's description of democracy as a political regime without a stable social referent (a condition they refer to as the "impossibility of the social"), Laclau and Mouffe revise traditional Marxist understandings of hegemony as a political strategy ultimately grounded in the sociological reality of class antagonism. Pursuing an anti-essentialist element in Gramsci's writings, they argue instead that class struggle, in its politicization of economic inequality, ought to be seen as one of many post-revolutionary democratic movements: "From the critique of political inequality there is effected, through the different socialist discourses, a displacement towards the critique of economic inequality. . . . The socialist demands should therefore be seen as a moment internal to the democratic revolution, and only intelligible on the basis of the equivalent logic which the latter establishes."[25] This analysis of socialism as a movement internal to the logic of democracy both inverts the familiar Marxist account and envisions potential alliances among those heterogeneous social movements usually seen as emerging from the 1960s: feminist, anti-racist, post-colonialist, ethnic, anti-capitalist, environmental, anti-homophobic. Though typically referred to as "new social movements," these diverse struggles are better understood as, in Mouffe's words, "new democratic movements."[26] The importance of this distinction is threefold: first, it emphasizes the continuity between modern society-based political movements and the democratic politicization of social relations (economic and domestic); second, it highlights the distinction between civil society and the state as being central to the self-understanding of those movements; third, it provides an anti-essentialist critique of modern identity-based political ideologies.[27]

The second implication of Lefort's argument is structural. As his own phrasing reveals, the name for the "empty place" that institutionalizes the theoretical "locus" of democratic "power" is the "public." The second chapter in *Sentimental Bodies* traces this structural observation through the historical writings of Hannah Arendt and Jürgen Habermas. Despite their differences, Arendt and Habermas agree with eighteenth-century theorists of republicanism that a society is democratic only if it provides sites of public opinion formation that are both accessible and influential. Habermas's recent, more theoretical writings extend this insight into the normative significance of official and unofficial public-sphere institutions to an analysis of the liberal welfare state as the context within which social movements operate. The problem with the welfare state project, Habermas argues, is that it "continues to be nourished by a utopia of social labor [that] is losing its power to project future possibilities for a collectively better and less endangered way of life."[28] This crisis results from two misconceptions: an overestimation of the nation-state's ability to regulate the international market economy and an underestimation of the state's ability to mobilize administrative power to political ends. Together, the systems of "money" (the capitalist market) and "power" (the administrative state) mediate and disable the "utopian" goal of the democratic revolutions—that of securing "forms of life that are structured in an egalitarian way and that at the same time open up arenas for individual self-realization and spontaneity."[29] Like Lefort, Habermas responds to this double bind by linking the expansion of public-sphere institutions to the process of democratization. Such institutions ideally allow social movements with "forms of organization that are closer to the base and self-administered" to critique and transform the "inner dynamic of subsystems regulated by money and power."[30] Expanding on this insight, Andrew Arato and Jean Cohen locate Habermas's analysis as a continuation of the "project of the democratic revolutions which created modern civil society." "The political issue," they conclude, "is how to introduce public spaces into state and economic institutions . . . by establishing a continuity with a network of societal communication consisting of public spheres, associations and movements."[31]

Sentimental Bodies draws on these political theoretical debates and recontextualizes them through reference to shifts in U. S. historiography begun by Bernard Bailyn and Gordon Wood nearly thirty years ago. Breaking with the liberal consensus historiography of the 1950s, Bailyn's and Wood's books reconstruct the ideological context of republicanism in terms that echo both Arendt and Habermas. The idea of founding a republic, Wood argues, "meant more for Americans than the simple elimination of a king and the institution of an elective system. It added a moral dimension, a utopian depth, to the political separation from England—a depth that involved the very character of their society."[32] Just as Lefort insists on the symbolic character of modern democracy, Wood argues that the republican "common interest was not, as we might today think of it, simply the sum or consensus of the particular interests that made up the community. It was rather an entity in itself, prior to and distinct from the various private interests of groups and individuals."[33] As suggested by his time frame (1776–1787), however, Wood also tends to interpret the ethos of collective "disinterest" inscribed within republicanism as indicative of a "classical politics" surpassed by the less "utopian" demands of modern liberalism: "Like Puritanism, . . . republicanism was essentially anti-capitalistic, a final attempt to come to terms with the emergent individualistic society that threatened to destroy once and for all the communion and benevolence that civilized man had always considered the ideal of human behavior."[34] Though nostalgically attached to this "anti-capitalist" version of republicanism, Wood's analysis equates the rise of economic liberalism with the origins of modernity. In doing so, it effaces the continued challenge posed to that liberalism by democratic forms of republicanism (including those of Lefort and Habermas). In accordance with this interpretation, Wood concludes by reducing the republican ideal of political "virtue" to John Adams's classical use of that term in order to justify a premodern and hierarchical politics of social deference.

In contrast, J. G. A. Pocock's *The Machiavellian Moment* (1975) focused on the continued and continuing impact of republicanism on both the theory and the practice of U. S. democracy. Pocock acknowledges that the ideal of republican virtue becomes, at times, a static and closed justification of social hierarchy. What interests him, though, is the equally consistent use of that ideal to justify an agonistic and open-ended public debate concerning what Laclau and Mouffe might call the hegemonic articulation of democratic associations.[35] Pocock's subsequent writings have emphasized this point: "If I had wanted to write a book called *The Catonian Moment*, I would have done so. I chose, however, to begin with Machiavelli, the better to make the point that 'virtue' in early modern times was invariably regarded as ambiguous and fragile, dynamic and problematic, and will probably continue to be so regarded until Western man gives up the belief that he/she is naturally a political animal."[36] Where Wood constructs an opposition between a republicanism that is categorically pre-modern and a modernity that is categorically liberal, Pocock stresses the tense coexistence of the two paradigms. Republicanism and liberalism thus emerge as contemporary and competing models of democratic self-government. Support for Pocock's argument appears in the variety of post-revolutionary *and* anti-deferential conceptualizations of "virtue" that inform the political and cultural discourse of the antebellum United States: Thomas Paine's argument for an egalitarian distribution of land and capital in *Agrarian Justice*, the men's and women's labor movements of the 1830s, the feminist "Declaration of Sentiments" written at Seneca Falls in 1848, Harriet Jacobs's refiguring of the sentimental novel in *Incidents in the Life of a Slave Girl*.[37] In each case, the significance of modern republicanism and the Machiavellian virtue it invokes consists in its attack on both the ideological and structural presuppositions of the liberal consensus: first, republicanism legitimates an unending struggle over the ideological inscription of virtue and corruption upon the text of the republic; second, it opens that struggle onto questions concerning the infrastructure of democratic citizenship.

Among the studies of the early republic influenced by Pocock are some of the most challenging recent accounts of that period's literary culture. Though their conclusions differ, Michael Warner, Jay Fliegelman, Larzar Ziff, and Christopher Looby have all argued that an attention to the dynamics of republicanism ought to lead to a re-evaluation of the assumptions central to the liberal account of modernity.[38] In *The Letters of the Republic*, Warner makes this claim most persuasively. Republicanism structures the way in which we think about the "styles of rationalization and progressive thinking that we call modernity," because the central terms of modernity originate only within the context of republicanism.[39] The circularity of this claim is central to Warner's subsequent argument. If the story of the rise of democracy is that of the differentiation of civil and state power, the liberation of the private individual, and the triumph of the national people, then how does that story account for the emergence in the same period of the very terms—"society," "individual," "people"—that make it intelligible in the first place. "How," Warner asks, "can we describe the history of the transformation without holding constant the value-terms of modernity?"[40] Warner's largely convincing argument assigns the institutions and ideologies of print capitalism a determining role in this historical drama. Like Wollstonecraft's "philosophic eye," the market-driven print technologies of the late eighteenth century allowed citizens to imagine forms of political authority that were rational and noncoercive to the degree that they were abstract and disembodied. Citizens, in other words, gained political power only insofar as they were able to represent their *local* and *embodied* experience as *universal* and *disinterested* through the mediation of print. As such, print acquired cultural meanings that provided (and continue to provide) what Warner refers to as a "metapolitics of speech": "[the cultural meanings of print] are the basis for deciding who speaks, to whom, with what constraints, and with what legitimacy."[41] The resulting antinomy between embodiment and abstraction—interestedness and universality—transforms the significance of the body within modernity. Modern republicanism positions the body not only *at*, but also *as* the vanishing point of the body politic.

The Politics of the Body

While this historical recovery of republicanism resulted in what Robert Shallope referred to in 1972 as a "republican synthesis," objections to that "synthesis" emerged—and, I would argue, predictably emerged—from within those social movements focused on the political significance of the body.[42] Most notably, feminist historians have argued that the ostensibly democratic republicanism of the 1780s and 1790s quickly and, for some, inevitably evolved into an anti-democratic theory of "republican woman-hood" that assigned separate and unequal roles to women and men.[43] Similar objections have been raised to Arendt's and Habermas's reconstructions of the eighteenth-century public sphere, as well as their uses of that reconstruction as a normative foundation for contemporary critical theory and practice.[44]

In the most general sense, these are the debates in which *Sentimental Bodies* participates. And Warner again provides a useful context. While the principle of self-abstraction that Warner locates at the center of republicanism suggests that the body appears within political discourse only through its negation, the practice of self-abstraction reveals that this principle operates differentially with respect to different forms of embodiment: "It is a ground rule of argument in a public discourse that defines its norms as abstract and universal, but it is also a political resource available only in this discourse, and available only to those participants whose social role allows such self-negation (that is, to persons defined by whiteness, maleness, and capital)."[45] If self-abstraction is the sine qua non of republican citizenship (the ethical caveat that makes "public space" an "empty place"), then "persons" with "bodies" can be only partial citizens—at best. In theory, this contradiction applies to any citizen. In practice, however, the burden of corporeality falls unequally on those persons with bodies marked as non-white, nonmale, and/or economically dependent. Citizens, according to Warner, are those persons whose bodies vanish at the boundary between private and public life, while subjects are persons whose eccentric corporeality disqualifies them from public life by rendering their bodies all too visible.

The severity with which Warner poses this power-ladened antinomy between abstraction and embodiment is accurate to some forms of republicanism. The ideal of virtue, for example, was often understood in precisely these terms. But it also forces him to encode all contemporary discourses focused on the political significance of the body as categorically liberal. The dialectic within republicanism between publication and embodiment thus becomes an opposition between republicanism and liberalism. Sentimentalism provides Warner with his privileged example: "The turn toward sentiment can be seen as a key element in the extension of the national imaginary to the female readership of novels and in the emergence of a liberal paradigm for appreciating printed texts."[46] I will return to this point in chapters 4 and 5. For now, I want to stress my agreement with Warner: discourses like sentimentalism position the body within republicanism as both a tool of domination and a site of contradiction. Where Warner focuses on the first of these two deployments of the body, I focus on the second. The body can provide a tool of domination—a means of excluding "persons" with "bodies" from citizenship—only if struggles over the structural boundaries of public life open onto ideological struggles over the political significance of the body itself. In making this claim, I draw and expand upon critiques of nineteenth-century sentimentalism inspired by the debate between Ann Douglas and Jane Tompkins in the mid-1980s, and continued by a variety of writers who agree with Douglas and Tompkins that sentimentalism involves, in Shirley Samuels's words, "a project about imagining the nation's bodies and the national body."[47] Karen Sanchez-Eppler's study of sentimental strategies within antebellum feminism and abolitionism provides one historical context for this shift in the body's political significance: "[A]ssumptions of a metaphorical and fleshless political identity were disrupted and unmasked through the convergence of two rhetorics of social protest: the abolitionist concern with claiming personhood for the racially distinct and physically owned slave body, and the feminist concern with claiming personhood for the sexually distinct and domestically circumscribed female body."[48] Sanchez-Eppler agrees with Warner that this "eruption of the body in antebellum culture" marks, for good or bad, a liberal inversion of the republican model of citizenship as disembodied and universal.

Similar claims could be made in relation to other, perhaps less familiar antebellum reform movements focused on the body, its sensations, and its relations. Temperance and anti-onanism campaigns, as well as opposition to corporal punishment in state institutions ranging from schools and prisons to the military, all deploy the rhetoric of sentimentalism in order to position the body as resistant, yet malleable matter—the liminal substance that, as Jonathan Elmer puts it, sentimental reform "both needs, and needs to regulate."[49] What the studies I draw upon tend to overlook, however, are the seventeenth- and eighteenth-century origins of these sentimental strategies.[50] The nineteenth-century culture of sentiment emerges out of early Enlightenment discourses that focus on the body as both a ground and a site of political debate. Janet Todd, G. J. Barker-Benfield, and Ann Van Sant all trace this modern understanding of the body to the materialist and sensationalist psychology of writers ranging from John Locke and Julian La Mettrie to Jean-Jacques Rousseau and Adam Smith.[51] While there are significant differences among these schools of thought, they share a commitment to what I would like to call the *disestablishment* of the body. No longer one of many phenomena ordered through pre-existing political, ethical, and theological systems, the body becomes the noumenal grounding of existence itself—a point of origin upon which political, ethical, and theological systems are then erected. The body, in Thomas Laqueur's words, is transformed from a "sign of" into a "foundation for civil society."[52] As Robyn Wiegman and others have suggested, one effect of this shift lies in the body's newfound ability to naturalize social and political inequalities through reference to the corporeal self-evidence of anatomical "differences" like sex and race.[53] Lauren Berlant makes this point nicely: "Wherever citizenship comes to look like a question of the *body*, a number of processes are being hidden. The body's seeming obviousness distracts attention from the ways it organizes meaning, and diverts the critical gaze from publicity's role in the formation of taxonomies that construct bodies publicly."[54]

While this point seems indisputable, the same shift in the location of the body also positions it as a site of political contestation, a public "question" whose answer may not be as "obvious" as Berlant implies. The sentimental abstraction of the body from its social and political environment, in other words, establishes the terrain upon which anatomy could become (sexual and racial) destiny—a "foundation for civil society." But it also sets forth the promise of an uncompromisingly democratic politics grounded in the autonomy of every body's sensations. The culture of sentiment thematizes this contradiction within both the body and the body politic by opposing what Barker-Benfield refers to as the autonomy of the individual's "spontaneous wish" to the heteronomous "code of manners" that makes that "wish" legible. Expanding on this contradiction, Barker-Benfield agrees with Laqueur, Wiegman, and others that the eighteenth century "invented the modern terminology of sex," but he adds that it did so with "an acute awareness of conflict." This sense of conflict appears within sentimentalism as a tension between "feeling" and "code" in the sentimental body: "The tension between feeling and code was intended to sharpen the emotional effect on the sensitive reader who, presumably, experienced the same conflict within herself."[55] Positioned as both the ground and the site of this conflict, the body of the reader mediated between the presumably autonomous experience of corporeal sensation, on the one hand, and the clearly heteronomous demands of social codification, on the other. In the most general sense, then, the abstraction of the body from its political and social environment both corresponded to and radicalized the democratic disestablishment of political authority. Just as the isolation of civil from state power could position "society" as the basis of political autonomy, the isolation of the body from society could locate "sentiment" as a grounding figure for personal autonomy.[56] In each case, the body and its sensations emerge as the site of the political problem of self-government—a problem now framed as involving the collective and consensual management of the body's expressive capabilities.[57]

When Lefort locates the political question of public space at the "heart of democracy," his metaphor is thus doubly accurate. First, it locates the politics of the body at the core of the republican body politic. Like the "bowels" whose regularity signifies for Wollstonecraft the progress of French republicanism, and the "human sensuous activity" that provides the dialectic counterpart to liberal idealism in Marx, the "heart" positions the body at the center of the "empty place" whose institutionalization marks the distinctive (and divisive) feature of modern democracy. Second, it figures the centrality of the body by drawing on the most powerful of all sentimental tropes, the heart. Understood as a site of authentic "feeling," the heart provides a universal and pre-political point of affective identification for individuals otherwise divided through the imposition of an ideological "code" that is, for any true sentimentalist, never "heartfelt." Yet this metonymic substitution of "heart" for "body" also points to sentimentalism's complicity with the ideology of individual and collective bodily refinement—the "sentimentalizing process"—that Barker-Benfield traces through eighteenth-century literary and political discourse. In Wollstonecraft, for example, the "heart" is the locus of a body politics capable of distinguishing the virtuous "multitude" from the odious "mob." Where the "agitations" of the "bowels" signify a lack of discipline within both the body and the body politic, the "natural feelings" of the "heart" link the "health" of the body to the "regeneration" of the body politic. This ideology of bodily refinement is sentimental because it gains its authority by simultaneously eliciting and reforming the sensations of the body—by both conjuring and exorcising the "excrementious humors" of the bowels. Even the most radical of nineteenth-century body politics operate on this sentimental terrain. In *Song of Myself*, for example, Walt Whitman's claim to be "no sentimentalist . . . no stander above men or women" leads him to criticize the ideology of bodily refinement: "I keep as delicate around the bowels as around the head and the heart." But this boast becomes meaningful only in the context of a sentimental literary culture committed to the public reform of both the body and the body politic. The "voices of sexes and lusts" that Whitman's poetry "unveils" are also "clarified and transfigured" by their publication within it.[58]

The sensations of the sentimental body thus provide what I would like to refer to as the republican "phenomenology of publication." Like Hegel's "phenomenology of the spirit," this phrase must be understood in both the objective and subjective genitive. The sensations of the body provide the referent for various technologies of publication, ranging from print to video capitalism (the historical manifestations of the republican "spirit"), while those technologies transform the historical significance of the body itself (the sensational manifestations of republican "phenomena"). And it is this dialectic between publication and the body that makes the rhetorical question J. G. Ballard poses in my epigraph to this introduction seem so typically modern and hopelessly archaic. His question is modern because it locates the body as a site of political struggle: "Will the body at last rebel, tip those vitamins, douches and aerobic schedules into Boston Harbor and throw off the colonialist oppressor?"

Ballard's portrayal of the body as an anti-colonial rebel aligns him with other modern (and postmodern) theorists. I will limit myself to three prominent examples: Michel Foucault, Elaine Scarry, and Judith Butler. For

Foucault, the modern "intensification of the body" positions it at the crux of the myriad "procedures of power that characterized the *disciplines*"—most notably the discourse of "sexuality." But the body also provides a point of resistance within those "procedures": "The rallying point for the counterattack against the deployment of sexuality ought not to be sex-desire, but bodies and pleasures."[59] For Scarry, the "sheer material factualness of the human body" allows it to lend to historical and cultural phenomena the "aura of 'realness' and 'certainty.'" But that body also contains the expressive capacity to disrupt the legibility of the "real": "To witness the moment when pain causes a reversion to the pre-language of cries and groans is to witness the destruction of language."[60] For Butler, the "fixity of the body, its contours, its movements" are fully "material," but this "materiality" also must be "rethought as the effect of power, as power's most productive effect." "Bodies," in other words, "matter" because the "unsettling of 'matter' can be understood as initiating new possibilities, new ways for bodies to matter."[61]

Like Ballard's rhetorical question, each of these accounts is typically modern because it positions the body as a site of political contestation. "Pleasure," "pain," and "matter" are the "feelings" Foucault, Scarry, and Butler use to designate the body's resistance to the "codes" of "discipline," "language," and "power." In contrast to these accounts, however, Ballard's question becomes archaic when it naturalizes the body as an uncontested ground of post-colonial liberation. (One wonders what his "Glossary of the Twenty-First Century" would look like.) In contrast to the "X-ray" that deploys the body as a screen for a scientifically mediated moral discourse, Ballard's "glossary" imagines a body that is revolutionary because it exists *outside* of that discourse. The problem with this formulation is not that it locates the body as a point of political resistance (a postmodern Caliban), but that it equates unmediated bodily expression with political freedom. As Berlant points out, this recourse to the body's self-evidence may "free" some individuals from some forms of political control, but that freedom is revolutionary in neither individual nor collective terms. And nowhere are the problems involved in this ideological deployment of the body's obviousness more self-evident than in the national archive Ballard mines for his historical allusion. The act of tossing British-owned chests of tea into Boston Harbor may have catalyzed colonial opposition to British rule, but it also inaugurated—or at least nationalized—that now typically "American" tendency to claim nationality by "playing Indian." Carefully decorated and displayed for publication in personal correspondence, newspapers, and broadsides, the rebel bodies of the colonists were artfully projected as indigenously "American." The "Rallying Song of the Tea Party" thus admonishes "Mohawks" like Sam Adams, John Hancock, and Paul Revere to rally against King George: "Our country's 'braves' and firm defenders / Shall ne'er be left by true North-Enders / Fighting Freedom's cause!"[62] This political display of the body

reveals its "revolutionary" potential, but it also highlights the careful mediation of the colonial claim to post-colonial autonomy through the management, subjection, and publication of "native" bodies.

I conclude with this observation not simply in order to pose the body as
essentially ideological—a dummy available for any act of political ventrilo-
quism. Like Marx's "human sensual activity," Ballard's figure of a "brutish"
and "unenlightened" body promises to prevent any such duplicitous body
politics by transcending the oppositions that I invoked at the beginning of
this introduction: literature and politics, theory and practice, ideology and
everyday life, civil society and the state, the body and the body politic. And
in doing so it does capture one utopian strain within modernity by figuring
the body as a revolutionary locus of uncodified affect. Ballard, in other
words, exploits the "liberatory" rather than the "repressive" side of the dialectic within sentimentalism between feeling and codification, between the
body and its public life. Without dismissing the power of this utopian (and
privatizing) gesture, my point is that it also presupposes a structural underdevelopment of the body that positions "feeling" in a relation of exteriority
to those public-sphere institutions within which "feelings" are contested
and codified. As Donald Lowe has suggested, this underdevelopment secures a body that is both critically utopian and deeply ideological: the "body
referent, the actual, lived body in the world, i.e., our own body, is coded
and realized by language, yet concurrently and in spite of that it is nevertheless always more than any concept, image or representation of it."[63] The
modernity of the sentimental body—"our own body"—lies in its ability to
embody this paradox, regardless of whether it is "free" or "repressed,"
"brutish" and "unenlightened," or "housed" and "sparingly nourished." By
emphasizing this structural point, *Sentimental Bodies* enacts a similar paradox. It traces the history of the modern body to a sentimental ideology that,
by naturalizing publicly mediated taxonomies through recourse to the im-
mediacy of "feeling," masks the political power located at the "heart" of
both the body and the body politic. It also deploys the body or, more precisely, the various sensations that bodies express as unpredictable points of structural resistance to the corporealization of those ideological codes.

As should be clear from these introductory remarks, one of the central concerns of *Sentimental Bodies* is to think critically about several clusters of
terms that cultural and literary historians tend to use descriptively. These
terms could be called the keywords of my argument: democracy, liberalism,
and republicanism; sensation, sentiment, and sentimentality; body and
mind; public and private; political and social; sex, gender, and sexuality.
They also include terms that appear too seldom in literary and cultural criticism, most notably *civil society* and *the state*. Readers will search in vain for

static definitions of any of these terms, except in the notes where I refer to
specific arguments and debates. Rather, I have tried to locate these concepts
within the texts and arguments out of which they emerge and from which
they can never be fully abstracted. In this sense, *Sentimental Bodies* is an
historical study. But it is also a study intended to raise questions about the
ways in which history has been (and is being) written. History thus enters
into the argument as a form of provocation to theory, while theory enters as
a provocation to history. Put another way, history serves the function of
defamiliarizing our theories of the present, while theory allows for the defa-
miliarization of our narratives of the past. If this formulation seems paradoxical, there is good reason for it. As Lefort points out, the democratic politicization of social relations transforms the act of writing history into a political
performance with its own generic, institutional, and economic limitations.
"Democracy," he writes, " . . . proves to be the historical society *par excellence*, a society which, in its very form, welcomes and preserves indeterminacy."[64] Taking Lefort's argument a step further, I would add that societies
and institutions are democratic to the degree that they understand history as
a story of the present, told and debated in relation to its multiple past(s).
While this disjointed form of "present-ism" strips history of its metapolitical
certainty, it also provides historiography with a relation to a future that is not
yet determined.

Having said this much, and at the risk of contradicting myself, I do want
to clarify my usage of the most vexed and central terms of this study: liberalism and republicanism. As Daniel Rogers and others have argued, these
terms name political ideologies that are often opposed in theory, but seldom
separable in practice.[65] This point seems indisputable. In this chapter, for
instance, I locate Wollstonecraft within a liberal tradition due to her effort
to essentialize and stabilize the structural opposition between political and
social life. In later chapters, she reappears as part of a republican tradition
due to her attention to the social (gender and class) inequalities hidden by
that opposition. This example teaches neither that liberalism and republicanism are hopelessly confused categories, nor that the analytic distinction
between them is simply (as Rodgers would have it) a reflection of a late-
twentieth-century paradigm shift with little historical relevance. Rather, it
teaches that liberalism and republicanism name two antithetical *and* inseparable possibilities inscribed within the larger idea of democratic self-government. In short, liberalism responds to the question of self-government by
grounding political authority in the representative and legislative apparatuses of the nation-state. When the power wielded by those apparatuses
becomes openly heteronomous (rather than transparent or neutral), liberalism tends to retreat. It reacts by preserving official forms of political opposition, while also shielding presumably non-political and private areas of life
from state power (intimate and economic relations, for example). Republi-

canism, in contrast, grounds political authority in public-sphere institutions located outside of the state apparatus. As a result, it tends to react to heteronomous state power with public-oriented reform movements whose targets may include political, economic, and intimate relations. *Sentimental Bodies* intentionally makes use of these relatively abstract and theoretical accounts of liberalism and republicanism in order to engage current debates within the fields of political, legal, and cultural studies. But it also locates those debates in the historical field out of which they emerge.

With these caveats in mind, I have divided *Sentimental Bodies* into three sections: "Sentiment and Citizenship," "Sentiment and Sex," "Sentiment and Sexuality." Each of these sections contains two chapters that link historical and theoretical argumentation by focusing on both the strategic usages of sentiment as a means of debating the politics of modern bodily relations *and* the epistemological assumptions that position the body as the sentimental grounding of that debate.

Part One: Sentiment and Citizenship. As a pair, chapters 2 and 3 expand on the theoretical and historical argument that I have outlined in this introductory chapter by situating *Sentimental Bodies* within the debates concerning liberalism and republicanism that dominate the historical field. These debates reflect two opposed understandings of the significance of the public sphere in the early republic. In brief, republicanism requires active citizens who participate within public debate and decision making, while liberalism tends to produce passive subjects secure in their ability to defend themselves against publicity. The conventional conclusion to this debate focuses on the triumph of liberalism, thus ignoring a variety of radical redeployments of republicanism ranging from nineteenth-century labor movements to late twentieth-century feminism. I argue, in contrast, that liberalism's normative relation to democracy requires that it maintain at least a theoretical commitment to participatory models of both citizenship and public space. I have titled this section "Sentiment and Citizenship" because both chapters ultimately locate the figure of "sentiment" as the dividing line between citizenship and subjection in the early republic. In the first chapter, I focus on that figure as it appears in the writings of Arendt and Habermas. For Arendt, sentiment refers to those (plebeian) bodies whose needs and desires threaten to destroy the public sphere as a site of political debate; for Habermas, the same threat contains the dialectic possibility of democratizing that site. In the second chapter, I extend this theoretical discussion to a reading of George Washington's "Farewell Address" as a text that mobilizes Washington's body (and eventually, his corpse) as both the ground and the site of debate over the meaning of nationality. The "Address" adheres closely to Arendt's classical understanding of republicanism by limiting democratic access to the public sphere, but it also subverts that limitation by allowing the general will to penetrate and divide Washington's body.

Part Two: Sentiment and Sex. The next two chapters are also paired. Where the first two focus primarily on the structural intersection of citizenship and sentiment, this second pair of chapters traces the complicated shift in the relations among sentiment, sex, and gender. As sentiment becomes increasingly associated with female bodies and middle-class norms of femininity in the late eighteenth century, it becomes available as a means of securing the structural boundary between public and private life along gender and class lines. This is the context that Warner assumes when he aligns sentimentalism, liberalism, and women's (nonpolitical) access to national identification. And it also reflects the ideology that Rousseau popularized in *Emile* when he posed and answered the question of the relation between anatomical sex and republican citizenship. In response to this now famous question, Rousseau argues that "woman" is designed "to please men, to be useful to them, to make herself loved and honored by them, to raise them when young, to care for them when grown, to counsel them, to make their lives agreeable and sweet."[66] Both chapters trace a genealogy of this antifeminist idea, while also situating that genealogy in the context of those early feminist demands for political and social equality that Rousseau encodes as "civil promiscuity."[67] In the first, I discuss female sentimentalism by looking at one typical example, Hannah Foster's *The Coquette*. Foster's novel, I argue, both resists and repeats sentimentalism's wedding of sentimental "feeling" and social "code" by deploying the category "woman" as a public and politically significant site of affective identification. In the second, I focus on Charles Brockden Brown's *Clara Howard* in order to explore the origins of the complementary nineteenth- and twentieth-century discourses that read male sentimentalism—including Rousseau's own—as an effeminizing and masochistic pathology. Both novels mark the unstable origins of the modern sex-gender system as they react to and against the sensationalist and materialist conceptions of an ungendered body out of which later gendered understandings of sentimentalism emerge.

Part Three: Sentiment and Sexuality. My final chapter and the afterword trace the distinction between sentimentality and sexuality that becomes central to nineteenth- and twentieth-century liberalism. Again, this shift is complicated. As antebellum social and political reform movements placed pressure on the structural boundaries of the republican public sphere, one liberal response both produced and silenced those subjects—persons and topics—unsuitable for public debate. The structural integrity of the public sphere, this form of liberalism argued, could be preserved only by restricting access to public debate, while also securing the sanctity of private life. The title "Sentiment and Sexuality" refers to this section's focus on the deployment and isolation of "sexuality" as one name for those topics, "sexual" or not, that emerged from this process as categorically private. In chapter 6, I begin with a reading of the first successfully prosecuted libel for obscenity in the United States, in order to trace the origins of modern legal and cultural understandings of obscenity to liberalism's attempt to police the political boundaries of the republican public sphere. I then move to Harriet Jacobs's *Incidents in the Life of a Slave Girl*, arguing that sentimentalism's relation to this policing is vexed due to its paradoxical understanding of the (sexual) body as simultaneously public and private. Committed in principle to uncensored publication as a means of linking publication and bodies, sentimentalism betrays that commitment in practice when it distinguishes between publicizable and obscene sentiments, between sentimentality and sexuality. In the afterword, I suggest that the significance of this contradiction between the structure and the ideology of sentimentalism (between republicanism and liberalism) cuts across both the body and the body politic. I do so by focusing on one powerful intersection of literary and political criticism where twentieth-century writers like Hannah Arendt and Ann Douglas take an anti-sentimental turn. For both, the story of (anti-) sentimentalism ends happily in a private space that collapses sentimentality with (homo)sexuality—the closet in which Billy Budd shares his "passionate" interview with Herman Melville's greatest anti-sentimental liberal, Captain Vere.

Part One

SENTIMENT AND CITIZENSHIP

2

United States Liberalism and the Public Sphere

A value which is normally good in itself is not
necessarily optimized when it is maximized. We have
come to recognize that there are potentially desirable
limits to the indefinite expansion of political democracy.
Democracy will have a longer life if it has a more
balanced existence.

(*Samuel Huntington,* The Crisis of Democracy,
1975)[1]

At Security Concepts, we believe an efficient police
force is only part of the solution. No, we need
something more. We need a twenty-four-hour-a-day
police officer, a cop who doesn't need to eat or sleep, a
cop with superior firepower and the reflexes to use it.

(RoboCop, *1987*)

Utopian Liberalism

When Klaatu and his robot companion Gort land in Washington, D.C., in
Robert Wise's *The Day the Earth Stood Still* (1951), their spaceship has
already circled the planet and, for the first of two times in the film, brought
the Earth to a standstill. Printing presses, telephone switchboards, radio and
television stations, public gathering places—all of the apparatuses for and
markers of the modern public sphere focus on the international significance
of the spaceship's arrival. "Every eye," as one announcer puts it, "every
weapon is trained on the ship." After much anticipation, Klaatu exits the
ship with a metallic offering in hand—a gift, he later explains, to aid in the
study of other planets. Mistaken for a weapon, the object is shot out of
Klaatu's hand by one of the soldiers surrounding the ship. Gort responds to
this act of aggression by instantly disintegrating all of the weaponry in the
area. In the following scene, Gort has encased himself in an impermeable
plastic shell, while Klaatu has been isolated in a military hospital where he
meets with the president's advisor, Mr. Harley. Klaatu informs Harley that,
due to the development of both nuclear weapons and interstellar rockets,
the Earth now threatens the security of other planets. As a representative of
those planets, Klaatu demands an audience not with the president, but with
representatives of all the nations of the Earth. Despite what has already

been presented as international public concern over Klaatu's arrival, Harley answers that such a meeting would be impossible; the British will meet only in Washington, the Soviets only in Moscow. Unconcerned with the politics of the Cold War, what he refers to as the "childish jealousies" and "petty squabbles of your planet," Klaatu suggests that he take his case to the public at large. Harley responds by imprisoning this democrat-in-teflon-drag in the hospital. Later that night, Klaatu escapes, adopts the pseudonym Mr. Carpenter, and rents a room in a local boardinghouse.

Set against the background of a manhunt throughout Washington, the remainder of the film consists largely of Klaatu's search for an appropriately rational, influential, and international public for his speech. This search eventually leads him to Professor Barnhart, an expert in "celestial mechanics," who agrees to assemble an audience of scientists and experts from other fields. As a preamble to his speech, Klaatu again brings the Earth to a standstill, this time by shutting off electricity to everything except airplanes and hospitals. Aided by Helen Benson, a secretary in the Department of Commerce, but betrayed by her insurance broker boyfriend, Klaatu is fatally shot by the military on his way to the climactic meeting. Carried back to the ship by the now liberated Gort, Klaatu returns to life and appears just as his audience is being dismissed. Klaatu delivers his speech with Gort by his side:

> The universe grows smaller every day, and the threat of aggression by any group anywhere can no longer be tolerated. There must be security for all, or no one is secure. This does not mean giving up any freedom, except the freedom to act irresponsibly. Your ancestors knew this when they made laws to govern themselves and hired policemen to enforce them. We of the other planets have long accepted this principle. We have an organization for the mutual protection of all planets, and for the complete elimination of aggression. The test of any such higher authority is, of course, the police force that enforces it. For our policemen, we created robots. Their function is to patrol the planets in spaceships like this one, and to preserve the peace. In matters of aggression, we have given them absolute power over us. This power cannot be revoked. At the first sign of violence, they act automatically against the aggressor. The penalty for provoking their action is too terrible to risk. The result is, we live in peace, without arms or armies, secure in the knowledge that we are free from aggression and war, free to pursue more profitable enterprises. We do not pretend to have achieved perfection, but we have a system and it works. I came here to give you these facts. It is no concern of ours how you run your own planet, but if you threaten to extend your violence, this Earth of yours will be reduced to a burned-out cinder. Your choice is simple: Join us and live in peace or pursue your present course and face obliteration. We shall be waiting for your answer. The decision rests with you.

Following a sympathetic exchange of glances with Helen, Klaatu re-enters the ship, which ascends and disappears as the hundred or so experts representing the nations of the Earth scatter. Unlike the first carpenter reborn to redeem humanity, Klaatu preaches not a covenant of grace, but a covenant of law. His threat is not eternal damnation, but instant disintegration.

In many ways, *The Day the Earth Stood Still* is atypical when compared to other Cold War films. It provides a relatively heterogeneous depiction of the nations of the Earth, and it is also the first 1950s science fiction film to portray an alien as other than malevolent. At points, it even undermines the Cold War political paranoia typical of such films by parodying those who, like the keeper of Klaatu's boardinghouse, hint that they know exactly where on Earth the spaceship has come from.[2] In other ways, however, *The Day the Earth Stood Still* remains quite typical. It is no coincidence that Klaatu's interplanetary mission sends him to the nation-state Hollywood consistently imagines as the focal point of alien invasions: Washington, D.C. Nor is it a coincidence that, throughout the film, the entire world seems to operate on Eastern Standard Time. More relevant to the present work, Klaatu's speech echoes the political theory that, though generally national rather than international (or intergalactic) in scope, informs other Cold War films. Just as *The Invasion of the Body Snatchers* concludes by deferring to the omnipotent authority of the FBI to eliminate the alien invasion, *The Day the Earth Stood Still* defers to the omnipotent authority of robots like Gort to eliminate aggression. And while the elimination of "body snatchers" and the elimination of "aggression" are obviously different goals, both result in a reduction of politics, or what political theorists refer to as the political, to what legal theorists refer to as the rule of law. Unconcerned with the political origin of the law, Klaatu articulates a simple opposition of law and violence, of responsible and irresponsible freedom. What begins as an international political moment inclusive of anyone concerned with the mitigation of violence becomes, through this opposition, a law-enforcing threat disseminated by experts and policed by robots. "By threatening danger," Klaatu reminds his listeners, "your planet faces great danger."

I begin with this summary of Wise's film because its opposing of law and violence isolates one prominent and specifically liberal strand within the fabric of post-World War II democratic political theory. In H. L. A. Hart's influential 1961 essay *The Concept of Law*, for example, the same opposition is cited in defense of the rule of law as the basis of a legal system in which a "secondary rule of recognition is accepted and used for the identification of primary rules of obligation."[3] As a supplement to "primary rules," which are oral, internalized, and generated spontaneously within civil society, "secondary rules" are, according to Hart, written, externalized, and generated through formal juridical procedures overseen by the state. Faced with the question of why anyone ought to obey the rule of law or, more accurately, laws generated in accordance with the rule of law, Hart echoes Klaatu on two counts. First, he shares with Klaatu an understanding of the world familiar to any reader of Thomas Hobbes. Hart bases his defense of the rule of law on a quasi-historical narrative in which a "pre-legal world" gives way to a "legal world" that, while "irksome at times," is "less nasty, less brutish, and less short."[4] Second, he repeats Klaatu's threat of lawless violence as part of a larger strategy to induce (voluntary) adherence to the "legal world." "Sanctions," Hart maintains, "are . . . a *guarantee* that those who would voluntarily obey shall not be sacrificed to those who would not. To obey, without this, would be to risk going to the wall. Given this standing danger, what reason demands is *voluntary* co-operation in a *coercive* system."[5] For both Klaatu and Hart, the effect of the opposition of law and violence is to reduce political questions concerning the content and origin of the law to juridical questions concerning its administration. For both, "publicity" functions not as a prerequisite for public debate and political action, but as a means whereby "human behavior is controlled by general rules publicly announced and judicially applied."[6] What is missing from either account is a sustained meditation on the potentially heteronomous force of the legal system, on the relations among the citizens who authorize the law, the state that enforces it, and the subjects who obey it.

Beginning with Cold War–era consensus historians such as Richard Hofstadter, Daniel Boorstin, and Louis Hartz, many of the histories of the United States provide a sociological basis for this strain of law-based and state-focused liberalism. The United States, consensus historians insist, is and always has been a liberal nation. The hyphen that links the nation to the state thus marks not a division between law and society, but a convergence of the two. At times such histories take on a utopian tone, as in Hartz's characteristic assertion that "given the totalitarian nature of Russian socialism, the hope for a free world surely lies in the power for transcending itself inherent in American liberalism." At other times, they take on a dystopian tone as in Sacvan Bercovitch's quasi-Marxist claim that "the same visionary appeal that makes 'America' into an ideological battleground also restricts the battle to the ground of American ideology."[7] In either case, a consensus exists that, loyalty oaths and red scares aside, the United States is immune to the political and civil struggles that motivate European history. Presented as descriptive, consensus historiography is itself prescriptive, if in no other ways than in its construction of a canon of U.S. culture grounded in the possessive individualism of John Locke, the wily pragmatism of Benjamin Franklin, and the sociological generalizations of Alexis de Tocqueville. The trick of consensus historiography consists less in its construction of such a canon, than in its identification of that canon with the history of the United States. In this sense, Klaatu himself would seem a consensus historian. As evinced by his final glance toward Helen (as well as his paternal relation with her fatherless son), neither Klaatu's personal desires nor his political prescriptions are alien to the intimate and legal structures of national life in the United States. In fact, his interstellar demands are presented as descriptive of his audience's collective history. "This does not mean giving up any

freedom," he claims, "except the freedom to act irresponsibly. Your ancestors knew this when they made laws to govern themselves and hired
policemen to enforce them." That Klaatu's prescriptions sound remarkably
like an internationalist variant of *The Federalist Papers* assures the film's
American audience that they will retain their national autonomy (and global
hegemony) even as they assimilate to an alien authority.

By posing law and violence, autonomy and heteronomy, liberalism and
totalitarianism as the complementary and exhaustive alternatives of contemporary political theory, the axioms of consensus historiography continue
to structure debate within fields as diverse as those of cultural criticism,
moral philosophy, and legal theory.[8] The prominence of this law-based and
state-focused liberalism should not be mistaken for its inevitablity, however. The antithesis of democracy may well be totalitarianism, as Claude
Lefort and others have argued, but the antithesis of liberalism is republicanism.[9] In an essay from 1981, J. G. A. Pocock usefully traces the latter antithesis to two competing paradigms within democratic political philosophy.
Typified by theorists ranging from Hobbes and Locke to Klaatu and Hart,
liberalism tends to divide society into public and private spheres, while
reducing the law-giving citizen to the law-abiding (or law-exploiting) subject of the state. Typified by Machiavelli, Rousseau or, in England, James
Harrington, republicanism tends to view society as unified through public
processes of political self-determination, while understanding the liberal
reduction of citizen to subject as a corruption of a specifically political virtue. "What mattered about a *repubblica*," Pocock writes, "was that its authority should be *pubblica*":

> Nevertheless, to lower the level of citizen participation in a republic could end by
> reconstituting it as a legal monarchy, in which every man's [sic] *libertas*, even his
> *bourgeoisie*, was protected by law which an absolute sovereign administered. . . .
> The juristic presentation of liberty was therefore negative; it distinguished be-
> tween *libertas* and *imperium*, freedom and authority, individuality and sover-
> eignty, private and public.[10]

Liberalism and republicanism share a theoretical commitment to the principle of popular sovereignty, a commitment that presupposes the distinction
between civil and state authority central to any democratic political theory.
They differ, however, in republicanism's greater emphasis on the public
sphere as the space within civil society where the people's sovereignty is
debated, contested, and exercised. In contrast to the liberal subject, the
republican citizen requires not only the negative liberty to withdraw from
legal coercion and state supervision, but also the positive liberty to participate in public processes of collective self-determination.

Though evidence of a varied and dynamic Anglo-American republicanism
has emerged through the work of those cultural and social historians

grouped around Pocock and the idea of the "republican synthesis," the significance and, at times, the very existence of that republicanism remains a source of debate.[11] Rather than further pursuing the vicissitudes of this well-known debate, this chapter will examine two early theoretical attempts to rethink its central terms. Hannah Arendt's *On Revolution* and Jürgen Habermas's *The Structural Transformation of the Public Sphere* both mediate the antinomies of Cold War ideology by focusing, with different emphases, on the history and ideology of republicanism: in Arendt's case, on the disappearance of the classical and revolutionary notions of political action within modern life; in Habermas's case, on the decline of the eighteenth-century conception of the public sphere as a space of critical debate concerning the exercise of civil and state power. Arendt and Habermas thus share an interest in the theoretical and normative relevance of the eighteenth-century democratic revolutions for contemporary political theory and practice. They differ, however, in their respective understandings of the location of political action within modern social relations, a difference that results in (and from) their opposed readings of eighteenth-century sentimental literary culture. Where Arendt figures the "flooding" of sentiments into the literary culture of the French Revolution as threatening to destroy the public sphere as a site of political debate, Habermas figures the same sentimental literary culture as opening the dialectical possibility of democratizing that debate. In charting these similarities and differences, I share with other writers an interest in assessing the relative merits of Arendt and Habermas as theorists of liberalism, republicanism, and modernity. My focus, though, rests on the theoretical significance of this contrast in relation to current revisionist accounts of republicanism and, in the chapters that follow, on the impact that those accounts ought to have on our understanding of the politics of sentimental literary culture in the United States.

Arendt and Classical Republicanism

To speak of liberalism and totalitarianism as anything other than antithetical political systems is to contradict the familiar axioms of Cold War or even post-Cold War democratic political theory in the United States. As one of the earliest and most significant exceptions to this generalization, Hannah Arendt's study of the eighteenth-century democratic revolutions provides an alternative to the either/or opposition of liberalism and totalitarianism. In what follows, I will ultimately agree with the chorus of critics who argue that Arendt's use of classical republicanism as a normative ideal is inadequate to the complexities of modern democracies. Yet I begin with *On Revolution* not simply in order to join that chorus. Rather, I start with it because of the provocative way in which it fails. Arendt's passionate defense of public life provides an incisive critique of modern liberalism's tendency to privatize the category of citizenship, while her willfully anachronistic recourse to classical republicanism as an alternative to liberalism reintroduces that very tendency. Arendt, in other words, argues perhaps more persuasively than any other critic for the type of fully pluralized and participatory public life that liberalism tends to devalue. But she also neglects the structural consequences of that argument when she looks to antiquity in order to draw a hard and fast line between public and private realms. For my purposes, this neglect is valuable because it highlights the theoretical difficulties of thinking through the category of the political in the historical context of a modernity that has politicized virtually all forms of sociality—including those economic, intimate, bodily, and domestic relations that Arendt insists are private. As such, Arendt's study usefully introduces two of the major themes that I will pursue both here and in later chapters: it maps the contested boundaries between and among competing notions of publicity and privacy; it focuses on the location of the body within a revolutionary body politic that distributes power along those lines.

Originally published in 1963, *On Revolution* draws on concepts Arendt had explored five years earlier in *The Human Condition*. In that previous argument, Arendt described and criticized the "rise of the social" as central to what she saw as the sacrifice of the classical ideal of political action within modernity. "The social realm," Arendt writes, "where the life process has established its own domain, has let loose an unnatural growth, so to speak, of the natural; and it is against this growth . . . that the private and intimate, on the one hand, and the political (in the narrow sense of the word), on the other, have proved incapable of defending themselves."[12] As in *On Revolution*, Arendt structures her argument around an opposition between public and private spheres (the title of the chapter in which this passage appears is "The Public and Private Realms"), but that opposition quickly accrues correlaries. Here, the primary opposition of public and private spawns a secondary, if not fully congruent opposition between political and social. Elsewhere, it takes on further significances: polis and *oikos*, polis and *bios*, polis and kinship, speech and violence, freedom and necessity, agonism and consensus, individual and mass, light and darkness.[13] The problem with these oppositional pairs is not that they are irrelevant to modern (or postmodern) life. They are, in fact, the oppositions that have structured much political thought and action in both Arendt's time and our own. Rather, the problem with each of these pairs is that Arendt never fully clarifes the relations that govern their interaction. In this passage, for example, does "nature" provide a stable referent to which "politics" can be opposed? Or does "nature" signify an unstable process (an "unnatural growth") that varies over time? If "nature" has a stable referent, then how does it become "political" in the first place? If it does not, then how can it be opposed to "politics"?

These ambiguities within *The Human Condition* have lead Arendt's critics to question both the historical and the theoretical implications of her championing of classical republicanism. Arendt clearly intends her stylized portrayal of the Greek and Roman polities to provide an antidote to the focus on economic and (to a lesser degree) domestic relations that dominates modern political theory—a focus that unites otherwise antagonistic thinkers such as Locke and Marx.[14] But, Arendt's critics ask, is a classical republicanism reliant on a rigorous depoliticization of those economic (slave-master) and domestic (gender) relations located within the household the only viable alternative to a political theory dedicated, in Arendt's apt phrase, to the "nation-wide administration of housekeeping?"[15] The opposition of polis and *bios*—of political and biological relations—may transform the modern idea of a "body politic" into an oxymoron, just as the distinction between polis and *oikos* logically renders the term "political economy" oxymoronic.[16] But Arendt's endorsement of those oppositions too quickly disregards the myriad and important ways in which the modern democratization of political relations has forced the body (like the household) to become not just a ground, but also a site of political contestation. While appeals to scientific expertise and legal authority (Klaatu and Hart) clearly marginalize politics as a democratic means of mediating social conflict, Arendt's recourse to a strict separation of political and social relations seems both unrealistic and antidemocratic within the context of a modern world that has deeply politicized all forms of sociality—including economics and intimacy. Even writers sympathetic to other aspects of Arendt's project are attentive to the problems inherent in her uncritical equivilence between economic necessity, domestic relations, mass psychology and, ultimately, the body itself. The "Arendtian body," as one of those critics puts it, is a "complex site of displacement, a dumping ground for those elements in Arendt's thought that remain un- or undertheorized."[17]

The complexity of this displacement is perhaps best captured by Arendt's own contradictory claims. "The character of the public realm," Arendt asserts in a passage that portrays the relation between public and private as somewhat permeable, "must change in accordance with the activities admitted into it."[18] But, she adds a few pages later, "there are a great many things which cannot stand the implacable, bright light of the constant presence of others on the public scene."[19] What are those "things" or, more precisely, what permanent characteristics constitute their "thing-ness"? In *On Revolution*, Arendt addresses this question by shifting the historical grounding of her argument. Rather than opposing classical and modern worlds, Arendt contrasts the French and American Revolutions as indicative of two possibilities within modernity. Unlike the French revolutionaries who "failed" because they framed "political" constitutions only to disregard them as overly "formalist" and "legalistic" when faced with the "social" demands of the

newly sovereign People, the American revolutionaries "succeeded" by framing and holding to a "constitution to lay down the boundaries of the new
political realm and to define the rules within it."[20] And though both revolutions theorized questions of political authority by seeking out an "absolute"
or "higher law" to anchor "man-made laws," only the American revolutionaries avoided the "absurdities" of the French Revolution by distinguishing
"clearly and unequivocally between the origin of power, which springs from
below, the 'grass roots' of the people, and the source of law, whose seat is
'above,' in some higher and transcendent region."[21] Like the classical politi-
cians of *The Human Condition*, Arendt's American revolutionaries protect
the sanctity of both the public and the private realms by abstracting political
from social issues. Any anxiety on their part concerning the relation between
politics and society is thus groundless since they, like a collective
Goldilocks, got revolution "just right," while the French revolutionaries al-
ternated and continue to alternate between revolutions that are too hot and
those that are too cold.

This is a glib summary of *On Revolution*, yet it is not unfaithful to the first
of Arendt's three interrelated and, at times, irreconcilable arguments. The
first argument is sociological and follows the consensus historiography in
making the untenable claim that, at the end of the eighteenth century, little
or no social inequality existed in the United States: "The reason for the
success and failure [of the revolutions] was that the predicament of poverty
was absent from the American scene but present everywhere else in the
world."[22] Arendt elsewhere qualifies this "sweeping statement," yet the contours of her argument mirror those of the consensus historians in asserting
that the American Revolution was a middle-class revolution with neither an
upper nor a lower class to create problems.[23] Arendt's second argument con-
tradicts and moves beyond her first by attempting to account for the realities
of slavery and class inequality in the United States. Faced with these historical glitches, Arendt shifts from the field of sociology to that of liberal political science and argues, in another echo of *The Human Condition*, that the
American Revolution succeeded because it sought neither to publicize private concerns nor to provide political solutions to social problems. Unlike
the French revolutionaries who allowed their "ocean-like sentiments"—
their sympathy with the sufferings of the poor—to drown "the foundations
of freedom," the American revolutionaries allowed "no pity to lead them
astray from reason, the men of the American Revolution remained men of
action from beginning to end, from the Declaration of Independence to the
framing of the Constitution."[24] By resisting any sympathetic identification
with the poor, the American revolutionaries maintained the boundary between the public and private realms: their "actions" kept "things" in their
proper places. The boundary thus established cut not only across the revolutionary body politic, but also through the revolutionary body. It divided

public from private realms, and political from social relations just as surely as it divorced reason from pity, rationality from sentimentality, and (in the more corporeal language of the eighteenth century) head from heart.

If Arendt's arguments were limited to these two, they would be difficult to distinguish from other Cold War attempts to rationalize modern state institutions through a reduction of political questions concerning the boundaries of public debate to juridical questions concerning the maintainance of those boundaries. This is the approach taken in the conclusion of that founding document of contemporary neo-conservativism that provides my first epigragh to this chapter, Samuel Huntington's contribution to the Trilateral Commission's "Report on the Governability of Democracies": "We have come to recognize that there are potentially desireable limits to the infinite expansion of political democracy. Democracy will have a longer life if it has a more balanced existence."[25] In contrast to Huntington's report, however, Arendt's third argument complicates her first two by suggesting that this reduction of political questions concerning democratic legitimation to legal questions concerning the "governability" of democracies betrays what she elsewhere calls the "revolutionary spirit." At this point, Arendt again shifts the field of her argument—neither sociology nor political science, but political theory—and introduces the metaphor of the mask or, in Latin, the *persona* into her discussion. In the Roman theater, Arendt explains, the mask or *persona* had a dual effect: "it had to hide, or rather to replace, the actor's own face and countenance, but in a way that would make it possible for the voice to sound through."[26] When this theatrical device entered legal terminology as a metaphor, Arendt continues, it was used to distinguish between the "private individual in Rome" and the "Roman citizen": Without his *persona*, there would be an individual without "rights and duties, perhaps a 'natural man'—that is, a human being or *homo* in the original meaning of the word, indicating someone outside the range of the law and the body politic of the citizens, as for instance a slave—but certainly a politically irrelevant being."[27] Like the "no man's land" that separates the public and private realms in *The Human Condition*, the *persona* has two functions.[28] It prevents the private sphere of social necessity from engulfing the public sphere of political freedom, while also guarding the sanctity of bodily and intimate relations from public scrutiny. This legal and political concept, according to Arendt, is exactly what the French revolutionaries lacked as their "passion for unmasking society" tore away "the mask of the *persona* as well, so that the Reign of Terror eventually spelled the exact opposite of true liberation and true equality; it equalized because it left all inhabitants equally without the protecting mask of a legal personality."[29]

At this point, Arendt's analysis remains within the contours of the liberal consensus. By substituting the Russian for the French Revolution, one could still place it in the lineage of Cold War political theory from 1950s McCarthyism to 1980s Reaganism. What is novel in Arendt's defense of the *persona*, though, is that it not only opposes the expansion of public discourse to include private concerns, but also supports a republican conception of the public sphere as irreducible to the state. While Huntington argues for the regulation of society even at the expense of reducing questions open to public debate to questions concerning the governing strategies of the state, Arendt argues for the maintenance of the public sphere as a space of political action and collective self-determination among what she refers to as the "body politic of the citizens." And though Arendt initially applauds the American revolutionaries for their resistance to social demands, her defense of the public sphere also leads her to polemicize against the American Revolution's subsequent "failure":

> Jefferson's drive for a place of public happiness and John Adams' passion for "emulation" . . . came into conflict with ruthless and fundamentally anti-political desires to be rid of all public cares and duties; to establish a mechanism of government administration through which men could control their rulers and still enjoy the advantages of monarchical government, to be "ruled without their own agency", to have "time not required for the supervision or choice of the public agents, of the enforcement of laws", so that their attention may be exclusively given to their personal interests.[30]

What Arendt fears, in this passage, is the modern reconstitution of what Pocock refers to as a "legal monarchy"—the transfer of Louis XIV's *l'etat, c'est moi* to what Ernst Bloch calls the "ultimate apologist illusion" of the modern nation-state: *l'etat, c'est nous*.[31] It is precisely this transference that both Huntington and Klaatu effect, the first through his attribution of "democracy" to the U.S. state, the second through his reduction of politics to an international legal system enabling the "pursuit of more profitable enterprises."

In her attempt to block this transference, however, Arendt recurs once again to an impermeable distinction between public and private spheres. This recourse indicates, somewhat paradoxically, her affinity with the law-based and state-focused liberalism that she otherwise powerfully attacks. This is the limitation of Arendt's critique. At times, she distinguishes between political and juridical conceptions of citizenship and, following that distinction, suggests the normative possibility of a participatory public sphere that critically regulates the legislative and administrative powers of even an adequately representative state. Aligning Thomas Jefferson's plan for a system of "elementary republics" or "wards" in the United States with the French *sociétés révolutionnaires* and the soviets of the Russian Revolution, Arendt approves of each of these apparently spontaneous manifestations of the "revolutionary spirit," arguing that what was suggested in each instance was "an entirely new form of government, with a new public space for freedom which was constituted and organized during the course of the revolution itself."[32] More often, however, Arendt's unwillingness to make such a distinction leads to a simplistic polemic against any interpenetration—political, juridical, or otherwise—of public and private spheres. "Nothing," she argues in one of her least palatable moments, ". . . could be more obsolete than the attempt to liberate mankind from poverty by political means; nothing could be more futile and dangerous."[33] And it is here that Arendt again adopts the premises of her ostensible antagonists. In 1937, for example, the President's Committee on Administrative Management responded to the economic consequences of the Depression by relying upon a similarly simplistic opposition of political and administrative concerns. "The forward march of American democracy," the committee concludes, "at this point in our history depends more upon effective management than upon any other single factor."[34]

Two damaging consequences follow from this second argument. First, Arendt agrees with the president's committee in abandoning questions of "social liberation" to those nonpolitical "technocrats" who, she claims, "know how to manage people and things in a sphere of life whose principle is necessity."[35] Second, she agrees with the committee in allowing the public sphere that she otherwise vigorously defends to become an increasingly insignificant and isolated subsystem within an increasingly administered society. The extent of this isolation of the public sphere from any social concerns becomes evident in positive form when she applauds Jefferson for drawing an analogy between Congress and heaven in a late letter to John Adams ("Jefferson's notion of true happiness comes out very clearly . . . [when he] concludes one of his letters to Adams as follows: 'May we meet there again, in Congress, with our antient Colleagues, and receive with them the seal of approbation "Well done, good and faithful servants.'"); and in negative form when she faults the Russian soviets for attempting to establish workers' councils in order to manage the factories. ("The fatal mistake of the councils has always been that they themselves did not distinguish clearly between participation in public affairs and administration or management of things in the public interest.")[36] In each case, Arendt's actor-citizens begin to look, at best, like angelic performers with nothing to say of any concern to earthlings like us or, at worst, like classical antagonists involved in a meaningless game of one-upmanship conducted on the Senate floor. In contrast to the theatrical *persona* that, when donned by the actor in Arendt's analysis, permits "the voice to sound through," the legal *persona* works in the same analysis to exclude "voices" that attempt, in any form, to politicize private issues, to speak of economic or domestic relations in the public sphere. The price of Arendt's classical conception of political action is its categorical irrelevance to the most pressing concerns of modern life. While she defends the public sphere, she does so only by making it a space of disembodied performance constituted through its opposition to the unspeakable (and unspeaking) bodies that mark its internal and external limits.

Habermas and Modern Republicanism

Published a year before *On Revolution*, Jürgen Habermas's first book, *The Structural Transformation of the Public Sphere*, both echoes and complicates Arendt's defense of the public sphere. Like Arendt, whose earlier work he cites, Habermas sees the "rise of the social"—the emergence of the category of "society"—as marking the specificity of modern as opposed to classical political forms. Also like Arendt, Habermas seeks to preserve the public sphere, as a space of political debate, from attacks by its conservative and liberal critics, both historical and contemporary. Taking John Stuart Mill's *On Liberty* as an intellectual turning point in the movement away from the revolutionary conceptualization of the public sphere as the site of democratic opinion formation ("the reasonable consensus of publically debating private persons"), Habermas follows Arendt in arguing that, with liberalism, the "political public sphere no longer stood for the idea of a dissolution of power; instead it was to serve its division; public opinion became a mere limit on power":

> The liberalist interpretation of the bourgeois constitutional state was reactionary: it reacted to the power of the idea of a critically debating public's self-determination, initially included in its institutions, as soon as this public was subverted by the propertyless and uneducated masses. Far from having united from the beginning so-called democratic with originally liberal elements (i.e., heterogeneous motives), the bourgeois constitutional state was interpreted under this dual aspect for the first time by liberalism.[37]

On the one hand, nineteenth-century conservativism (Hegel's *Philosophy of Right* serves as Habermas's example) undermines the democratic public sphere by reinterpreting public opinion as merely subjective, and then sublating it into the objective totality of the bureaucratic state.[38] On the other hand, nineteenth-century liberalism (Mill's *On Liberty*) undermines the same public sphere by reinterpreting public opinion as (again) subjectivism and opposing it to a legislative state intended to protect personal liberties and private interests.[39] Arendt and Habermas agree that this shifting conception of the public sphere leads to a strengthening of the administrative *and* legal power of the state. They also agree that this theoretical turn toward the state results from the revolutionary appearance of the "propertyless and uneducated masses" in public.

These points of agreement elide significant differences, however. Where Arendt portrays the social demands of the "masses" as essentially nonpolitical (a symptom of the erosion of political freedom by social necessity), Habermas represents those same demands as evidence of a structural transformation in the position of the public sphere in relation to civil and state authority. "With the rise of a sphere of the social," Habermas writes, " . . . the theme of the modern (as opposed to the ancient) public sphere shifted from the properly political tasks of a citizenry acting in common . . . to the more properly civic tasks of a public engaged in critical debate."[40] Habermas thus differs from Arendt in criticizing her idealization of classical republicanism, as well as her endorsement of the binarism between political and social relations typical of both classical and liberal political theory. In an essay from 1976, Habermas makes this difference clear. Though he agrees with the normative value of Arendt's distinction between conceptions of sovereignty as violence and as speech, Habermas objects to her stylized image of the classical polis as purely political and nonviolent: "Arendt pays the price of screening all the strategic elements out of politics as 'violence,' severing politics from its ties to the economic and social environment in which it is embedded via the administrative system, and being incapable of coming to grips with the appearances of structural violence."[41] Where Arendt insists on the structural autonomy of political and social life (an insistence that preserves the public sphere only as an increasingly isolated space accessible to those few avatars of classical political virtue), Habermas locates the public sphere as a point of mediation between state and society. As a metaphor, the term "public sphere" stands in for those diverse civic institutions in and through which political debate critically regulates the powers of the state (the "administrative system") on the one hand, and civil society (the "economic and social environment") on the other. Viewed from this perspective, Habermas's subsequent writings further pursue the project of modernity by calling for a democratization of the institutions of public opinion formation. Using the shorthand of those writings, the public sphere institutions that Habermas endorses mobilize the communicative value of "solidarity" endemic to the "lifeworld" against the systemic steering mechanisms of "power" (the administrative state) and "money" (the capitalist economy).[42]

When translated into the language of the American Revolution, these contrasts between Arendt and Habermas become even starker. Like the Federalists of the 1790s, Arendt reacts to the popular social movements of her day by driving a wedge between (classical and American) republicanism and (modern and French) democracy. "The republican form of government," she insists, "recommended itself to the pre-revolutionary political thinkers not because of its egalitarian character (the confusion and confused equation with democratic government dates from the nineteenth century) but because of its promise of great durability."[43] Like the Federalist's opponents (the Anti-Federalists and, later, the Democratic and Republican Societies), Habermas resists this antinomy between republicanism and democracy by deferring to the synthesizing force of public opinion. This synthesis could be understood as both republican and democratic because public opinion ideally recognized only those opinions authorized by critical debate among the people at large. "The *publicum*," Habermas explains, "developed into the public, the *subjectum* into the [reasoning] subject, the receiver of regulations from above into the ruling authorities adversary."[44] Again, the crux of this transformation lies in its distinction between civil and state authority. Where Arendt secures the impermeable boundaries of the public sphere by placing those "activities connected with sheer survival" under the supervision of the state, Habermas understands those same boundaries as permeable to social demands originating within either economic or domestic relations.[45] This reformulation of the binarisms common to both classical republicanism and modern liberalism draws on Hegel's division of society into three spheres: the family (the "intimate sphere" in Habermas and Arendt), civil society, and the state.[46] But it also modifies Hegel by charting (and endorsing) the historical development of the public sphere from an unofficial network of cultural institutions (coffee houses, literary salons, an occasional mollyhouse) into an official site of public-opinion formation and democratic legitimation (parliaments, congresses): "The public sphere in the political realm evolved from the public sphere in the world of letters; through the vehicle of public opinion it put the state in touch with the needs of society."[47]

Immanuel Kant's *Critique of Practical Reason* provides one well-known instance of this republican insistence that it is the public sphere (rather than the state) that is, in Hegel's words, "inherently rational."[48] Hegel's resistance to this republican "principle of publicness" emerges when he discusses the relations among philosophy, rationality, and the state.[49] The "owl of Minerva" flies at "dusk" because philosophy, according to Hegel, is not "pursued in private like an art, but has an existence in the open, in contact with the public, and especially, or even only, in the service of the state."[50] As I will argue in chapters 4 and 5, Kant's critical philosophy follows a different flight plan. His search for a means of securing a form of political power that is both rational (universal) and practical (nonheteronomous) leads him away from the imposition of a legalistic "categorical imperative." Rather, Kant pursues a republican line of argumentation by positing a contingent accord between the objective rationality of just legislation and the subjective autonomy of moral judgment. As Kant's later writings emphasize, the resulting antinomy between political power ("politics") and moral autonomy ("right") can be resolved only through critical debate conducted in public. "In this regard," Kant writes, "I propose another affirmative and transcendental principle of public law, the formula of which is: 'All maxims which *stand in need* of publicity in order not to fail their end, agree with politics and right combined.'"[51] One typical (and Hegelian) reading of this maxim locates Kant alongside Klaatu and Hart in a liberal tradition focused on the rational authority of the rule of law (only later to critique this legal formalism as lacking historical and ethical specificity). Yet Kant's own emphasis on "publicity" as the synthesis of "politics" and "right" places him in a republican tradition that grounds political and moral authority not in the law, but in public debate concerning what the law ought to be. And though Kant (like Arendt) vacillates over the question of who and what constitutes the boundaries of the public sphere (at times, only philosophers seem involved), his repeated references to the "human heart" suggest an at least potentially inclusive, if humanist, answer.[52]

Kant, of course, is not alone in grounding political and moral authority in critical public debate itself grounded in the "heart." His metaphor becomes convincing (and legible) only in the context of an already existing sentimental culture that depended for its political impact upon the same subordination of the (potentially) heteronomous power of the law to "heartfelt" claims mediated by public debate. For Arendt, this sentimental culture provides further evidence of the modern collapse of public and private spheres. The novel, she insists, is the "only entirely social art form" because it publicizes those domestic (economic and intimate) concerns better left within the walls of the household.[53] Habermas, in contrast, locates the sentimental novel as the "authentic literary achievement" of the eighteenth century, not because it conflates public and private spheres (nor because it enshrines a personal life void of political significance), but because it constructs a personality that is generated in private *and* oriented toward the public:

> Subjectivity, as the innermost core of the private, was always already oriented to an audience (*Publikum*). . . . Thus, the directly or indirectly audience-oriented subjectivity of the letter exchange or diary explained the origin of the typical genre and authentic literary achievement of that century: the domestic novel, the psychological description in autobiographical form. Its early and for a long time most influential example, *Pamela* (1740), arose directly from Richardson's intention to produce one of the popular collections of model letters.[54]

The contradictions within this sentimental ideal of literary authenticity are well known. As Henry Fielding revealed when he rewrote *Pamela* as *Shamela*, a virtuous serving-girl's unconscious sensations (Pamela) could easily be "shammed" by a designing and upwardly mobile literary strategist (Shamela). Indeed, the "audience-oriented subjectivity" of the early novel makes the two characters virtually indistinguishable, since both agree that the publication of privatized bodily and intimate relations transforms those relations into strategic sites of class and gender warfare. Oscar Wilde makes a similar point at the end of the nineteenth century in *The Importance of*

Being Earnest. Asked by Algernon if he may read her diary, Cecily responds by highlighting the self-interest that informs her self-disclosures: "Oh, no. You see, it is simply a very young girl's record of her own thoughts and impressions, and consequently meant for publication. When it appears in volume form I hope you will order a copy."[55]

Still, Habermas's argument remains important. The distinctive feature of the eighteenth-century culture of sentiment undoubtedly lay in its repeated descriptions of intimate bodily sensations: tears and fainting spells, blushes and disgust. "Shammed" or not, such descriptions structured the politics of sentimentalism by distinguishing between personal and political relations, while also linking the two through acts of publication. Whether strategic or expressive, the volumes dedicated to Shamela, Cecily, and others created a public trained to interpret the political significance of the most intimate details of everyday life. And though Habermas sometimes writes as if the forms of intimacy generated within the eighteenth-century bourgeois home provided an unproblematic point of origin for Pamela-like subjects (a tendency indicated by the ease with which he equates "psychology" with "domesticity" in the passage above), he more often attends to the ideological implications of such claims. "Book clubs, reading circles, and subscription libraries," he writes, " . . . formed the public sphere of a rational-critical debate in the world of letters within which the subjectivity originating in the interiority of the conjugal family, by communicating with itself, attained clarity about itself."[56] Addressed to an audience so general that it was literally unrealizable (or realizable only literarily), this process of "clarification" was Janus-faced. It enabled a false universalization of historically specific norms ("heartfelt" or not) by equating their publication with their inherent rationality (their "humanity"). But it also encouraged public debate concerning those norms. And while the literary character of that debate could limit its participants to those trained in the arts of abstract argumentation, it also held out the possibility of publicizing otherwise privatized forms of social domination. The continuing relevance of the latter possibility is evinced by the publicist orientation of post-revolutionary social movements, ranging from the "moral suasion" typical to antebellum reformers to the best-known slogans of contemporary feminist and queer activism ("The personal is political" and "Silence = Death").[57] Despite their ideological diversity, such movements all originate as acts of structural transgression, as attempts to politicize social concerns that both classical republicanism and modern liberalism would prefer to keep off the public stage.

This last point needs to be clarified. Habermas's more recent writings demonstrate his affinity with new social movements like the German Greens. They are, Habermas writes, "the only ones to demand that the inner dynamic of subsystems regulated by money and power be broken, or at least checked, by forms of organization that are closer to the base and self-administered."[58] Yet it would be difficult (to say the least) to imagine either Richardson or Kant as environmental, feminist, or queer activists. In later chapters, I will describe this discrepency between the theory and practice of eighteenth-century republicanism as producing a gap between the structure and ideology of sentimentalism—between its structural commitment to the publication of bodily and intimate experience on the one hand, and its ideological commitment to the codification of that experience as private on the other. In response to the same discrepency, Habermas makes two related arguments. The first exploits a theoretically useful tension between the abstract ideal of the public sphere as a space of unfettered debate and the historical reality of its constitution through any number of social constraints (including gender, class, race, and education): "However exclusive the public might be in any given instance, it could never enclose itself entirely and become consolidated as a clique; for it always understood and found itself immersed within a more inclusive public of all private people. . . . The issues discussed became 'general' not merely in their significance, but also in their accessibility: everyone had to *be able* to participate."[59] The boundaries of the eighteenth-century public sphere were historically exclusive, even at their most democratic. But an inability either to justify or to theorize those exclusions generated a dialectic between theory and practice that eventually destabilized those same boundaries. "The public of the first generations," Habermas writes, "even when it constituted itself as a specific circle of persons, was conscious of being part of a larger public."[60] The "liberalist interpretation" of the public sphere could stall this dialectic by channeling the needs and desires of a citizenry through the legislative and administrative institutions of the state. Yet the same liberalism would remain haunted by its democratic origins as long as that state sought its legitimacy through reference to the people at large.

Habermas's second argument is more complicated and attempts to explain the historical basis of this theoretical tension. In this argument, Habermas locates the discrepancy between formal inclusiveness and practical exclusiveness as a gap between two conceptions of the public sphere: the public sphere in the world of letters (the *literarische Offentlichkeit*), and the public sphere in the political realm (the *politische Offentlichkeit*). On the one hand, the public sphere could be thought of as a space of open debate among equals, a space where "privatized individuals in their capacity as human beings communicated through critical debate in the world of letters, about experiences of their subjectivity."[61] For Habermas, this first literary model of the public sphere provides an ideal of communicative rationality that is both democratic and normative. In theory, its idealization of a common humanity originally generated within the bourgeois home could lead to a progressive elimination of privatized (or naturalized) relations of domination.[62] Following this path, democratic republicans never tired of pointing out that any form of domination corrupts citizens' political virtue by under-mining their ability to participate as equals in public debate. In theory, then, the same ideal also led to a notion of political freedom in the public sphere as inseparable from social equality in the private sphere. Thomas Paine's critique in "Agrarian Justice" of the monopolistic tendencies of industrial capitalism, for example, draws on this first model of the public sphere. Re-publicanism, Paine argues, necessitates an egalitarian distribution of prop-erty and capital since an inegalitarian distribution, by "breaking the spirit of the people," transforms the republican citizen into a subject of the state, one who "has nothing to do with the laws but to obey them."[63] Mary Wollstone-craft's argument in *A Vindication of the Rights of Woman* for egalitarian divorce laws and women's citizenship similarly relies on this first model of the public sphere. When women are deprived of "civil and political rights," the resulting inequality threatens the virtue of all citizens: "They may be convenient slaves, but slavery will have a constant effect, degrading the mas-ter and the abject alike."[64]

On the other hand, the public sphere could also be conceived of as a space of debate limited to those (property-owning, white, male) individuals capa-ble of exercising control over their private households, a space in which "private people in their capacity as owners of commodities communicated through rational-critical debate, concerning the regulation of their private sphere."[65] For Habermas, this second political model of the public sphere is ideological since it maintains a false identification of "bourgeois" and *homme*.[66] In practice, it leads to a privatization of relations of domination since domination or, more specifically in this case, economic, gender, and racial domination provides the unacknowledged infrastructure for participa-tion in public debate. In practice, then, it also leads to an Arendtian notion of political freedom in the public realm as inseparable from (or irrelevant to) social inequality in economic and domestic relations. As Habermas notes, this encoding of both the capitalist market and the patriarchal family as pri-vate anchored the bourgeois understanding of the public sphere: "The fully developed bourgeois public sphere was based on the fictitious identity of the two roles assumed by the privatized individuals who came together to form a public: the role of property owners and the role of human beings pure and simple."[67] In his *Report on Manufactures*, Alexander Hamilton follows this second model of the public sphere when he rebuts Jeffersonian and agrarian republican arguments that large-scale manufactures corrupt citizens' politi-cal virtue. Dismissing such arguments for an independent and equal citi-zenry, Hamilton claims that republicanism depends upon capitalist manu-facture since only the latter produces and utilizes the resources "favorable to national independence and safety."[68] As historians Linda Kerber and Mor-ton Horowitz point out, Federalist jurists' and theologians' attacks on egali-tarian divorce and marital property laws during the 1790s also support this second conception of the public sphere.[69] Though both Paine and Hamilton are republican theorists, Paine's republicanism logically requires the expansion of the democratic principles of liberty and equality to economic and domestic relations, while Hamilton's republicanism relies on a state-sanctioned privatization of those same relations.

If Habermas's two arguments seem familiar, there is good reason for it. A tension between normative theory and historical practice has haunted republican political discourse at least since Marx identified communism as its greatest "specter" in 1848.[70] Like the early Marx, Habermas responds to this tension by reinscribing it as a dialectic between democratic theory and bourgeois practice, between the citizen understood as "one human being among others," and the citizen understood as "an owner of goods and persons."[71] This tension is dialectical because, Habermas suggests, it enables its own transcendence: "On the basis of the continuing domination of one class over another, the dominant class nevertheless developed political institutions which credibly embodied as their objective meaning the idea of their own abolition, . . . the idea of the dissolution of domination into that easygoing constraint that prevailed on no other ground than the compelling insight of a public opinion."[72] Habermas consequently interprets later working-class movements like Chartism as evidence of an emerging "plebeian public sphere" that nevertheless remained "oriented toward the intentions of the bourgeois public sphere," while his more recent writings extend this argument to social movements such as feminism: "Bourgeois publicness . . . is articulated in discourses that provide areas of common ground not only for the labor movement but also for the excluded other, that is, the feminist movement."[73] In reference to similar movements in the United States, historians Sean Wilentz and Christine Stansell have charted the republican basis of democratic claims to economic (and gender) equality through the mid–nineteenth century.[74] For these reasons, Habermas maintains the literary model of the public sphere as a normative ideal with which to critique both the eighteenth-century bourgeois (and masculinist) public sphere and its later transformations. For the same reasons, writers like Pocock continue to emphasize the persistence of republicanism in their attempts to subvert the dominance of consensus historiography in the United States. "What went on in the eighteenth century," Pocock writes, "was not a unidimensional transformation of thought in favor of the acceptance of 'liberal' or 'market' man, but a bitter, conscious and ambivalent dialogue."[75]

Also like the early Marx, however, Habermas tends at times to resolve the dialectic between democratic theory and bourgeois practice in a narrative that becomes alternatively utopian and dystopian. Through a contrast with the eighteenth-century literary public sphere, much of the second half of Habermas's book argues that capitalism's restructuring of public-sphere institutions like the print media combined with the expansion of the administrative state to produce forms of publicity that were "manipulative" rather than "critical." Like his Frankfurt School mentors, Habermas is thus left with a narrative of decline as his eighteenth-century ideal devolves into the dystopian reality of the nineteenth and twentieth centuries:

> Originally publicity guaranteed the connection between rational-critical public debate and the legislative foundation of domination, including the critical supervision of its exercise. Now it makes possible the peculiar ambivalence of a domination exercised through the domination of a nonpublic opinion: it serves the manipulation *of* the public as much as legitimation *before* it. Critical publicity is supplanted by manipulative publicity.[76]

This narrative is historically plausible, as anyone familiar with the market-driven and uncritical utopianism surrounding new public-sphere technologies like the Internet and MTV knows. But it also leads Habermas to a theoretical impasse. On the one hand, he leaves behind his earlier portrayal of eighteenth-century public sphere as ambiguous—both democratic and bourgeois, normative and ideological—by writing as if the institutions of eighteenth-century publication forced their participants to practice what they theorized; on the other hand, he writes as if the nineteenth- and twentieth-century transformations of the public sphere installed structures solely designed to legitimate bourgeois hegemony. Having greatly simplified his earlier arguments, Habermas concludes by advancing an undifferentiated eighteenth-century model of the public sphere as both theoretically and historically normative. Like Arendt's stylized image of the classical polis, the latter then provides an ideal point of contrast in comparison with which the later manifestations of the public sphere become purely ideological.

Critics of Habermas have attacked *The Structural Transformation of the Public Sphere* on both of these points. Writing of the French Revolution, Joan Landes suggests that Habermas's representation of the eighteenth-century public sphere as normative is itself ideological in its inattention to gender as the dominant category through which the boundaries of the revolutionary public sphere were policed.[77] In the United States, this argument gains support from the axiom with which Paine himself begins "Agrarian Justice": "It is wrong to say God made *rich* and *poor*; He made only *male* and *female*."[78] Mary Ryan expands on this criticism in an American context when she argues that the second half of Habermas's book overlooks the revolutionary appearance of women and other marginalized groups in public during the nineteenth century.[79] Beyond an historicist revision of *The Structural Transformation*, both Landes and Ryan extend their insights to a political critique of Habermas's theorization of modern republicanism. Relying on the totalizing argument that "the bourgeois public is essentially, not contingently, masculinist," Landes portrays her revision as unmasking Habermas's normative claims as essentially ideological.[80] Ryan, in partial contrast, portrays her own revision not as a demystification of Habermas's norms, but as a supplementary challenge to his history. The latter approach has been pursued further by political theorists such as Nancy Fraser and Seyla Benhabib. While both portray the "official public sphere" as, in Fraser's words, "the prime institutional site for the construction of the consent that defines the new, hegemonic mode of domination," they also reject this "Gramscian moral" in favor of an immanent critique.[81] "A critical model of public space," Benhabib concludes, "is necessary to enable us to draw a line between juridification . . . on the one hand, and making public, in the sense of making accessible to debate, reflection, action, and moral-political transformation, on the other. To make issues of common concern public in the second sense means making them accessible to discursive will formation."[82]

A full accounting of these debates among Habermas's critics is beyond either the reach or the requirements of my argument. What remains important within those debates, however, is that their participants share with Habermas a common debt to the language of republicanism. When Benhabib asserts that "the struggle to make something public is a struggle for justice," she is repeating one of the truisms of eighteenth-century republicanism.[83] When Fraser adds that "an adequate conception of the public sphere requires not merely the bracketing, but rather the elimination, of social inequality," she follows the radical forms of republicanism typical of writers like Paine and Wollstonecraft.[84] For my purposes, then, the importance of Habermas's reconstruction of the modern public sphere is that it raises a set of questions that Arendt's analysis forecloses—questions concerning the relations between and among competing conceptions of public and private life. In the chapters that follow, the answers to these questions will draw on oppositions familiar from Arendt: corporeality and nationality in George Washington's "Farewell Address"; sensation and sentiment in Hannah Foster's *The Coquette*; rationality and sentimentality in Charles Brockden Brown's *Clara Howard*; sentimentality and sexuality in Harriet Jacobs's *Incidents in the Life of a Slave Girl*. In this sense, all of the writers I discuss share with Arendt a will to secure the boundaries of the public sphere by determining the proper content of public and private life. But they also differ from her when they allow the pressure of democratic claims to political inclusion central to modern republicanism to blur the boundaries of public debate. As I have tried to suggest through the contrast of Paine and Hamilton, modern republicanism in no way ensures a democratic politics (in fact, republicanisms operate and have operated in many ways to preclude such a politics). But the democratic basis of modern republicanism does provide two guiding assumptions that will inform my readings in the following chapters: that modern liberalism reacts against the democratic potential of eighteenth-century republicanism by representing and administrating a depoliticized citizenry through an increasingly depoliticized state; that the effects of this depoliticization are felt not only across the body politic, but also within the newly politicized bodies of its citizens.

Coda: Dystopian Liberalism

The summary of republicanism that this chapter offers is tendentious, as many readers will have recognized. In reviewing the writings of Arendt and Habermas along with selected criticisms of those writings, I have overlooked a more troubling and thorough critique most frequently associated with those postmodern theorists Habermas too quickly refers to as "young conservatives." While this label covers writers ranging from deconstructive cultural critics grouped around the figure of Jacques Derrida to social-systems analysts like Nicholas Luhman, it is generally reserved for Habermas's most formidable antagonist: Michel Foucault.[85] Like both Arendt and Habermas, Foucault understands the project of modernity as transforming the political significance of the body itself. In contrast, however, Foucault views the modern body neither as best left outside of the public realm altogether (Arendt), nor as the material site of an audience-oriented subjectivity engaged in public debate (Habermas). Rather, the modern "intensification of the body" positions it as a target of discipline and control—an "object of knowledge and an element in relations of power." The body thus becomes, in Foucault's words, the transfer point between an "anatomo-politics of the body" on the one hand, and a "bio-politics of the population" on the other: "The old power of death that symbolized sovereign power was now carefully supplanted by the administration of bodies and the calculated management of life."[86] From this perspective, the focus on the expressive and liberatory potential of the body within eighteenth-century sensationalist discourses like sentimentalism becomes a cultural means to the political end of greater normalization. If the public institutions that mediate the modern discourses of the body all require unequal and nonconsensual forms of exchange (confession, medical science, demographics), then the completion of the project of modernity involves little more (and nothing less) than the completion of this process of normalization. The "continual and clamorous legislative activity" of modern political revolutions, Foucault concludes, "were the forms that made an essentially normalizing power acceptable."[87]

Foucault's own position on the question of modernity is more complicated than this passage implies, and I will return to these complications in my final chapter. For now, I allude to the less nuanced version of Foucault's argument because it does capture one critique of republicanism hardwired into the popular imagination. Skeptical of the utopian liberalism of films like

The Day the Earth Stood Still, this critique responds by reducing political subjectivity to little more than a reflex of the state apparatus, while limiting social activism to legal argumentation. While the latter of these two tendencies can be seen in the courtroom heroics of so many recent films (*Philadelphia* and *The People vs. Larry Flint* are two good examples), the former is best captured in the film that I want to turn to in this coda: Paul Verhoeven's *RoboCop* (1987).

RoboCop is set in the Detroit of the near future and opens in the boardroom of "Omni Consumer Products" (OCP), a corporation that specializes in restructuring and profiting from previously "nonprofitable sectors of the economy"—hospitals, space exploration, police, prisons. Before deploying the million workers required to begin its next project (the contruction of the utopian metropolis of the future, "Delta City"), OCP must first eliminate the "criminal element" of "Old Detroit." With this goal in mind, the head of the "Security Concepts" division of OCP (Dick Jones), introduces his version of Klaatu's Gort: "a twenty-four-hour-a-day police officer, a cop . . . with superior firepower and the reflexes to use it." Designed for "urban pacificiation," "Enforcement Droid 209" promises to rid Old Detroit of crime in forty days. In a test run in the boardroom, E. D. 209 guns down one of OCP's executives who quickly dies, stretched over the scale model of Delta City. Disappointed and concerned with lost profits, the chairman of OCP turns to a younger executive's plan for a cyborg that combines the technology of E. D. 209 with the street smarts of a human police officer. OCP's search for the cyborg's organic component ends when a cop named Murphy is killed by Clarence Boddicker, the coke-snorting leader of the "criminal element" of Old Detroit. Murphy dies on the operating table of an OCP hospital. Deprived of his memory, but equipped with an LED readout and a very large gun, he is resurrected as RoboCop.

When juxtaposed to *The Day the Earth Stood Still*, *RoboCop* clearly can be read as a critical response to the triumphant liberalism of the earlier film. *The Day the Earth Stood Still* envisions a utopian future based on three premises: the rule of law as a means of ensuring social justice; a state that enables the "pursuit of more profitable enterprises"; a police force of robots that flawlessly identify and eliminate illegal acts. *RoboCop*, in contrast, remains skeptical on each of these three counts. First, the rule of law in Old Detroit functions not to provide justice, but to enable OCP's privatization of public concerns. In his opening speech, the Chairman of OCP highlights this failure by suggesting that E. D. 209 will "give something back" to a community already deprived of essential public services due to "shifts in the tax structure ideal for corporate growth." Second, the "pursuit of more profitable enterprises" in Old Detroit is a project common to the "law-abiding" and "criminal" populations. "No better way to make money than free enterprise," shouts one of the members of Boddicker's gang in a statement that mirrors OCP's slogan, "Good business is where you find it." This ideological similarity is also played out in the plot of *RoboCop*, much of which revolves around the discovery of a conspiracy between Dick Jones's "crime management program" and Boddicker's plans for greater profits in Delta City. The new metropolis will provide, in Jones's seductive phrase, "virgin territory for the man who knows how to open up new markets." Third, Gort's postmodern progeny—E. D. 209—spectacularly fails to accomplish its objectives. In contrast to mere machines like Gort and E. D. 209, cyborgs like RoboCop are able to draw on what the movie refers to as a "lifetime of on-the-street law-enforcement programming." This distinction is again played out in narrative terms, as RoboCop's climactic arrest and shooting of Dick Jones coincides with the reconstruction of his human identity. With the help of Murphy's female ex-partner Ann Louis (*RoboCop*'s more muscular version of Helen Benson), RoboCop escapes a police chase engineered by Jones, rediscovers his human identity and, in the final scene, refers to himself as "Murphy."

Each of these three points marks *RoboCop* as a critique of the earlier film. The first two highlight the corruption of the rule of law by the state's concessions to corporate capitalism, while the third holds out the idea of the human as a source of moral resistance to corporate control. By the end of the film, however, the first two seem insignificant since RoboCop ultimately secures the alliances among OCP, the state, and the police. In his final encounter with Dick Jones, RoboCop circumvents his fourth, secret directive that "any attempt to arrest a senior officer of OCP will result in shutdown," yet he remains programmed to "serve the public trust, uphold the law, protect the innocent." Like Gort and E. D. 209, RoboCop functions not to question, but to enforce the law—no matter how that law is generated or authorized. "Jones runs OCP," Boddicker reminds RoboCop, "OCP runs the cops. You're a cop." Again, this limitation is played out narratively. By killing Jones and Boddicker, RoboCop eliminates the enabling premise of Boddicker's syllogism. Yet the same action locates corporate corruption in the film's two Dicks (a pun Verhoeven seems fond of), thus personalizing what had been a broadly structural critique of OCP's takeover of Old Detroit. RoboCop's fourth directive not to arrest a senior officer of OCP not only remains in place, but also becomes irrelevant due to the elimination of OCP's one corrupting element. Having focused on a single instance of conspiracy between OCP and the state through RoboCop, the film thus concludes by rendering moot its initial, more general questioning of the politics of corporate capitalism. As Fred Glass argues, the final scene marks the reintegration of RoboCop into the corporate family.[88] When asked by the grateful and suddenly benevolent chairman of OCP, "What's your name, son?" RoboCop responds "Murphy." Granted recognition as "human" by the corporate patriarchy, RoboCop will enable Delta City to proceed on schedule. It seems inevitable that he will be instrumental in protecting OCP's now legal *and* depoliticized colonization of Old Detroit.

At times, the distinction between robot and human that marks *RoboCop's* third critical difference from *The Day the Earth Stood Still* seems equally insignificant. The technological differences which separate E. D. 209 from RoboCop are less than insuperable and, in one battle between the two, even those differences are reduced to RoboCop's greater aptitude in walking down stairs. More often, however, *RoboCop* hinges on the distinction between robot and cyborg. Where Gort is a flawless judge of the distinction between legality and illegality, E. D. 209 seems qualitatively incapable of rendering such judgments. In contrast, RoboCop is able to act judiciously, though only after he experiences a dream of his past life as Murphy. This experience undermines the premise of RoboCop's corporate creator: "He doesn't have a name. He has a program. He's product." And it eventually leads RoboCop to reconstruct his human identity by accessing the police files of Murphy and visiting his suburban home. As perhaps the only technophobic scene in an otherwise technophilic movie, this visit is worth looking at more closely. Guided through the house by the pre-recorded sales pitch of a real estate agent displayed on computer terminals in each room, Robo-Cop experiences a series of flashbacks to memories of Murphy's wife and children whom, as he later tells Ann Louis, he could "feel" but not "remember": his son asking him to spin his gun like the TV cop "T. J. Lazer"; his wife and son carving Halloween pumpkins; his wife greeting him at their bedroom door. The pathos of this scene stems not from the utter banality of Murphy's family life (what Habermas calls the "quiet bliss of homeyness" typical of bourgeois privacy), but from his impotence when acting as "Murphy" to prevent its destruction.[89] Apparently angered by the computerized sales pitch, RoboCop smashes one of the computer terminals on the way out of the house. Both home and family, it would seem, are or should be free from the juridical-corporate alliances that RoboCop embodies and enables. It would be difficult to imagine either Gort or E. D. 209 acting similarly.[90]

As the film's only representation of what Habermas and Arendt refer to as the intimate sphere, Murphy's now-vacant suburban home thus motivates RoboCop's pursuit of the illegal enterprises common to Jones and Boddicker, to OCP and organized crime. Murphy's intimate life, in other words, generates and shelters a human subjectivity resistant to OCP's ideological control. If this is the difference between *The Day the Earth Stood Still* and *RoboCop*, however, then it is again a slight difference. Though motivated by apparently spontaneous "feelings" which the audience has already "remembered" for him, RoboCop's own "memories" of Murphy's life are themselves accessible only through two sources: the police computer and the cop show that his son associated with him. When RoboCop finally identifies his human component as "Murphy," he is actually quoting from the police data bank. When his female partner makes the same connection, she does so because RoboCop spins his gun like "T. J. Lazer." While the "feelings" associated with these "human" memories motivate RoboCop's resistance to OCP's control, the memories themselves are both legally authorized and mass-mediated. For this reason, *RoboCop* is less a critique of *The Day the Earth Stood Still* than it is a postmodern parable concerning the construction of human subjectivity within the liberal utopia of the earlier film. Murphy's family life provides RoboCop with what Habermas refers to as "a saturated and free interiority" that the film itself represents as a form of ideological programming.[91] Like Gort, RoboCop is the ideal instrument of the liberal rule of law; as "Murphy," he is also its ideal subject—"Part Man, Part Machine, All Cop." While the citizens of the 1950s nuclear public sphere could at least choose between liberalism and "obliteration," those making that decision in the 1980s are offered no choice. RoboCop's only advice to the public is directed to schoolchildren: "Stay out of trouble." When Ann Louis is gunned down and pleads for help at the end of the film, the defeated tone of RoboCop's reply does little to undermine its content: "They'll fix you. They fix everything."

Ultimately, then, there is a critical difference between the two films, as there is between Habermas and many of his postmodern critics.[92] Like *The Day the Earth Stood Still*, *RoboCop* uses the threat of lawless violence to induce adherence to the existing law. In contrast, though, *RoboCop*'s violence is not centralized in a future threat of total "obliteration," but is diffused throughout a society already pervaded by the "criminal element." Like the repetitious reports of random violence on the nightly news, this diffusion further disables any collective resistance to the rule of law by constructing a fully paranoid and depoliticized subject rendered loyal to the state. This loyalty is assured through the political strategies of what Michael Taussig calls the "nervous system."[93] Taussig's Hegelian metaphor is altogether appropriate in this context. For Hegel, the state operates as the central nervous system of the national body politic; it is the "mind" that provides the "universal end and known objective" for the administration of civil and familial relations.[94] Taussig both adopts and inverts Hegel's metaphor: the state ensures its centrality by maintaining a sense of nervousness that turns it into the only reliable source of national security. As I have suggested in my discussion of Arendt and Habermas, liberal political theory from Klaatu to RoboCop or, more accurately, from *The Federalist Papers* to the National Security State relies on this reduction of the political citizen to the legal subject. As I have also suggested, republican political theory provides a counterpoint to that reduction by distinguishing between the public sphere and the state on the one hand, and the political citizen and the depoliticized subject on the other. The problem with *RoboCop*'s postmodern parable is not that it maps the myriad paths along which the triumphant liberalism of *The Day the Earth Stood Still* can turn into a strategy of domination—a cartography already familiar from Arendt and Habermas. The problem is that it pursues that critique with neither the earlier film's utopian justification, nor any alternative vision of potential resistance to the dystopian liberalism that it ultimately reinscribes.

3

The Patriot's Two Bodies: Nationality and Corporeality in George Washington's "Farewell Address"

> In a word, I want an *American* character, that the powers of Europe may be convinced we act for *ourselves* and not for *others*; this in my judgment, is the only way to be respected abroad and happy at home and not by becoming the partizans of Great Britain or France, create dissensions, disturb the public tranquillity, and destroy, perhaps for ever the cement wch. binds the Union.
>
> *(George Washington to Patrick Henry, October 9, 1795)[1]*

> Consecrated by the ashes of Washington, none would be so barbarous as to lay a hostile hand upon an edifice which, while it enclosed the representatives of the people, held, at the same time, the sepulchre of him whom all civilized men united to honor. Long as . . . the capitol would stand . . . it would stand longer for being known to all the world as the tomb of Washington.
>
> *(Debates in Congress, 1832)[2]*

Representing Washington

Anticipating retirement after his first term as president, George Washington asked his friend and confidante James Madison to draft a farewell address in 1792. That draft runs just over three pages and focuses on publicizing Washington's commitment to the national union and the Constitution of 1787, his decision not to run for a second term, and his solicitude for his "fellow-citizens."[3] After a second term that, according to the final version of the "Address," he had been impelled to accept after "mature reflection on the then perplexed and critical posture of our affairs with foreign nations," Washington again sought a close advisor to draft a farewell address in 1796.[4] This time the advisor was not Madison who subsequently had alienated his

Federalist supporters by aligning himself with Thomas Jefferson, Philip Freneau, and the cause of democratic republicanism in both France and the United States. Instead, Washington chose Alexander Hamilton, the man whom the emerging Republican Party held primarily responsible for the corruption of the nation or, as Jefferson put it at the time, the man who was "so bewitched and perverted by the British example, as to be under thorough conviction that corruption was essential to the government of the nation."[5] When he solicited Hamilton's assistance, Washington sent him a series of detailed instructions along with a copy of Madison's earlier draft. The seventeen pages Hamilton added (and Washington revised) set forth a recognizably Federalist program by advocating political isolation from both republican France and monarchical Britain, while also linking the earlier draft's emphasis on union to the state's sanctioning of a nationalized market economy. Published in the Claypoole's *Daily American Advertiser* on September 9, 1796, the final version of the "Address" is generally seen as synthesizing the political views of Washington, Madison, and Hamilton.

As seems inevitable with the texts of those North American Creoles now referred to as the "founding fathers," there remains a good deal of debate over who dominates this synthesis. Through a retrospective identification of a founder's authorial intent with the general will of the nation, such controversy quickly becomes politically invested. This intertwining of hermeneutics and politics may be most familiar to late twentieth-century readers from the neo-conservative use of the concept of "Framers' intent," but it is neither new nor invariably conservative. In 1859, for instance, Horace Binney's *An Inquiry into the Formation of Washington's Farewell Address* employed a series of metaphors that merge Washington and Hamilton as co-authors or co-founders in an antebellum attempt to unite Northern economic interest with an implicit polemic for North-South union: "This would point to an allotment of the soul and elemental body to Washington, and the arranging, developing, and informing spirit to Hamilton,—the same characteristic that is found in the great works he devised for the country, and are still the chart by which his department of the government [the Treasury] is ruled."[6] Binney's quasi-Aristotelian metaphor figures Washington's "soul and elemental body" as the maternal vessel for Hamilton's paternal "spirit." Typical of this genre, the *Inquiry* locates the historical origin of nationality in the "body" of a founding author that, in turn, harbors (and is haunted by) a variety of political "spirits." Similarly "informed" (and haunted) by the spirit of that founder, Binney then assumes that his otherwise arcane scholarship has national significance. Some interpreters might argue that Binney misrepresents the true author(s) of the "Farewell Address," but few would dispute his more basic assumption that the political stakes in the project of establishing authorship involve the identity and future of the republic.

Binney's rhetoric thus confirms one frequently repeated axiom concerning modern nation formation. As Craig Calhoun succinctly puts it, "ideologists of nationality almost always claim it as an inheritance rather than a contemporary construct."[7] But Binney's identification of nationality with founding intentionality is not simply a sign of post-revolutionary filiopietism. The intrusion of politics into arguments about authorship affects not only historically belated readers of the "Address," but also Washington, Hamilton, and Madison. Like Binney, the authors of the "Address" mobilize the founding figure of "Washington" as a symbol through which competing political claims concerning the nation may be articulated. "[S]ome sentiments which are the result of much reflection," the final version of the "Address" reads, " . . . will be offered to you with the more freedom, as you can see in them the disinterested warnings of a parting friend who can possibly have no personal motive to biass his counsel" (3–4). Whoever authors the representations of nationality in the "Farewell Address" does so with this authorization of "Washington" as "parting friend." In a toast drunk two years prior to the "Farewell Address," the Democratic Society of Wythe County, Virginia, employs a similar rhetorical strategy to different political ends: "George Washington—May he be actuated by republican principles and remember the spirit of the constitution, or cease to preside over the United States."[8] Like the author(s) of the "Address," the toasters honor the symbolic figure of "Washington," but only if the historical actions of Washington remain true to the "spirit of the constitution." And while this constitutional spirit clearly differs from the spirit of capitalism invoked by the *Inquiry*, the toasters share with Binney the symbol "Washington" as the corporeal-textual site where political differences are negotiated and resolved. Like so many founding figures ("Jefferson," "Jay," "Franklin," "Hamilton," "Madison"), "Washington" names not (only) a biographical and historical person, but (also) a public space where the abstraction of nationality becomes realizable through symbolic acts of political and cultural representation.

I begin with this local controversy concerning the authorship of the "Farewell Address" because it raises and highlights the more general question of who authorizes representations of nationality—a question that preoccupied eighteenth-century republican political theorists and that Jean-Jacques Rousseau posed most dramatically in *The Social Contract*. To the question of which comes first, the nation or its representation, Rousseau responds with a paradox. "Sovereignty," he explains, "for the same reason that it is inalienable, cannot be represented; it lies directly in the general will, and will does not admit of representation."[9] Like the chicken's egg, the "general will" provides a point of national origin that is, in short, not one. Simultaneously sovereign and unrepresentable, the "general will" fragments the corporate image of the nation as a representable political body. While the immediate targets of Rousseau's attack are the French monarchists who incarnated sovereignty in the mortal body of the king, its effect is to politicize all forms of representation, monarchical or democratic. "The basis of our political systems," states the "Address" in its most Rousseauist moment, "is the right of the people to make and to alter their Constitutions of Government" (8). This line of reasoning disincorporates sovereignty by shifting the locus of the general will from either the monarch's body or the representative institutions of the nation-state to unofficial apparatuses of public opinion formation located outside of the state.[10] That this republican disestablishment of political authority should trouble Washington is no surprise. The second of his two terms as president coincided with the rise of both organized political dissent within the borders of the United States, and an oppositional press whose barbs were aimed not at the British court, but at the newly formed nation-state. As Washington put it in a letter posted to Jefferson two months prior the publication of the "Address," these developments led to the "grossest, and most insidious mis-representations." "By giving only one side of the subject," he explains, partisan newspapers like Benjamin Bache's *Philadelphia Aurora* and Philip Freneau's *National Gazette* portray him "in such exaggerated and indecent terms as could scarcely be applied to a Nero; a notorious defaulter; or even to a common pickpocket."[11]

Washington's complaint is understandable, though its address to one of the men responsible for the rise of the oppositional press and multiple party system is a notable irony.[12] Given the republican commonplace that sovereignty is irreducibility to representation, national symbols like Washington inevitably become subject to (and subjects of) unofficial public debate. The marks of the "Address"'s vexed relation to this structural inevitablity appear in its twofold displacement of questions of sovereignty to those of representation. Though republican in its affirmation of the priority of sovereignty to any act of representation, the "Address" simultaneously speaks of the existing Constitution as "sacredly obligatory" and admonishes "every individual to obey the established Government" (8). Though equally republican in its conception of a publicly active citizenry, the "Address" also imagines a state energetic enough to "confine each member of the Society within the limits prescribed by the laws and to maintain all in the secure and tranquil enjoyment of the rights of persons and property" (9). My previous chapter described these tensions as typical of republican and liberal tendencies within democratic political theory. In the "Address," the two intersect in the corporate image of "Washington," an image that becomes, in Slavoj Zizek's apt phrase, "the real thing"—the consumable "Nation-Thing" that anchors national identity.[13] Like the mortal body of the monarch, the "thing-ness" of Washington's body threatens to disrupt the equation of the nation and the state, of the citizen and the subject. In contrast to the monarch's Christic body, however, Washington's patriotic body disavows that threat by linking popular sovereignty to state representation, not by translating mortality into divinity.[14] This disavowal teaches two lessons concerning the shift from a theocratic to a democratic polity. It reveals the centrality of the corporate image of the nation as an indivisible body politic to the nationalist fantasy of *e pluribus unum*, while it also points to the revolutionary emergence within that body of a division between civil and state authority. Civil society, in this sense, names the unofficial national and transnational spaces where citizens simultaneously assent to and resist the subjectifying operations of modern nationalism.

Republicanism, Liberalism, Nationalism

Cultural and literary historians have recently begun to focus on the relation between nationality and nationalism as discrete forms of political identification in the early republic. Rather than conflating national and nationalist discourses, these studies mark a disjunction between a republican understanding of the nation as requiring political participation and a liberal understanding of nationality as an effect of political representation. In *The Letters of the Republic*, Michael Warner provides a useful, if stylized version of this contrast. Only liberalism, he suggests, could conceive of nationality as an effect of representations made meaningful through what Benedict Anderson refers to as "imaginary identifications": "You can be a member of the nation, attributing its agency to yourself in imaginary identification, without being a freeholder or exercising any agency in the public sphere. Nationalism makes no distinction between such imaginary participation and the active participation of citizens. In republicanism that distinction counted for everything."[15] As I suggested in the last chapter, two consequences follow from this contrast. While the liberal tradition tends to understand liberty in largely negative terms as freedom from state coercion and legal constraint, the republican tradition understands it positively as necessitating an equality of condition among citizens. And while liberalism thinks of liberty as occurring naturally in those private spaces unoccupied by the law, republicanism requires an investigation of the civil institutions (economic and domestic) that enable and disable citizens' participation in public debate. In the best-known genealogy of modern republicanism, J. G. A. Pocock has charted this concern with civic equality through debates on the national distribution of arms and property.[16] Warner's contribution focuses on access to the institutions of print and publication as enabling (and structuring) citizens' ability to participate in the formation of public opinion. In either case, the distinction between nationality and nationalism serves to highlight the crucial difference between a republican citizenry that authorizes political power and the liberal subjects who obey that power.[17]

In the late eighteenth century, this antagonism between republican and liberal understandings of nationality emerged most famously in the debates over the ratification of the Federal Constitution. Drawing on *The Spirit of the Laws*, opponents of the Constitution tirelessly repeated Montesquieu's warning that a republic would be corrupted if its territorial boundaries expanded to such a degree that citizens could be governed only as subjects.[18] In an essay from the Pennsylvania ratifying convention, for example, the dissenting minority echoes Montesquieu in their first objection to the Constitution's centralization of political power in the nation-state: "We dissent, first, because it is the opinion of the most celebrated writers on government, and confirmed by uniform experience, that an extensive territory cannot be governed on the principles of freedom, otherwise than by a confederation of republics, possessing all the powers of internal government, but united in the management of their general and foreign concerns."[19] Writing in support of the Constitution, Madison anticipates and responds to this argument in *Federalist 10* by redefining republicanism as representative government. Since a popular democracy is impossible, he asserts, "[a] republic, by which I mean a government in which the scheme of representation takes place . . . promises the cure for which we are seeking."[20] The effect of this redefinition is to provide the conceptual framework within which a republican or, synonymously for Madison, a representative government could be legitimated. This redefinition marks a move toward modern liberalism by reducing the participatory institutions of the public sphere to the representative institutions of the state. It also marks the origin of modern nationalism, characterized by its injunction for the citizen to identify with the nation while minimizing his or her ability to influence the meaning of that identification. In contrast to the republic of letters, the empire of law locates sovereignty not in unofficial spaces of public opinion formation (newspapers, literary and reading societies, coffee- and meetinghouses, political parties, citizens' associations), but in the representative and bureaucratic institutions of the nation-state (congresses, parliaments).

Traditional readings of the "Farewell Address" uncritically repeat this reduction of the public sphere to the state.[21] In his influential 1961 study *To the Farewell Address*, for example, Felix Gilbert reads the "Address" teleologically as marking the origin of the "basic issue of the American attitude toward foreign policy: the tension between Idealism and Realism." The "Address," according to Gilbert, integrates the "idealist" demands of popular sovereignty—understood as the rise and representation of the "will of the people" in the concerns of the nation-state—with the "realist" demands of international "power politics"—understood as competition between those states.[22] Like Binney, Gilbert incorporates the "idealist" and "realist" positions in the "Address"'s (two) authors: Washington embodies the "idealist" position; Hamilton acts as a "realist" proponent of an "aggressive imperialist program." Combined, these respective contributions to the "Address" represent the truth of American political thinking about foreign policy as it extends "beyond any period limited in time."[23] In reaching this conclusion, Gilbert rightly argues that the justifications for political isolation seem divided historically along Washingtonian and Hamiltonian lines. Where Washington's instructions to Hamilton hold out the promise that "if there be no engagements on our part, we shall be unembarrassed, and at liberty at all times to act from circumstances, and the dictates of justice, sound policy, and our essential interests," the "Address" itself rests its advocacy of isolationism on the more rigorously "realist" axiom that it is "folly in one nation to look for disinterested favours from another. . . . There can be no greater error than to expect, or calculate upon real favours from nation to nation"(17).[24] But Gilbert's reading does more than simply mark this split between Washington and Hamilton. It also generates an isolable category called "American foreign policy" in order to transform an historical debate within the "Address" into an ahistorical truth about international relations represented by the "Address." The appendix of Gilbert's study plays out this isolation textually by reproducing only those sections of the "Address" and its drafts that are "concerned with foreign policy."[25]

This retrospective isolation of the category "American foreign policy" relies on two misconceptions concerning republicanism's location of popular sovereignty in the public sphere. First, it assumes an understanding of the public sphere as a space delineated by the territorial boundaries of the nation-state. This first assumption overlooks the transnational and cosmopolitan character of much eighteenth-century political and cultural debate. "Liberty," argued John Stewart (a member of the Republican Society of Charleston), "is the gift of God to mankind and wheresoever a violation is attempted, it is the bound duty of man, as a Citizen of the World, and a member of the Society of Man, to resist it."[26] The context of this argument is a letter to Citizen Genet, the French minister charged in 1793 with securing American support for an extension of the 1778 Treaty of Alliance between the two revolutionary republics. Genet responded to the chilly reception of a Washington Administration more interested in maintaining neutrality toward all European powers by threatening, in Hamilton's words, to "appeal from the President of the United States to the People."[27] For Federalists like Hamilton, this republican circumvention of state power undermines the security and integrity of the nation. Washington supports this interpretation when he repeatedly credits Genet with "fathering" the subversive Democratic and Republican Societies "for purposes well known to the Government; that they would shake the government to its foundation."[28]

As a member of one such Society, Stewart offers a different view. "It is time," his letter continues, "to supersede the prejudices and errors of local juris-prudence when they militate the diminution of Natural Right, and the pro-longation of slavery and oppression." The scandal occasioned by Genet along with the XYZ Affair, the Bavarian Illuminati hysteria, and the passage of the Adams Administration's Alien and Sedition Acts later in the decade all attest to the interdependence of the categories "foreign" and "domestic" in early debates concerning nationality.[29]

Second, Gilbert's isolation of the category "American foreign policy" leads to a rhetorical analysis that assumes as historically self-evident an opposition of "domestic" and "foreign" that the "Address" must polemically construct. As a result of this second assumption, such analyses treat the "Address's" two major themes—its advocacy of political isolation and its warning against political sedition—as separate issues. Again, this oversight erases the transnational context of both "domestic" and "foreign" politics in the late eighteenth century. In a famous letter to the Italian republican Philip Mazzei, for instance, Jefferson reports that "an Anglican, monarchical, and aristocratical party has sprung up, whose avowed object is to draw over us the substance, as they have already the forms, of the British government."[30] Jefferson's criticism of the emerging Federalist party both foreshadows and differs from later forms of nationalism. When Ralph Waldo Emerson fa-mously admonishes the "American scholar" to disregard the "courtly muses of Europe," he intentionally draws on the Whig language of anti-aristocratic republicanism in order to police the national boundary between "domestic" and "foreign."[31] When Jefferson issues a comparable warning against "mon-archical" and "aristocratical" British influence, his point is not to isolate the United States from Europe, but to produce an alliance between supporters of republicanism on both continents. The "Address," in contrast, invokes the threat of "foreign influence" in order to nationalize the "Citizen of the World" as an "independent Patriot": "As avenues to foreign influence in innumerable ways, such [foreign] attachments are particularly alarming to the truly enlightened and independent Patriot. How many opportunities do they afford to tamper with domestic factions, to practice the arts of seduc-tion, to mislead public opinion, to influence or awe the Public Councils!" (15).[32] By defining the "independent Patriot" in opposition to "foreign influence" and domestic "arts of seduction," the "Address" responds to the cosmopolitan demands of republicanism (or monarchism) by policing the national boundary between the "foreign" and the "domestic," between the loyal subject of the nation-state and the alienating or seducing citizen of the republic.

The historical events leading to this redefinition of both nationality and citizenship are well documented: the radicalization of the French Revolu-

tion during the first half of the 1790s; Washington's "Proclamation of Neutrality" toward both France and Britain following Citizen Genet's visit in
1793; James Monroe's embrace of the French Republic in his diplomatic
capacity in 1794; the use of Federal power to quell the Whiskey Rebellion
in 1794; the ratification of the Jay Treaty with Britain in 1795. Of these, the
last provides the most immediate and significant context for the "Address."
Sent by Washington to secure British compliance with the Treaty of 1783,
John Jay, the anglophile Chief Justice of the Supreme Court, negotiated a
new treaty that drew contrary responses from Federalists and Republicans.
For Federalists, the Treaty's commercial alliance with Britain and political
neutrality toward both France and Britain merely confirmed Washington's
"Proclamation of Neutrality," a position later reconfirmed in the "Address."
For Republicans, the same treaty signaled a further betrayal of the republican cause in France, along with a new international alliance with the forces
of monarchical reaction in Britain. In a letter to a local paper justifying their
proposed burning of Jay in effigy, the Republicans of Fayetteville, North
Carolina, again draw on the cosmopolitan language of republicanism in
order to articulate their complaint: "[r]umor has it that persons inimical to
liberty, who wish to subvert the ties existing between America and France,
mean to try to repel the execution of this just action; It is hoped that the
spirit which ever characterized the true friends to a democratical government will be prevalent on the occasion, and shew these satellites of anarchy
that tar and feathers will be the recompense for their good intentions."[33] A
toast of the Joint Societies of New York provides a pithier version of the
same objection: "May the *cage*, constructed to coop the American Eagle,
prove a trap for none but *Jays* and *King*-birds."[34] For Republicans, the
treaty's doctrine of "neutrality" did not simply confirm the already existing
boundaries of the nation-state. Rather, it constructed those boundaries by
encoding republicanism in both France and the United States as a transnational threat to national sovereignty.

   The "Address" could have responded directly to these criticisms of the Jay
Treaty, as Washington himself did in personal letters to Hamilton and Gouverneur Morris.[35] But it did not. Instead, it challenges the structural basis of
republicanism by interpreting the very publicness of citizens' political dissent as evidence of their conspiratorial designs against the nation. This is
hardly a novel strategy as indicated by Washington's previous attacks on the
Democratic and Republican Societies as "self-created" and as the offspring
of Citizen Genet after the Whiskey Rebellion.[36] Like the oppositional press,
the Societies are "self-created" because they lack state authorization; they
are a result of "foreign influence" because "enlightened and independent"
patriotism requires loyalty to the state. In 1796, the "Address" intensifies
and condenses this strategy. After repeating Madison's three-page statement

of Washington's reasons for declining reelection, the final version of the "Address" proceeds with an interruption and explanation:

> Here, perhaps, I ought to stop. But a solicitude for your welfare, which cannot end but with my life, and the apprehension of danger, natural to that solicitude, urge me on an occasion like the present, to offer to your solemn contemplation, and to recommend to your frequent review, some sentiments, which are the result of much reflection, of no inconsiderable observation, and which appear to me all important in the permanency of your felicity as a People. (3)

What begins in 1792 as a publication of the need for the "election of a Citizen, to administer the executive government" becomes, in the 1796 version, an occasion for national instruction. This disjunction between publicist and didactic or, to use Homi Bhabha's terms, "performative" and "pedagogical" modes of address within the "Address" is highlighted by Washington's own rhetorical positioning.[37] Solicitous of "your welfare," the "I" that offers its "sentiments" in the "Address" stands apart from public debate. I will return later to this "I" that is one apart from the "People." For now, let me stress that this shift does not, in itself, signify a move from republicanism to liberalism, from nationality to nationalism. But it does mark out the space within which the final version of the "Address" will reconstruct the cosmopolitan citizen of the republic as the nationalist subject of the liberal state.

The Meanings of National Union

When the "Address" resumes its argument in 1796, it begins by exploiting the gap between performance and pedagogy central to all forms of national discourse. "In proportion as the structure of a government gives force to public opinion, it is essential that public opinion should be enlightened" (12). As Bhabha notes, this gap between "enlightened" and "unenlightened" public opinion within the "narrative address of the nation, turns the reference to a 'people' . . . into a problem of knowledge that haunts the symbolic formation of modern social authority."[38] By positioning Washington's patriotic first-person outside of this problematic, the "Address" conducts a political lesson concerning national union intended to exorcize this democratic specter. Along with a "love of liberty," the "Address" asserts, "[t]he Unity of Government which constitutes you as one People is now dear to you. It is justly so; for it is a main pillar in the edifice of your real independence" (4). This initial claim nicely captures the process Bhabha refers to as the "splitting of the national subject." If "Unity of Government" stresses "unity," then "government" remains subordinate to the "constituting" people; if it stresses "government," then the people remain subordinate to a "unity" that precedes and "constitutes" them. In the first case, "real independence" relies upon a structural distinction between civil and state authority, thus opening the possibility of the people unifying against the government in public attempts to reconstitute themselves as a body politic; in the second case, "real independence" collapses that distinction by interpreting civil disobedience as disloyalty to the nation-state. The first reading presumes a Rousseauist and republican interpretation of the national social contract as an ahistorical fiction; the second presumes a Lockean and liberal interpretation of the social contract as an historically locatable event.[39] The first figures the social contract as, in Etienne Balibar's phrase, a "contract of association"; the second figures it as a "contract of subjection," an "ideological artifact destined to divert the benefits of the contractual form to the profit of an established power."[40]

As the passage continues, the ambiguity between these antithetical forms of address remains:

> But as it is easy to foresee, that from different causes and from different quarters, much pains will be taken, many artifices employed, to weaken in your minds the conviction of this truth; as this is the point in your political fortress against which the batteries of internal and external enemies will be constantly and actively (though often covertly and insidiously) directed, it is of infinite moment, that you should properly estimate the immense value of your national Union, to your collective and individual happiness. (4)

What begins as a recommendation to support "Unity of Government" becomes, by the middle of the paragraph, a recommendation backed by threats. "Internal and external enemies," the "Address" promises, will attack the individual reader's and collective people's "political fortress." Yet the "Address" specifies neither how the people can identify those "enemies," nor what sort of "politics" constitutes their "fortress." This ambiguity seems less a confusion than, at this point at least, a strategy. By interpellating the people into the "Address" as an effect of the "Unity of Government" while allowing the ambiguity in that phrase to remain, the "Address" creates an initial consensus between Republican and Federalist factions. A Republican like Jefferson could read the "Address" as advocating citizens' participation in those unofficial public-sphere institutions that constitute "national Union," while a Federalist like Hamilton could read it as advocating subjects' identification with and support for the representative institutions of the nation-state. In the first case, the "enemy" would be anyone who attempted to collapse the structural distinction between popular sovereignty and political representation, between the founding power of the people and the governing power of the state. In the second case, the "enemy" would be anyone who attempted to attack the nation-state as the sole legitimate representation of the people.

Having raised the political stakes without further clarifying the rules of the game, the "Address" continues to defer any clarification, while devoting the next five paragraphs to an elaboration of two motivations for supporting "Unity of Government." "For this," the "Address" argues, "you have every inducement of sympathy and interest. Citizens by birth or choice, of a common country, that country has a right to concentrate your affections. The name of *American*, which belongs to you, in your national capacity, must always exalt just pride of Patriotism, more than any appellation derived from local discriminations. With slight shades of difference, you have the same religion, manners, habits and political principles" (4–5). Though elaborated at length in Jay's contributions to the *Federalist Papers*, this claim of "sympathy" as a means of nationalizing "appellation[s] derived from local discriminations" is passed over in the "Address." Economic self-interest, not sympathy or affection, provides the signified for the national signifier "American." Only the former establishes what the "Address" refers to as an "indissoluble community of interest as one *nation*": the South, "benefitting by the Agency of the *North*, sees its agriculture grow and its commerce expand," while the North relies on the South for the "precious materials of manufacturing industry." The West in turn provides a "valuable vent for the commodities" of the Eastern importers and manufacturers, while the East supplies the West with products "requisite to its growth and comfort" (5–6). Resonant with Hamilton's merchantilist arguments of the early 1790s, this grounding of national union in an expanding market economy reduces civil to economic society. As republicans ranging from Jefferson and Paine to Marx and Habermas argue, one effect of this reduction is to legitimate forms of economic power that undermine democratic access to the public sphere. But the "Address" does not advocate capital development on these anti-democratic grounds. Rather, it figures capitalism as the necessary means to the synthesis of "Republican Liberty" and "National Union." Like sympathy, capital guarantees a patriotic and harmonious civil society that ideally complements the (noncoercive) power of the nation-state.

Of course, there would be no reason for the "Address" to continue were powers of sympathy and capital sufficient to ensure national union. It could conclude with its two recommendations, or perhaps with its third, to "let experience solve" any problems that arise (6). But sympathy, capital, and experience are all insufficiently national concepts since none of them map neatly onto the territorial boundaries of the nation-state: "experience" always threatens to become "local"; "capital" opens the nation onto the demands of "foreign" markets; "sympathy" leads to dangerously "passionate attachment[s] of one Nation for another" (14). So rather than ending here, the "Address" proceeds to enumerate the "causes which may disturb our Union" and, at this halfway point, commits itself to the Federalist reading of the phrase "Unity of Government." Ironically, it is here that the "Address" produces what I referred to earlier as its most Rousseauist moment: "The basis of our political systems is the right of the people to make and alter their Constitutions of Government." "But," the "Address" adds, "the Constitution which at any time exists, 'till changed by an explicit and authentic act of the whole people, is sacredly obligatory upon all. The very idea of the power and the right of the people to establish government presupposes the duty of every individual to obey the established government" (8). This theoretical sleight of hand promises to heal the split in the national subject. It weds the republican emphasis on constitutional founding to the liberal demand for patriotic obedience by reducing the institutions of public opinion-formation to those of the "established government": Since the "continuance of UNION" is the "primary object of Patriotic desire," there is good reason to consider "mere speculation in such a case . . . criminal" (6). The "Address" does invoke the theoretical principle of popular sovereignty, but only in order to reconstruct the law-making people as law-abiding subjects. Leaving aside for the moment the speculative possibility of an "explicit and authentic act of the whole people," the only response left for those who desire the "name of *American*" is obedience to the (national) laws and government that currently exist.

Predictably then, the remainder of the "Address" consists largely of an extended attack on all threats to what Washington calls the "*American* character" in the letter to Patrick Henry that provides the first epigraph to this chapter. Unofficial sources of public opinion-formation lead to the proliferation of "combinations and associations, under whatever plausible character, with the real design to direct, counteract, or awe the regular deliberation and action of the constituted authorities" (8). In response to those who, like the Democratic and Republican Societies, would argue that both local associations and transnational alliances are the basis of republican liberty, the "Address" echoes the *Federalist Papers*.[41] While the "passions" which fuel such associations may be inseparable from the postlapsarian "love of power" which "predominates in the human heart" and while such associations may be beneficial in "Government of a Monarchical cast," the establishment of popular government renders this "spirit of party" both unpatriotic and potentially pernicious: "[I]n Governments purely elective, it is a spirit not to be encouraged. From their natural tendency, it is certain there will always be enough of that spirit for every salutary purpose. And there being constant danger of excess, the effort ought to be, by force of public opinion, to mitigate and assuage it" (11). Civil and political associations organized to balance the power of the nation-state are, according to the "Address," desirable within limits. As Richard Hofstadter has observed, the "Address" does accept the concept of "saluatory" political opposition—and it is this grudging acceptance that marks the emerging two-party system late in the 1790s.[42] Beyond such limits, though, political and civil associations serve only to compromise the nation-state's claim to be representative. Since the official institutions of the nation-state already represent the *"American* character," both irregular political dissent and the oppositional press that disseminates that dissent must be, at best, superfluous or, at worst, an invitation to what the "Address" typically pairs as foreign "influence and corruption" and domestic "riot and insurrection."

Corporate Nationalism

As Alexis de Tocqueville would argue forty years later, the strategies of containment that the "Address" employs in order to disable civil and political dissent suggest one possible (and dystopian) future for eighteenth-century republicanism. By defining public criticism of the representative institutions of the nation-state as both natural *and* undesirable, the "Address" produces the nationalist paranoia recognizable more vividly in the Adams administration's Alien and Sedition Acts in 1798 or, later, in the post–World War II National Security State.[43] Since citizens cannot know that their political passions and patriotic desires are identical with the interests of the nation-state, and since such an identification is nevertheless the a priori assumption of the state's claims to be representative, citizens must constantly purge themselves of any opposition to the state. As Washington suggests in a letter to Henry Lee, this lesson applies even to the (duped) members of the Democratic and Republican Societies, who share with later victims of "false consciousness" the flaw of "mean[ing] well, but know[ing] little of the real plan."[44] "Against the wiles of foreign influence," the "Address" warns, ". . . the jealousy of a free people ought to be *constantly* awake; since history and experience prove that foreign influence is one of the most baneful foes of Republican Government" (15). If citizens fail—as they inevitably will—to remain *"constantly* awake" against the "wiles of foreign influence," to transform themselves voluntarily into subjects of the nation-state, then the logic of corporate nationalism leads to their involuntary transformation by (nonelective) state institutions. Citizens, argued education and prison reformer Benjamin Rush in 1787, must be converted into "republican machines. This must be done if we expect them to perform their parts properly, in the great machine of the government of the state."[45] As Michel Foucault, Ronald Takaki, and Thomas Dumm have all suggested in different contexts, the liberal nation-state emerges out of this equation of republican government with political paranoia and subjectifying institutions.[46]

But the "Address" also provides a republican critique of the tutelary and disciplinary mechanisms of the nation-state. While it does argue for the reduction of citizens to subjects, the "Address" also maintains a reliance on the "force of public opinion" to mediate between the nation and the state. "The effort ought to be," the "Address" asserts, "by force of public opinion, to mitigate or assuage" the "spirit of party" or "faction." This is the primary and most general contradiction in the "Address," as it is of all liberal nationalist political theory legitimated through public appeals to popular sovereignty. As I argued in my previous chapter, the concept of public opinion could reconcile republicanism and democracy only if it recognized, in Habermas's words, "those opinions authorized by critical debate among the people at large."[47] Between the Scylla of localism and the Charybdis of cosmopolitanism, the "Address" carves out this public space of "enlightened and independent" patriotism. And one effect of such patriotism may be the voluntary (or involuntary) purification and subjection of citizens' bodies. But that outcome cannot be vouchsafed within a printed text like the "Address" that both participates in and solicits public debate. "Will it be proper," Washington worries, " . . . that the State Printers will give it a place in their Gazettes—or preferable to let it be carried by my private Secretary to that Press which is destined to usher it to the World & suffer it to work its way afterwards?"[48] The problem with this dilemma is that it offers no good choice. In either case, the "Address"'s orientation toward a printed-mediated "World" allows unofficial public debate to hollow out state authority. And it does so in two ways. It reasserts the distinction between civil and state authority since the "Address," as one of many newsworthy attempts to enlighten public opinion, cannot operate as a suture between the two. And it maintains the disjunction between the local or (trans)national citizen and the nationalist subject by producing a citizen attentive to the potential corruption of the state, rather than a state attentive to the potential disloyalty of its subjects.

The "Address," in other words, grounds its argument for the conversion of citizens into subjects not in the official institutions of the nation-state, but in the unofficial institutions of the public sphere. By appealing to a people whose responses it can neither represent nor prescribe, the "Address"'s polemic thus reaches its limit at the moment when it attempts to lend its pedagogy the "force of public opinion." Marked once in the public orientation of that pedagogy, this limit is marked again in the figure of "Washington." Where the body of the monarch theoretically incarnates God's will, Washington's patriotic body ideally incorporates the people's will. As a symbol of national union, that body functions in the "Address" to erase the distinction between civil and state authority central to any democratic political regime. In place of that distinction, Washington's body secures an organic conception of the nation as an indivisible whole. This symbolism reacts against the revolutionary disincorporation of society—a coup literalized in the decapitation of the King—by reinstituting what Claude Lefort refers to as the "corporeality of the social": "The attempt to incorporate power in society, society in the state, implies that there is nothing, in a sense, that can indicate an externality to the social and to the organ that represents it by detaching itself from it."[49] The utopian appeal of this symbolism lies in its substitution of a (vicarious) experience of national embodiment for either the abstraction of world citizenship or the more local demands of everyday life.[50] Corporate nationalism promises to realize the true interests of the people, to end all partisan debate and, ultimately, to reduce the (trans)national public sphere to the nation-state that "Washington" represents. As even a narcoleptic citizen like Rip Van Winkle could recognize, this promise of national security also implies a political debt: a national identification with Washington's "*American* character" may simply substitute one King George for another.

Yet Washington's patriotic body remains incapable of fulfilling this nationalist promise. Just as the theocratic synthesis imaged in the monarch's body allowed for antinomian agitation, the democratic synthesis promised by the patriotic body remains vulnerable to civil opposition. Because it defers to the authority of public opinion, the "Address" distinguishes between citizenship and subjection, even as the incorporating image—and symbolic authority—of "Washington" threatens to collapse that distinction. This resistance to the demands of national incorporation opens the "Address" to criticism by those whom it interpellates not as Washington's subjects, but as his "fellow-citizens." Washington may fantasize in a letter to Henry Knox that "the great power above would, erect a standard of infallibility in political opinions." But he also acknowledges that this fantasy remains unrealizable for "inhabitants of this terrestial globe" like us.[51] Deprived of any such divine authorization, Washington's patriotic body thus harbors a necessarily incomplete list of secular "spirits": Hamilton's "informing spirit," the Virginia toasters' "spirit of the constitution," the "Address"'s "spirit of party," the North Carolina Republicans' "spirit which ever characterized the true friends of democratical government." This collection of antagonistic "spirits" opens the possibility that, as Jefferson suggests, Washington signed without authoring the "Address," that his signature merely authorized a "bewitching" ghostwriter like Hamilton. Perhaps, as the "Address" itself comes close to affirming at several points, Washington's "fallible judgment" led or misled him into "unconscious" errors (2, 18, 19). Haunted by such uncanny possibilities, the "Address" reacts at this point not, in liberal fashion, by realigning Washington with the nation-state but, in republican fashion, by reassuring the citizen of Washington's political virtue. His public-oriented sentiments, the "Address" asserts, focus only on "your welfare" and "felicity"; they are the result of "much reflection"; they derive from "good intentions"; they are "natural" to one who views the United States as the "native soil of himself and his progenitors for several generations" (2,3,19).

The problem with these assurances is that they provide both points of identification and sites of argumentation. Regardless of claims concerning the integrity of Washington's sentiments—his paternalistic solicitude, his theoretical reflections, his good intentions, his political reputation, his nativist pedigree—such claims cannot close off debate concerning the truth value of those sentiments. Jay Fliegelman is half right when he describes this epistemological indeterminacy as typical of republican personality structures: "[A]n individual's actions are meaningful only insofar as they are revelatory of a specific personality or moral character; moral character is meaningful only insofar as it is vouchsafed by sincerity; sincerity is credible only insofar as it can be directly or indirectly experienced, and then preferably by an unseen witness to private behavior."[52] The "Address"'s republican recourse to Washington's character produces a narrative regress that is, as Fliegelman suggests, theoretically infinite. But that regression leads to public sphere institutions as sites of democratic opinion-formation, not to an inaccessible or invisible private life. As the democratic voice of the people replaces the theocratic voice of God, the problem inherent in the "witness" Fliegelman imagines is not that he or she must remain "unseen," but that the resulting evidence will remain subject to further investigation and debate. Testifying to the "*American* character" of the historical Washington, the symbolic figure of "Washington" works to foreclose such debate. Yet that very symbolism also reintroduces an antithesis between corporeality and nationality into the patriotic body. The "Address" may offer Washington's bodily image as a means of ideological synthesis. But that image quickly dissolves since Washington's body names both a ground and a site of debate. While Washington may assure Henry Lee that "the arrows of malevolence . . . never can reach the most vulnerable part of me," his claim to an "*American* character" renders even the most (in)vulnerable and private parts of his patriotic body public property.[53]

"Washington," as the "Address" figures him, admits as much in his final remarks: "How far in the discharge of my official duties, I have been guided by the principles which have been delineated, the public records and other evidences of my conduct must witness to you and the world. To myself, the assurance of my own conscience is, that I at least believe myself to be guided by them" (18). This conclusion assures the reader of Washington's political virtue, even as it hints at a dissonance between his intentions and the cosmopolitan citizen's judgment of those intentions. The latter possibility, in turn, undermines the "Address"'s attempt to figure "Washington" as an a priori validation of its pedagogy. "You and the world," the "Address" asserts, will have to judge both the public merit of and the political impetus behind Washington's intentions and sentiments. As one "citizen" among his (trans)national "fellows," even Washington remains uncertain concerning his intentions since, as the "Address" puts it a page later, he can be only "unconscious of any intentional error" (19). This gap between Washington's "conscious intent" and his "unconscious errors" opens a publicly mediated space of critical reflection between the citizens who judge Washington's sentiments and the subjects who identify with them. Like the patriotic read-

ers of the "Address," Washington remains unconscious not of his own intentions, but of his fellow citizens' judgment of those intentions. Or more precisely, his uncertainty concerning that judgment leads him to question his
own intentions. Washington's "unconscious" is, in this sense, democratic
rather than psychoanalytic. It houses not subversive memories, but seditious
citizens. By deferring to public opinion to determine the symbolic meaning
of "Washington," this "unconscious" locates the unofficial institutions of
local and (trans)national public spheres at the divided and inscrutable heart
of Washington's patriotic body.

In its republican moments, the "Address" thus conjures what might be
called the political unconscious of liberal nationalism. "Public opinion"
names the democratic spirit that disrupts any certainty regarding the merit
of the "Address"'s polemic. It replaces "Washington" as a symbol linking the
nation to the state with the sovereignty of the people as expressed and debated within local and (trans)national public spheres; and it subordinates the
"Address"'s claims for the personal integrity of Washington to public debate
concerning those claims. By locating the ontological basis for such knowledge in the unofficial institutions of public opinion-formation, the "Address"
deploys a logic of national disincorporation opposed to its own nationalist
attempts to use "Washington" as a symbolic relay between the nation and
the state. The significance of this deployment lies in its displacement of an
ontology of national identity with what Jacques Derrida playfully refers to as
a "hauntology"—a series of mediating "specters" that open and structure
debate concerning the oppositions that inform both the "Address" and its
liberal nationalist readings.[54] Since, for example, any knowledge of the
boundary between "domestic" and "foreign" must be adjudicated not by the
nation-state, but by debate in the (trans)national public sphere, the opposition of "domestic" and "foreign" becomes epistemologically unrepresentable
and indeterminate. Similarly, the "Address" destabilizes its opposition between the "arts of seduction" and those of "education," between the "e-
ducer" who leads the pedagogical subject "in" and the "se-ducer" who leads
that subject "out." In either case, such oppositions cannot be used to prescribe the limits of the public sphere since, outside of the public sphere,
there can be no epistemologically or politically legitimate means of anchoring those oppositions. Perhaps, one could argue, Washington's sentiments
are "foreign" to those of the people. Perhaps Washington acts not as an
"educator," but as a "seducer" of the nation.

Perhaps. But to argue that Washington's sentiments *may* be "foreign" or
that Washington *may* be a "seducer" is not to argue that they *are* "foreign"
or that he *is* a "seducer." Each of the latter arguments, by identifying and
representing the nation through the figure of Washington, would merely
invert and reinscribe the logic of national incorporation that the "Address"
subverts in its democratic and republican moments. Just as one reader might

argue that Hamilton's economic programs (his "realism") corrupt the virtue of Washington's representative sentiments in the "Farewell Address," another might argue that Washington's sentiments (his "idealism") corrupt the virtue of Hamilton's draft as representative. Beyond their obvious differences, these two readers would share a nationalist understanding of the nation as a genealogical medium through which founding spirits are passed in the form of an inheritance from one generation to the next. In contrast to both of these arguments, I have pursued the simpler though, in a sense, less obvious point that Washington's public-oriented sentiments in the "Address" are neither representative nor, strictly speaking, representable. Like any of the sentimental letters of the early republic, they are oriented not toward a representation of the people or nation, but toward participating in the public deconstruction and reconstruction of what the "Address" refers to as "national Union." Like many of those letters, they mobilize a series of unstable oppositions—"corruption" and "virtue," "foreign" and "domestic," "seduction" and "education"—and do so in order to negotiate and influence these deconstructions and reconstructions. The structural effects of this equivalence between Washington's sentiments and those of his "fellow-citizens" account for the ideological contradictions within the "Address." Even as the "Address"'s republicanism forces it to vie for ideological authority with other print-mediated publications (*The Rights of Man* or *National Gazette*, *Charlotte Temple* or *The Coquette*), its liberalism leads it to disavow that structural equivilence by drawing a line between "American characters" like "Washington" and their "un-American" doubles like "Paine" and "Freneau."

Disincorporating Washington

During congressional preparations in 1832 for the centennial anniversary of Washington's birth, the utopian lure of corporate nationalism structured a day's debate over a resolution to remove Washington's bodily remains from Mount Vernon to Washington, D.C. Though never acted upon due to protests by Washington's family, the disinterment and reburial of his remains had already been proposed and approved in 1799. Overlooking the opposition between state and familial authority that scuttled the previous resolution, Representative Hunt of Vermont argues that the Congress of 1832 would be simply reaffirming the earlier decision:

> No act can be done by the Government that would have so deep and permanent a moral influence in uniting the people and cementing the union of this confederacy, as the placing of these sacred remains at the base of this durable edifice, so that it may serve not only as the seat of national legislation, but also as the mauso-

leum of the father of his country. The same pure feelings of veneration which
dictated and responded to the resolutions of '99, still continue alive and unabated
throughout the country, and a more propitious time for executing the duties of that
resolve will never hereafter occur.[55]

Other representatives agree with Hunt's filiopietistic alignment of national
union, national legislation, and the nationalization of Washington's remains.
"Let us erect here an altar," argues Sutherland of Pennsylvania, "around
which our countrymen may assemble together, and mutually swear to per-
petuate the institutions established by the services and patriotism of Washington."[56] That Washington's last will and testament explicitly opposes such
a spectacle is of little consequence. Confronted with Washington's "express
desire" that his "corpse may be interred in a private manner, without parade,
of funeral Oration," Drayton of South Carolina barely hesitates: had Washington "foreseen that the Federal Legislature would desire to dispose of his
relics in a mode more suited to his name and fame, the whole tenor of his life
forbids the assumption that he would have opposed their wishes."[57]

In one sense, Drayton is right. The proposed removal of Washington's
corpse literalizes the ideology of national incorporation and, in doing so,
promises to provide Washington with the *"American* character" that both he
and the nation "want." As Representative Mercer of Virginia puts it in the
second epigraph to this chapter, "Long as . . . the capitol would stand . . . it
would stand longer for being known to all the world as the tomb of Washington." For those who support the removal, Washington's body acts as a "relic"
intended to identify the public sphere with the legislative action of the representative nation-state. Washington becomes, for Drayton, whatever the
"national legislature" wishes "Washington" to be, while his body ensures,
according to Mercer, the longevity of the capitol itself. This identification
transforms the public sphere into a depoliticized space of national consensus
through what Sutherland imagines as a monumental loyalty oath to "Washington." And while this fetishistic deployment of Washington's corpse
guards against the threat of national disincorporation, it also reveals a paradox that Lefort locates in the post-revolutionary image of the body politic:
"It is an image which, on the one hand, requires the exclusion of the malevolent Other and which, simultaneously, breaks down into the image of a
whole and a part that stands for the whole, of a part that paradoxically reintroduces the figure of the other, the omniscient, the omnipotent, benevolent
other, the militant, the leader, the Egocrat."[58] As an image and a part of the
whole, the "Egocrat" affirms and transgresses this depoliticizing vision of
the body politic. When aligned with the modern state, the body of the
"Egocrat" functions as the external part that comprises (and compromises)
the internal completion of the nation as an organic whole. The resulting
paradox emerges as Washington's body is called upon both to symbolize

national union and to silence national debate. In 1832, 109 of the 185 representatives enacted this paradox by debating and voting for the resolution
while, predictably, decrying the lack of unanimity as a sign of the entry of
"politics" and "divided sentiments" into an issue that rightfully transcends
politics and unites sentiments. Mercer, for example, protested against "all
reference to the politics of the day, which was marked by [Washington's]
untimely death."[59]

Of the seventy-six representatives who voted against the resolution, many
display a similar adherence to the logic of corporate nationalism, albeit on a
smaller scale. For many of the Southern representatives, the problem with
the resolution is not that it attempts to identify national sovereignty with the
nation-state, but that it identifies it with the wrong state. Assenting Northern
representatives like Dearborn and Everett of Massachusetts raise the specter of national alienation by suggesting that Mount Vernon and, with it,
Washington's "sacred remains" could be made subject to the whims of international commerce: "There is no security that Mount Vernon will remain in
the property of the present family. Such is the state of our laws, that it may
be sold at auction, and those sacred remains may be purchased by a for-
eigner."[60] Southern representatives like Thompson of Georgia respond with
the equally alarming possibility that those "sacred remains" could eventually
rest in the foreign soil of the North: "Remove the remains of our venerated
Washington from their association with the remains of his consort and his
ancestors, from Mount Vernon and from his native State, and deposite [sic]
them in this capitol, and then let a severence of this Union occur, and be-
hold! the remains of Washington on a shore foreign to his native soil."[61]
Though ideologically divided along regional lines, these Northern and
Southern nationalists implicitly agree that disagreements concerning the location of Washington's corpse engage a debate concerning the proper location of national sovereignty. What unites the manifest paranoia of a Northern nationalism with the incipient paranoia of a Southern nationalism is the
assumption that the dislocation of Washington's corpse threatens national
sovereignty. For both, the greatest threat would seem to be staged in the
story of a Mount Vernon gardener who, according to Representative Burges
of Rhode Island, plotted to transport "to Europe the bones of Washington,
and there [offer] them for sale, as relics, to the disciples or the fanatics of
freedom in the Old World."[62]

That this story invokes the specter of republican internationalism is no
coincidence, of course. The figure of the gardener condenses three points of
conflict in the debates of the 1790s: the ideal of agrarianism as a source of
political virtue; the civilizing (or corrupting) effects of the international market; the subversive (or liberating) spread of European radicalism. As such,
that figure could indicate the persistence of those debates well beyond the
eighteenth century. But recent histories of the republicanism suggest other-

wise, as does Burges's narration of the gardener's failure ("[H]e entered the tomb; but, in the darkness of the night, and under the excitement of a horror natural to the deed, he bore away [the remains] of another, by mistake.")[63] In *The Letters of the Republic*, for example, Michael Warner follows Habermas's early writings in locating the consolidation of liberalism and the representative nation-state in the 1830s, while Lauren Berlant focuses on Hawthorne's tales of the 1830s in *The Anatomy of Nationalist Fantasy*. J. G. A. Pocock's historical studies also tend to stop in the early decades of the nineteenth century. As a critical supplement intended to complicate such histories, I close by citing two further evidences of the survival of a republican understanding of nationality even within the debates over Washington's remains. For Representative Collier of New York, the "diversity of sentiment" evinced in Congress does not signify a greater need for the resolution. Rather, it presents "of itself sufficient reason why the resolution ought not to pass."[64] Diverse sentiments, for Collier, are not a problem to be resolved through a logic of national incorporation, but are the basis of debate concerning national union. Though a member of the original committee which authored the resolution, Representative Clay of Alabama seconds Collier's objection. "Respect ought to be paid to the opinions and feelings of others," Clay argues, "and [I] for one could not consent to celebrate the centennial anniversary of the birthday of Washington in a manner openly at war with the wishes of Washington's own state."[65] Both Collier and Clay leave open the possibility of a "unity of sentiments" that would validate the identification of the nation and the state, but both defer that possibility to a future that must remain, for the present, indeterminate.

The response of Representative Gordon of Virginia offers a different and more substantial objection: "Since the art of printing had been invented, pillars and monuments were but idle records. Letters were the best, the enduring monument. They held the names and the deeds of Washington, and would hold them forever; and it was vain to attempt, by an empty pageant, unchristian in its character, and in every way in bad taste, to add any thing to Washington's immortality."[66] Gordon's objection to the project of nationalizing Washington's remains could be read as a simple relocation of that project from monumental to literary forms of publication. In his final letter to Hamilton before the publication of the "Address," Washington requests the inclusion of a section on education for reasons that seem to foreshadow this shift: "I mean Education *generally* as one of the surest means of enlightening & givg. just ways of thinkg to our Citizens, but particularly the establishment of a University; where the Youth from all parts of the United States might receive the polish of Erudition in the Arts, Sciences & Belle Letters." Trained in this "Seminary" located at the "Seat of the General Government," these "youths" will learn that "there was not that cause for those jealousies & prejudices which one part of the union had imbibed against another part."[67] Like Emerson and the Young Americans who were

Gordon's contemporaries, Washington seems to imagine that the "polish of erudition" and "beauty" of "Belle Letters" will act as antidotes to the partisan passions and biased publications that threaten to divide the nation both from itself and from the state.[68] "Polish" and "beauty" thus provide the filtering apparatuses that winnow the wheat of national identity from the chaff of political and social movements intent on national and transnational debate. Gordon's equation of "letters" with "enduring monuments," as well as his elite dismissal of "bad taste" certainly indicate his own participation in this now familiar form of literary nationalism.

At the same time, Gordon's equation of letters with monuments is also reversible since monuments, like letters, are vulnerable to reinscription and reinterpretation. In attempting not to incorporate, but to disincorporate the nation through a reading of the "Farewell Address," I have exploited precisely this reversibility. The "Address" says that the nation and the state should meet in the figure of "Washington," that local, national, and transnational public spheres ought to be reducible to the nation-state; yet, the "Address" can say nothing about what the nation is since its participation within the republic of letters requires that the identity of the nation be determined only through public debate. That "letters" serve as the metaphor for the permeable boundary through which "sentiments" enter this debate indicates both of these possibilities. Understood as a filtering device, letters could serve as a barrier to participation in the republican public sphere. As Roger Chartier concludes of the French Revolution, the dividing line between the people and the public ultimately "ran between those who could read and produce writing and those who could not."[69] And Washington notes a similar division when he observes that the "ignorant savages" currently at war with the United States "have no press thro' which their grievances are related": "It is well known that when one side only of a Story is heard, and often repeated, the human mind becomes impressed with it, insensibly."[70] This much is true. Understood as an expressive medium, however, letters also provided a universalist vision of a republican public sphere open to any body's sentiments. As indicated by the sensationalist psychology that informs Washington's analysis of the press's power (as well as his conflation of oral and written discourse), republican letters disseminate "stories" that become influential through the "impressions" they "insensibly" leave on readers and listeners. And as Washington knew from his own experience with the press, increased participation within the unofficial institutions of public opinion formation could produce stories that turned the nation away from nationalist representations—regardless of their accuracy, beauty, or polish. The literary form of this dialectic between representation and participation—between the stories disseminated within the literary public sphere and the minds and bodies upon which they are "insensibly" "impressed"—constitutes the unofficial nation-space to which I now turn.

Part Two

SENTIMENT AND SEX

4

Corresponding Sentiments and Republican Letters: Hannah Foster's *The Coquette*

Enlightenment is man's release from self-incurred
tutelage. Tutelage is man's inability to make use of
his understanding without the direction of another.
Self-incurred is that tutelage when its cause lies
not in lack of reason but in lack of resolution and
courage to use it without the direction from another.
  (Immanuel Kant, "What is Enlightenment?,"
  1784)[1]

"Lord bless you, my dear girl," cried the teacher
smiling, "have you a mind to be in leading strings all
your life time. Prithee open the letter, read it, and
judge for yourself."
  (Susanna Rowson, Charlotte Temple, *1791)*[2]

Loose Letters

In a letter posted to her husband on August 14, 1776, Abigail Adams includes news of an illicit romance that keeps one of John's revolutionary colleagues, Elbridge Gerry, from returning immediately to Philadelphia: "I expected Mr. Gerry would have set off before now, but he finds it perhaps hard to leave his Mistress—I wont say harder than some do to leave their wives. Mr. Gerry stood very high in my Esteem—what is meat for one is not for an other—no accounting for fancy. She is a queer dame and leads people [in] wild dances."[3] The inclusion of this gossipy tidbit in a letter otherwise focused on the education of "learned women" and the political benefits of their "literary accomplishments" may seem anomalous. According to the editors of the Adams's correspondence, the "Watertown belle" who attracted Gerry could neither read nor write and perhaps, one could argue, she signifies for Abigail the threat posed by the prevailing inadequacy of female education in the month-old republic. Despite the physical separation occasioned by the pressures of the Revolution, Abigail and John continue their romance through the mediation of the post, while the same pressures force Gerry and the "belle" to choose between romance and revolution, between personal and political life. Perhaps, another could argue, Abigail's news signifies her jealousy of the very lack of education that enables the "belle" to demand Gerry's physical presence since, she hints, John finds it easier to abandon a literate wife than Gerry does to leave an illiterate mistress. Perhaps, a third might argue, Abigail's news signifies an identification with the "belle" and, through her, that "queer dame" "fancy" whose "wild dances" invoke the "rebellion" Abigail earlier had warned that the "Ladies" were prepared to "foment." "If perticuliar care and attention is not paid to the Laidies," Abigail threatens in a famous letter posted on March 31, 1776, "we are determined to foment a Rebelion, and will not hold ourselves bound by any Laws in which we have no voice, or Representation."[4]

As if aware of these multiple readings of her news, Abigail begins her next paragraph with an apostrophe to the post. "But hush," she writes, "Post, dont betray your trust and loose my letter."[5] Thematized most playfully here, anxieties concerning loose letters and the reliability of the post recur throughout Abigail and John's correspondence. "I have one favor to ask," John writes on July 3, 1776, "that is, that in your future Letters, you would acknowledge the Receipt of all those you may receive from me. . . . By this Means I shall know if any of mine miscarry."[6] On November 27, 1775, Abigail notes that "All Letters, I believe, have come safe to hand."[7] Given the immediate context of the Adams's correspondence, this anxiety concerning the circulation of letters once out of "hand" or, in this case, between "hands" is certainly understandable. The quality of colonial post roads varied greatly, and postal riders could be hired by different groups with different ends in mind.[8] Two years earlier in 1774, for example, agents of the Tory press in the United States exploited these irregularities by intercepting, publishing, and parodying letters to Abigail in which John referred to the "Fidgets, the Whims, the Caprice, the Vanity" of his Whig colleagues in the Continental Congress.[9] The anxiety produced by such unauthorized publications only intensified after the outbreak of war with England. "It is not prudent," John warns six days after signing of the Declaration of Independence, "to commit to Writing such free Speculations, in the present state of Things."[10] If loose letters threaten to place the fate of the nation in the wrong hands, then Abigail and John respond appropriately. They recognize that the success of the Revolution demands either that personal letters not circulate inadvertently in public or, failing that, careful editing of any personal opinions conveyed in potentially public letters.

This self-understanding of the national circulation of personal letters accords with either of two conventional models of the relation between personal and political life, between letters as vessels for personality and the public sphere as a sphere of letters. On the one hand, modern liberalism tends to conceive of personal life as private and inviolable, as a network of intimate practices freed from the abstract and alienating requirements of political life. On the other hand, republicanism is often said to interpret personal life as virtuous or corrupt depending on its identity with or difference from political life. The first depoliticizes the sort of personal sentiments expressed in the Adams's letters by relegating them to a private sphere subject to juridical protection and/or constraint. The second repoliticizes sentimental letters, though only after mandating their identity with the public. For liberalism, in short, the personal is not a public concern; for republicanism, the personal is immediately political. While most of the recent histories of the revolutionary and post-revolutionary United States acknowledge these two analytically distinct conceptions, they tend to resolve the contradiction through a narrative that pits them against one another, then announces the victory of liberalism. Regardless of whether the moment of victory is located in the writing of the Constitution in 1787, the juridification of the Constitution in *Marbury v. Madison*, or the rise of Jacksonian democracy in the 1830s, liberal consensus historiography assumes that the republican insistance on publication as the means of linking personal and political life fades from view. Such histories may applaud or condemn the victory of liberalism, but all assume that republicanism and liberalism are mutually exclusive and complementary alternatives within the political and social history of the United States.[11]

It would be a mistake, however, to subscribe to either of these two understandings of the politics of the personal or, in this case, the politics of the public circulation of personal letters. The liberal separation of personal and political life, as well as the republican identification of the two, reduce both the complexity of Abigail Adams's apostrophe to the post and, on a more general level, the significance of the category of letters in the early republican period. As Jürgen Habermas points out in *The Structural Transformation of the Public Sphere*, the institution of the post fits both historically and symbolically into a genealogy of the eighteenth-century public sphere conceived as a sphere of letters. Historically, the post emerges along with press institutions and commodity markets at the beginning of the eighteenth-century as an unofficial public medium for the circulation of news in the form of "news letters." Just as the post, Habermas argues, could develop fully only once the "regular opportunity for letter dispatch became accessible to the general public," the press could come into existence only once "the regular supply of news became public, that is, again accessible to the public."[12] Benjamin Franklin's career as republican newspaper printer and postmaster in Philadelphia provides only one example of the historical linkage between the two institutions. Positioned at the economic intersection of the press and the post, Franklin characteristically exploited both for his own profit.[13] That an accessible post could also be understood as politically crucial to the public sphere as a site of democratic self-determination is evinced in a 1791 address to Congress by none other than Elbridge Gerry. "However firmly liberty may be established in any country," Gerry argues in a debate over rising postal rates, "it cannot subsist if the channels of information be stopped."[14]

The symbolic relation between the public sphere and the post is more complicated. Theorists of the eighteenth-century public sphere like Gerry conceived of the post not simply as an institution enabling (or disabling) the publication of personal sentiments. They also understood it as an institution capable of transforming the structural relation between personal and political life. Evidence of this faith emerges most clearly in the contemporary popularity of epistolary correspondence—of both letter writing manuals and the sentimental novels that grew out of them. Prior to the revolutionary establishment of a state-sanctioned political public sphere accessible only to privileged individuals (white freeholders, patriarchal heads of families, male citizens), these manuals and novels carved out unofficial public spaces of literary and political debate theoretically accessible to all individuals regardless of status. In contrast to the limitations that the requirements of representation imposed on participation within the political public sphere, this literary model of the public sphere promised to secure a space in which, as Habermas puts it, the "rational-critical public debate of private persons with one another flowed from the wellspring of a specific subjectivity."[15] Letters symbolized this possibility because they ideally allowed for the unfettered publication of bodily and intimate experience. As such, the literary public sphere both relied upon and demanded public-oriented and public-mediated personality structures. "From the beginning," Habermas argues, "the psychological interest increased in the dual relation to both one's self and the other. . . . The diary became a letter addressed to the sender, and the first-person narrative became a conversation with one's self addressed to another person."[16] This intersubjective understanding of self-other relations locates personal and political life as neither opposed along lines of private and public, nor identical to one another. Rather, personality and politics are internally linked and mediated through the publication and circulation of letters.

This literary model of an accessible and influential public sphere lay at the ideological core of eighteenth-century republicanism, just as it continues to haunt the political imaginary of late-twentieth-century liberalism. As Alexis de Tocqueville was among the first to argue, the effects of this ideology are often twofold. It installs both the utopian, normative possibility of a democratic polity within which unofficial civil associations enable individuals to check the official political power of the nation-state, and the dystopian, nor-malizing possibility of a political power able to deploy the ideology of self-government even in the absence of such associations.[17] My last chapter argued that these two possibilities co-exist in Washington's "Farewell Address," and that they ultimately mark a division within Washington's body as a site of national identification. In modified form, they reappear in Abigail Adams's apostrophe to the post. On the one hand, that apostrophe demands that the post "Hush," that it silence her unorthodox speculations by not circulating her personal letters in public. Faced with a critical divergence between official and unofficial forms of publication, Abigail mandates a strict and unmediatable opposition of personality and publicity. In this sense, her withdrawal of personal from public opinion might seem a typically liberal response to the republican call for the equation of the two. On the other hand, the same apostrophe also demands that the post not "loose" her let-ters, that it facilitate the public circulation of her sentiments only in author-ized channels. As indicated by the very structure of this appeal to the "post," Abigail responds to the possibility that her letters may stray not by eschew-ing publication altogether, but by maintaining a republican faith in what Mary Favret refers to as the "ideal Post Office."[18] This structural ideal prom-ises not unmediated personal communication, but the literary mediation of both personal opinion and political power.

That both of these readings are suggested by Abigail's letter is itself sig-nificant. While John encourages her to "write by post," and while he notes that in their personal correspondence she "shine[s] as a Stateswoman," he elsewhere undercuts both her literary and her political authority.[19] "As to your extraordinary Code of Laws," John writes in response to her threat of sororal rebellion, "I cannot but laugh":

> We have been told that our Struggle has loosened the bands of Government every where. That Children and Apprentices were disobedient—that schools and Col-ledges were grown turbulent—that Indians slighted their Guardians and Negroes grew insolent to their Masters. But your letter was the first Intimation that another Tribe more numerous and powerfull than all the rest were grown discon-tented. . . . Depend upon it, We know better than to repeal our Masculine sys-tems.[20]

Even as John notes the rhetorical and political affinities between Abigail's threat and the rebellion he and his colleagues were fomenting through simi-lar means in Philadelphia, he responds to that threat with a dogmatic asser-tion of "masculine" dominance. In a more serious letter to James Sullivan on May 26, 1776, John repeats this dogmatism in response to the question "Whence arises the Right of the Men to govern the Women, without their consent?": "Depend upon it, Sir, it is dangerous to open so fruitful a Source

of Controversy and altercations. . . . There will be no end of it."[21] John's
attempt to mute the question Abigail raises typifies contemporary conservative reaction to the possibility of democracy in the early republic. And it
leaves Abigail with two options. Either she can continue to limit the audience for her threat of rebellion to John as her husband and official representative, or she can circulate her threat to a general public including, among
others, "Children," "Apprentices," "Indians," "Negroes," "Watertown
belles," "queer dames" and, again, her husband, John.

Like many of her contemporaries, Abigail remained torn between these
two options. "I think it my duty," she writes on June 3, 1776, "to attend with
frugality and oeconomy to our own private affairs. . . . Here I can serve my
partner, my family and myself, and injoy the Satisfaction of your serving
your Country."[22] In accordance with the ideology variously referred to as
"domestic feminism" and "republican motherhood," Abigail organizes her
life with John by separating their spheres of influence. The private, domestic, and familial affairs that fall under her control ideally complement the
public and (trans)national affairs that fall under his supervision.[23] Echoing
the eighteenth-century legal doctrine of "coverture," Abigail's self-understanding of her "duty" renders her politically invisible, except as represented by her husband.[24] The boundary between personal and political life
is thus drawn and secured along gender lines. Abigail's earlier demand for
"representation" and "voice" undoubtedly works against this structure of
political exclusion. But its address to John mitigates the force of that demand
by producing a now familiar compromise between civic activity and state
representation, between republican citizenship and sexual subjection.
"Women and dependents," Habermas notes, "were factually and legally excluded from the political public sphere, whereas female readers as well as
apprentices and servants often took a more active part in the literary public
sphere."[25] Only an institutional reduction of the critical function of the public sphere to the representative function of the state—a reduction, in Habermas's terms, of the literary to the political public sphere—would be needed
at this point to produce the (hetero)sexist ideology of separate spheres that
has dominated the history of liberalism in the United States.

At the same time, the structure of Abigail's letters points to their incom-
patibility with the ideology they otherwise espouse. If read as addressed
directly to John, the letters remain a private complaint of personal injuries
caused by "Masculine systems," or perhaps even a private concession to
those systems. In either case, Abigail's complaint to John reinscribes the
anti-democratic structure of representation within the political public
sphere. If read as addressed indirectly to John through the mediation of the
post, however, the letters become newsworthy—public-oriented attempts to
educate *her* country as to the political injustice of "Masculine systems" or, at
worst, public-oriented attempts to educate an audience limited to John. In

either case, Abigail's complaint mobilizes the egalitarian promise of the literary public sphere against the inegalitarian practices of the political public sphere. While the first reading is consistently legible in the letters and indicates Abigail's understanding of her sexual identity as assigning her a gendered "duty," the second is by no means illegible and indicates her contradictory understanding of her political identity as expressively linked to her ungendered desire or, as the protagonist of Mary Wollstonecraft's *Maria* puts it, her "active sensibility, and positive virtue."[26] While the first leads to an ideology of separate spheres characteristic of liberalism, the second leads to a civil egalitarianism characteristic of democratic republicanism. While the first understands personal letters, when circulated in public, as "lost" and reacts to that loss by reaffirming the boundary between personal and political life, the second understands them as "loosed" and reacts by investigating the civil and state institutions that police that boundary.

Given Abigail Adams's contradictory status as a lettered woman within a simultaneously patriarchal and republican political culture, her anxieties concerning the post's loose circulation of her correspondence are neither anomalous, nor simply personal. Rather, they are an effect of a structural antagonism within republicanism between literary and political models of the public sphere, between civil and state authority. The third chapter of this book traced this antagonism to an antithesis between corporeality and nationality within Washington's patriotic body. This chapter and the next investigate the effects of that same antagonism on the sexed and sexualized body. Here, I turn specifically to Hannah Foster's 1797 epistolary novel, *The Coquette; or, The History of Eliza Wharton*, as exemplary of the contradictions within the genre of female sentimentalism. Like many sentimental novels, *The Coquette* explores the political relations among sex, gender, and citizenship by narrating the seduction and death of a young, unmarried, middle-class woman. As in Richardson's ur-texts of the genre (*Pamela* and *Clarissa*), Foster stages that seduction as an eroticized struggle for control over the public circulation of personal letters. "I do not think you seducible," Mrs. Richman tells Eliza, "nor was Richardson's Clarissa, till she made herself a victim, by her own indiscretion."[27] *The Coquette*, in this sense, resembles novels like *Pamela* and *Charlotte Temple* in its attempt to educate young readers in the ideological and structural requirements of republican womanhood. But it also differs from such novels in its fuller thematization of the costs of the reduction of the literary to the political public sphere or, in short, the reduction of a republican citizenship to republican womanhood. The structural possibility of loose letters, I will argue, produces not only the dystopian plot of *The Coquette* as a warning to young readers to avoid the seductive perils of indiscrete correspondence, but also the utopian basis of the novel's critical potential as one among many sentimental letters loosed in the early republic.

Fantasies of Sex and Gender

As critics have often noted, Foster's claim on her novel's title page that *The Coquette* is "founded in FACT" is both a convention of eighteenth-century fiction and, in this case, more than simply conventional.[28] Nine years prior to her literary resurrection as Foster's protagonist, Eliza Wharton, Elizabeth Whitman arrived at the Bell Tavern in Danvers, Massachusetts, gave birth to a stillborn child and died two days later of puerperal fever. At the time, her possessions were few, consisting of a little money, clothes for herself and the baby, three rings, six silver spoons, and the eighteenth-century equivalent of a laptop with modem—a writing case with paper, pens, and sealing wafers. Reprinted in newspapers throughout New England, the initial account of Whitman's death appeared in the *Salem Mercury* on July 29, 1788:

> Last Friday, a female stranger died at the Bell Tavern, in Danvers. . . . The circumstances relative to this woman are such as to excite curiosity, and interest our feelings. She was brought to the Bell in a chaise. . . . She remained at this inn till her death, in expectation of the arrival of her husband, whom she expected to come for her, and appeared anxious at his delay. . . . Her conversation, her writings and her manners, bespoke the advantage of a respectable family and good education.[29]

The curiosity excited by the death of this "female stranger" only intensified once she was identified as Elizabeth Whitman, daughter of the Reverend Elnathan Whitman and descended, on her mother's side, from Connecticut's political and social elite. "Once Whitman's identity was revealed," writes literary historian Cathy Davidson, "ministers, journalists, and freelance moralists industriously made *meaning*—their meaning—of her otherwise incomprehensible life."[30] Like the heroines who follow in her wake, Whitman provides the body that serves as both a ground and a site for sentimental pedagogy. The news of her death furnishes, in the words of one anonymous essayist, "a good moral lecture to young ladies."[31]

Still, questions remained as to what the moral of that lecture would be. For those writers whom Davidson refers to as "morally conservative," Whitman's seduction and abandonment spoke for themselves. Her death exemplified the pernicious effects of both unrealistic marital aspirations among women and novel-reading as a source of those aspirations. "She was a great reader of romances," the *Massachusetts Centinel* asserted, "and having formed her notions of happiness from that source, became vain and coquetish." A similar etiology informs the *Boston Independent Chronicle*'s account: "She refused two as good offers of marriage as she deserved because she aspired higher than a clergyman's wife; and having coquetted till past her prime, fell into criminal indulgences."[32] By equating novel-reading and "coquetry," these journalistic accounts trace Whitman's death to her failed reading strategies. Seduced by the rewards meted out to Pamela-like heroines, Whitman follows the well-worn path of other female quixotes and Madame Bovarys. She mistakes sentimental fiction for fact and, in doing so, misreads the gender and class narratives that mediate her relation to the future. Her death thus produces a "moral lecture" through the negative example of her romantic disregard for the reality of her social status. Even had Whitman been born to a social position superior (or inferior) to that of a "clergyman's wife," however, these accounts imply that novel-reading would remain problematic since novels maintain only a counter-factual relation to the real. The aspirations novels inspire are to be understood, in other words, not only quantitatively as less than realistic, but also qualitatively as the very negation of the real.

By condemning novels in this categorical fashion, the journalistic accounts frame Whitman's death as a result of an epistemological confusion between fiction and reality, produced, in turn, by a generic confusion between the ontological claims of novels and news as antithetical forms of public discourse. Such generic attacks on the novel were ubiquitous in the early republic, and accord with one conservative variant of republican political theory. As Michael Warner has argued, critics of the novel "endlessly avowed a fear that fiction would detach readers' sentiments from the social world of the polity, substituting a private drama of fancy."[33] For this form of republicanism, the problem with such a substitution is that it entails a division of personal and political life, of personality structures ("readers' sentiments") and structures of publicity ("the social world of the polity"). Fiction threatens, in other words, to fracture the personal-political unity promised by the two linchpins of republicanism: virtue and publication. Sentimental seduction narratives like *The Coquette* consequently mark a tension within republican letters: they promise to wed the sentimental and the social through literary publication, but consistently fail to produce this virtuous conclusion. Seduction plots thus reveal what Warner refers to as the "ideological ambivalences surrounding the personality type of modernity."[34] Despite Foster's claim that her heroine's experiences are "founded in FACT," *The Coquette* and other early novels can only simulate the factual by publishing fictions grounded in specific social and generic conventions. This contradiction inspires contemporary defenses of novel-writing, as well as attacks on novel-reading. Both uphold, in Warner's words, "an ideal of republican literature in which publication and the public sphere remain identical; both worry that the environment of fictitious identification might no longer entail public knowledge or civic activity."[35]

This characterization of the anxiety produced by the novel's confusion of fact and fiction neatly summarizes one republican polemic against imaginary forms of political identification. But it also assumes a series of oppositions

(virtue and fancy, reality and fiction, polity and personality) that was under-
going significant revision in the late eighteenth century. The novel itself
contributes to that revision since, as Habermas suggests, it can be read not
only as subverting republican virtue by embracing the fanciful or fictive, but
also as attacking the very distinction between fiction and reality that informs,
for example, the generic distinction between novels and news: "The reality
as illusion that the new genre created received its proper name in English,
"fiction": it shed the character of the *merely* fictitious. The psychological
novel allowed anyone to enter into literary action as a substitute for his [sic]
own, to use the relationships between the figures, between the author, the
characters, and the reader as substitute relationships for reality."[36] While
Warner aligns this structure of substitution with the rise of liberalism as a
political regime based on imaginary (and privatized) identifications between
personal and public life, Habermas tells a different story. Rather than evincing a turn away from "public knowledge" and "civic activity," the novel's
realist fictions support the development of a literary sphere emerging within
civil society as a public (and imaginary) space conducive to unofficial critical
debate. "The privatized individuals coming together to form a public,"
Habermas argues, "also reflected critically and in public on what they had
read, thus contributing to the process of enlightenment which they together
promoted."[37] In contrast to Warner, then, Habermas views fiction not (only)
as corrupting, but (also) as democratizing public debate. The threat posed to
classical republicanism by the novel thus results more from its recoupling,
than from its decoupling of fancy and virtue, of fiction and fact, of personal
sentiments and public discourse. "Fancy," in this sense, exists not as a simple negation of the real, but as an imaginary projection, as Judith Butler puts
it, of the "not *yet* real."[38]

According to this second account, the novel neither dismisses all claims to
newsworthiness, nor forgoes all participation in public debate concerning
the social and generic conventions that constitute reality. Rather, it initiates
an alternative regime for the production of the real or, in the case of sentimental novels like *The Coquette*, for the production of what the *Salem Mercury* refers to as "our feelings" concerning the public significance of events
like Elizabeth Whitman's death.[39] Nowhere is the importance of such "feelings" more evident than in the scenes of reading that populate early novels.
In the most-read, banned book of the Enlightenment, for instance, the
philosophical heroine (Therese) concludes her narrative by recounting the
seductive "effects of reading and painting."[40] Having tired of her pragmatic
preference for masturbation (illicit sensual pleasure without the risk of pregnancy), Therese's lover (the Count) provides her with his library of erotica
and proposes a wager. If she can peruse the collection every morning for two
weeks without resorting to "manualism," the library is hers. If she fails, she
must accept a "divorce from manualism."[41] Insulted at the Count's low opin-

ion of her self-control, Therese accepts the wager, only to fall prey to the sensations inspired by the books and paintings five days later. "As my imagination began to be ignited," she reports, " . . . I threw off the sheets and covers and, without pausing to think whether or not the door of my room was secured, I prepared to imitate all the positions I saw."[42] The Count and Therese maintain an ideological commitment to "secrecy" as a means of ensuring sensual pleasure without disrupting the "order of society," but this mise-en-scène highlights the novel's structural betrayal of that commitment.[43] Like other sensational and pornographic novels, *Therese Philosophe* targets its heroine's and reader's bodies as sites of personal transformation and political critique. Both the bedroom's open door and the novel's publication reveal that Therese's fired imagination and the vice it provokes are neither private nor solitary.

The structural kinship between the pornographic and sentimental novel will be the subject of my sixth chapter. For now, suffice to say that this second understanding of the relations among publication, sensation, and the novel informs the critical re-evaluation of what Jane Tompkins refers to as the "sentimental power" of fictions like *The Coquette*.[44] In the most important application of these insights to the writings of the early republican period, Cathy Davidson argues that an attempt to refute earlier journalistic narratives of Whitman's death motivates Foster's own project of sentimental (re)education. Unlike most early novels, *The Coquette* contains no generic attack on either novels or novel-reading.[45] For Davidson, this absence pinpoints Foster's modification of previous narratives of Whitman's death and, through those narratives, arguments concerning the civil and political status of women in the early republic.[46] Taking Foster's Wharton as both an historical representation of Whitman and a fictional point of identification for all women readers, Davidson views *The Coquette* as a counter-hegemonic attack on those "ministers, journalists, and free-lance moralists" who, in publicizing their sentiments concerning Whitman's death, made "their meaning" of that death. *The Coquette*, Davidson suggests, critiques the sexual double standard, debunks the cult of domesticity, and provides a rare opportunity for the novel's readers to see, "in print, women very much like themselves."[47] The last of these three claims is the most significant because it anchors Davidson's objection to earlier feminist criticisms of the novel as, in Nina Baym's words, an "unqualified picture of woman as man's inevitable dupe and prey."[48] The problem with such analyses is not that they are inaccurate to a plot that does end in Eliza's seduction and death, but that they ignore the vicissitudes of what Therese calls the "effects of reading." Admonishing feminist critics to focus on the novel's "interstices" or, in short, to read between the lines, Davidson argues that Foster covertly attacks the "patriarchal culture" of the 1790s by "expos[ing] its fundamental injustices through the details and disasters of the plot."[49]

As one crucial basis of that culture, the institution of marriage is the most obvious target of this attack. In contrast to the news accounts that trace Whitman's death to her failure to marry wisely, Foster's novel allows its readers to shift the blame to Wharton's male suitors. Positioned between the "attentive and sincere" reverend (Mr. Boyer) and the "gay and polite" libertine (Major Sanford), Eliza faces a dilemma common to eighteenth-century heroines. Again, *Therese Philosophe* is exemplary. Just as that narrative begins by noting two contradictory "passions" that war within Therese ("the love of God and the love of sensual pleasure"), Eliza's first letter opens by opposing her "obedience to the will and desire of [her] parents" to her "pleasure . . . upon leaving [her] parental roof" (5).[50] Foster aligns the former with Boyer and the latter with Sanford, but she quickly complicates this conventional opposition by committing several of Eliza's early letters to a questioning of why Boyer and Sanford should be her only two marital choices or, indeed, why she should be married at all (24). "What a pity," Eliza writes in a letter to Lucy Freeman, " . . . that the graces and virtues are not oftner united! They must, however, meet in the man of my choice; and till I find such a one, I shall continue to subscribe my name Eliza Wharton" (22). This "subscription" allows Eliza to maintain the patronym that she inherits from her now dead father. As such, it places her momentarily outside of paternal (or fraternal) control. In a letter to her mother, Eliza repeats this assertion of autonomy in reference to Boyer: "[I]f I must enter the connubial state, are there not *others*, who may be equally pleasing in their persons, and whose profession may be more conformable to my taste?" (39). The singular appearance of a third suitor for Eliza toward the middle of the novel—Mr. Emmons, a "respectable merchant" from the city—seems to have no other narrative function than to highlight the possibility of marital choices beyond either Boyer or Sanford (62).

Such modifications are not definitive, of course. Labeling Eliza "a spoiled and artful flirt who refuses good marriage offers," Baym echoes both the *Chronicle*'s identification of Eliza as a "coquette" and Lucy Freeman's response to Eliza's objection to Boyer. "His situation in life," Lucy writes to Eliza, "is, perhaps, as elevated as you have a right to claim" (27). In contrast to both Baym and Lucy, Davidson encourages the reader to side with Eliza. Her refusals of Boyer and Sanford thus become signs not of her "coquetry," but of her commitment to an emerging redefinition of marriage as a purely contractual relationship grounded in mutual affection and heartfelt sentiments, rather than economic or kinship structures.[51] Eliza's "coquetry," in this sense, typifies what Davidson sees as the sentimental (and romance) novel's "reappropria[tion] of choice" for female protagonists and readers: "By reading about a female character's good and bad decisions in sexual and marital matters, the early American woman could vicariously enact her own courtship and marriage fantasies. She could, at least in those fantasies, view her life as largely a consequence of her own choices and not merely as the product of others in her life."[52] By highlighting the unpredictable (and liberatory) effects of such readerly identification, Davidson skirts Baym's claim that Eliza's story produces "[f]rom a woman's point of view . . . a demoralized literature."[53] While Baym here assumes an immediate identity between the female reader and the seduced and abandoned Eliza, Davidson points to the element of fantasy that mediates any identification between that reader and Eliza as a potentially representative protagonist. By positing fantasy as the mediating link between identity and publication, Davidson positions the reader as an agent capable, through the force of fantasy, of choosing to identify with Eliza as an independent agent, without choosing to identify with Eliza's death as the narrative outcome of that autonomy. Fantasy, in other words, renders the reality of Eliza's seduction and abandonment potentially unreal. As Lucy points out in one of the novel's many self-reflexive moments, the topics of Eliza's letters ("a bleeding heart, slighted love, and all the *et ceteras* of romance") chart only one of many narrative possibilities (107).

This insight into the political significance of fantasy enables Davidson to read *The Coquette* as historically continuous with nineteenth- and twentieth-century feminism. Rather than simply initiating a privatized "cult of true womanhood," *The Coquette* utters what Davidson refers to as a "smothered cry for female equality, a cry faintly but subversively heard in those sentimental novels . . . that remained steady sellers into . . . the dawnings of America's first full-fledged feminist movement."[54] But the same insight also points to a weakness in Davidson's portrayal of Foster as, in short, a democratic feminist in conservative republican drag. The problem with this assessment lies neither in its pathos nor its anachronism, but in its failure to extend Davidson's insight concerning the phantasmatic nature of identification to her own critical practice. Davidson notes the naivete of nineteenth-century readers who viewed *The Coquette* as a roman à clef and attempted, in their critical fantasies, to determine its significance by establishing the historical identities of the fictional characters (Aaron Burr or Joel Barlow as Major Sanford, for example). But she also repeats that strategy by reading the novel sociologically and attempting, in her critical fantasy, to determine its significance by establishing the historical context and probable response of the "early American woman reader."[55] In accordance with Foster's assertion that the novel is "founded in FACT," nineteenth-century readers located the factual in specific historical personalities; in accordance with the same assertion, Davidson locates the factual in a generic historical (and national) personality. While Baym and Davidson explicitly disagree as to the effect that *The Coquette* had and has on the "female reader," they implicitly agree that the "female reader" is a useful and realistic critical fiction with which to interrogate the novel's political implications.[56]

This fiction of the "female reader" is obviously a commonplace of much feminist criticism. And as a strategy within a larger project aimed at the retrieval of novels written by women, it seems to me unobjectionable. As a tool for reading those novels, however, the category of the "female reader" becomes problematic both theoretically and historically. In theoretical terms, the problem with this sort of critical essentialism is that it repeats the novel's own encoding of fiction as fact. By identifying the real as primary (in this case, the "fact" of the "female reader"), it misidentifies fantasy as secondary in relation to the real (in this case, as a "strategy" used by the "female reader" to avoid the "demoralizing" conclusions of seduction narratives). "This formulation," Judith Butler argues, ". . . operates through an implicit understanding of *fantasy* as that which both produces and is produced by representations and which, then, makes possible and enacts precisely the referent of that representation."[57] Fantasy, according to this implicit understanding of representation, both precedes and proceeds from the real, producing a paradoxical logic of identification best captured in Davidson's claim that Foster allowed "early readers" to see, "in print, women very much like themselves." By positioning "print" as the mediating term between "early readers" and "women," Davidson opens a gap between publication and identification that could lead to an interrogation of fantasy as the means by which fictive narratives like *The Coquette* interpellate "early readers" as "women." By asserting an immediate identity between "early readers" and "women," however, Davidson equates publication and identification. In doing so, she produces an uncritical fantasy of identification that becomes convincing only when, in Butler words, its "own phantasmatic status is eclipsed and renamed as the real."[58]

In historical terms, the theoretical problems raised by this foreclosure of fantasy are doubly significant since the late eighteenth century marks a pivotal moment in the development of the generic category of the "female reader." Historians Londa Schiebinger and Thomas Laqueur have established that the democratic revolutions in France and the United States coincided with a shift from a one-sex model of the human body as differing only by degree along an "axis whose telos was male" to a two-sex model of "radical dimorphism, of biological divergence."[59] "An anatomy and physiology of incommensurability," Laqueur writes, "replaced a metaphysics of hierarchy in the representation of woman in relation to man."[60] In response to the revolutionary assertion that the "mind has no sex," eighteenth-century anatomists discovered a direct correspondence between bodies and minds, between sex and gender. "The essence of sex," explained one French physician in 1775, "is not confined to a single organ but extends, through more or less perceptible nuances, into every part."[61] In the United States, Benjamin Rush's *Lectures on the Mind* both confirmed this conclusion and drew from it a now familiar political moral. "I hold it to be essential," Rush asserts, ". . . that there should exist exactly those degrees of inferiority and contrast between the two sexes which have been described. Many of the disorders, not only of domestic, but of political society, I believe originate in the inversion of this order."[62] Alongside contemporary ideologies based in racial logics of embodiment that reconciled the egalitarian promise of republicanism and the economic reality of chattel slavery, sexual dimorphism provided a justification for gender inequality. As Nancy Armstrong and Robyn Wiegman have suggested, sentimentalism's focus on bodies and affect contributes to this naturalization of sexual difference when it reduces the politics of gender relations to the corporeal "reality" of the sexed body. From *Pamela* to *Emma*, Armstrong concludes, sentimental fiction transforms "political information into the discourse of sexuality."[63]

Given these varied objections to the critical fiction of the "female reader," the problem with Davidson's account of sentimental novels like *The Coquette* is that it replicates Foster's own contribution to the dimorphic logic of the modern sex-gender system. Repeating Baym's often-cited description of sentimentalism as writing "by and about women," Davidson stages the interpretive controversy over Elizabeth Whitman's death as a battle between opposed communities of male "moralists" and female "readers." Of the seventy-four letters that make up *The Coquette*, fifty-eight mediate homosocial relations between women, while only six mediate heterosocial relations between women and men. For Davidson, this preponderance of letters written to and from women indicates the novel's public affirmation of what she refers to as "woman-talk: women confiding, chiding, warning, disagreeing, and then confronting one another." Davidson here notes the agonistic nature of such "talk," but her argument resolves any dissention through reference to the apparently self-evident category "woman."[64] By using this category to unify the "talk" of the politically and economically diverse characters who make up *The Coquette*, Davidson overlooks the problem that lies at the center of both the novel and much critical response to it—that of wedding sentimentality and sociality by deploying the category "woman" as a public site of readerly identification. "From the melancholy story of Eliza Wharton," writes Lucy in her final letter, "let the American fair learn to reject with disdain every insinuation derogatory to their true dignity and honor. Let them despise, and for ever banish the man, who can glory in the seduction of innocence and the ruin of reputation" (168). While Davidson and Baym read this concluding moral as addressed to an already existing "female reader," I will argue that it constructs that category by encouraging a fantasy of identification between the republican citizen whose "mind has no sex" and the sentimental subject for whom anatomy is (only) in the process of becoming destiny.

Sex, Gender, and Horsemanship

Like the figures of the "coquette" in the journalistic accounts of Elizabeth Whitman's death and the "Watertown belle" in Abigail Adams's letter to John, the figure of Eliza as seducible positions her at the boundary of the "American fair." If read teleologically, Foster's account of her heroine's indiscretions secure that boundary by delineating the norms of "dignity and honor" that ideally protect republican women against the designs of male seducers like Sanford. But this reading does not tell the whole story. It is certainly significant that Foster highlights the duplicity of the sexual double standard by positioning Eliza between Boyer and Sanford as symmetrically undesirable male suitors. If nothing else, this narrative deviation from the earlier news reports expands the boundaries of the "American fair" by complicating any facile categorization of Whitman as a "coquette."[65] But this deviation itself relies upon a second, arguably more significant pair of oppositions. Foster locates Eliza amid a chorus of specifically middle-class women (Lucy Freeman/Sumner, Julia Granby, Mrs. Richman) flanked, on one side, by aristocratic women like the "agreeable" but "soulless" Miss Laurence and, on the other, by lower-class women typified by the circus performers who appear as part of Lucy's censorial reflections on public entertainments (21, 34). Just as Boyer and Sanford mark the two extremes Eliza must negotiate in her search for a republican husband, Miss Laurence and the circus performers mark the extremes she must avoid if she is to move from the margins to the center of republican womanhood. Both Eliza and the reader must learn to defend their "dignity and honor" from the "snares," as Rowson puts it in her preface to *Charlotte Temple*, "not only of the other sex, but from the more dangerous arts of the profligate of [their] own."[66]

The pitfalls of an identification with characters like Miss Laurence are relatively straightforward. In contrast to the middle-class women who provide the novel's moral center, Miss Laurence is as bad a reader of generic and social conventions as the news reports made Whitman out to be. Educated in aristocratic fashion, she lacks the insight necessary to plumb the immoral and impoverished reality behind the fortune-hunting Sanford's "superficial, ensnaring endowments" (58). Foster leaves little doubt as to where such misguided faith in the class-based conventions of public representation leads: Miss Laurence winds up unhappily married to a second "fortune hunter," Mr. Laiton (98). At the opposite end of the social spectrum, the circus performers present a more complicated and revealing set of problems. In a none-too-subtle warning to both Eliza and the reader, Lucy prefaces her comments on the circus by cautioning against tragic drama. "Death," she writes in reference to a performance of *Romeo and Juliet*, "is too serious a matter to be sported with! An open grave cannot be a source of amusement to any considerate mind!" (112–13). She then quickly moves to the circus performers whom she condemns not, like Miss Laurence, for their excessive attention to the conventions of public representation, but for their inattention to those same conventions. "The circus," Lucy observes, "is a fashionable resort of late, but not agreeable to me":

> I think it inconsistent with the delicacy of a lady, even to witness the indecorums, which are practiced there; especially when the performers of equestrian feats are of our own sex. To see a woman depart so far from the female character, as to assume the masculine habit and attitudes; and appear entirely indifferent, even to the externals of modesty is truly disgusting, and ought not to be countenanced by our attendance, much less by our approbation. (113)

The letter concludes by recommending an antidote to both the theater and the circus. The "rational and refined amusement" of "Mr. Bowen's museum," Lucy suggests, "will bear frequent review without palling on the taste" (113).

Foster positions Miss Laurence and the circus performers antithetically: Miss Laurence's aristocratic education makes her too conventionally feminine (vulnerable to men of "show and fashion"), while the problem with the circus performers is that they do not appear to be feminine enough ("indifferent, even to the externals of modesty"). But together these two extremes allow Foster to achieve one of the prerequisites of any successful ideology—to portray an historically specific code of behavior (middle-class femininity, in this case) as universal. Miss Laurence and the circus performers fall outside the category of the "American fair" due to their inappropriate enactments of the relation between sex and gender, not because of their respective class positions. As Armstrong suggests, this depoliticization of class difference through reference to naturalized gender conventions is typical of both the sentimental novel and contemporary middle-class reform movements. In his "Thoughts upon Female Education," for instance, Rush provides what could be taken as a gloss of Miss Laurence's romantic fate. Upper-class educational practices, he argues, exaggerate gender difference by depriving women of the "useful branches of literature," thus rendering them susceptible to the "intrigues of the British novel" and the "refinements of Asiatic vice."[67] In his *Lectures on the Mind*, Rush supplements this argument for educational reform by fixing its limit at the anatomical division between male and female bodies: "There is an original difference in the bodies and minds of men and women, stamped upon both in the womb by the hand of nature. This difference shews itself in childhood, independent of precept and/or example; e.g., who ever saw a boy amuse himself with a doll? or a girl anticipate riding on horseback, by straddling or riding a stick?"[68] That the specter of female equestrianism haunts both *The Coquette* and the *Lectures* is as striking as it may be coincidental. Like Lucy, Rush conjures the image of female masculinity (and male femininity) in order to portray emerging middle-class gender conventions as universal, as a reflection of anatomical facts rather than an effect of political relations.

This comparison disguises an important difference, however. Foster may agree with Rush that gender conventions are grounded in the (sexed) body, but Lucy's judgment of taste is not as simple as his anatomy lesson. For Rush, the question of the relation between the body and the body politic—between sex and gender—is merely rhetorical. Sex (the "original difference in the bodies and minds of men and women") naturally expresses itself as gender (girls play with dolls, boys straddle sticks). Because this relation exists "independent of precept and/or example," any critical discussion of either sexual or gender (cross-)identification can only lead to utopian speculation: "The notion started by the ingenious and eloquent female author of *The Rights of Women*, that all the difference between the talents and the virtues of the two sexes is the effect of *education*, is as hypothetical as Helvetius's notion of all the variety in human talents depending on the same cause."[69] In contrast to this biological determinism, Lucy portrays the relation of sex and gender as mediated by neither anatomy nor nature, but by taste. Equestrianism is unsuitable to the "female character" not because it is counter-factual (she testifies that women may straddle sticks), but because it is distasteful. This substitution of aesthetic for anatomical judgment both reframes the question of the relation between sex and gender, and provides one typically sentimental answer. In response to democratic feminists like Mary Wollstonecraft and Olympe de Gouges who attacked the masculinist foundation of contemporary republicanism, many social conservatives drew upon the discourse of manners, refinement, and taste in order to shore up patriarchal gender conventions. It is this counter-revolutionary discourse that Norbert Elias refers to as "civilizing" and G. J. Barker-Benfield as "sentimentalizing."[70] Edmund Burke's *Reflections on the Revolution in France* provides a notable example of this conservative defense of sentimental refinement, while Foster's deployment of the language of taste and disgust positions *The Coquette* within the same political field.

As a metaphor for aesthetic sensibility, taste is perhaps most familiar from Immanuel Kant's *Critique of Judgment* where it tends to be shorn of any sentimental residue. "The Iroquois Sachem" who "was pleased in Paris by nothing more than by the cook shops" demonstrates, according to Kant, his inability to distinguish between two forms of taste: the sensual and the aesthetic.[71] While the former confirms the truism that "everyone has his own taste (the taste of sense)," only the latter can justify a "rightful claim upon everyone's assent."[72] Yet the rigor with which Kant polices this distinction (a rigor that leads him at times to abandon the sentimental altogether) disguises an historical (and etymological) continuity between sensual and aesthetic judgments. Kant exploits the metaphor of taste precisely because it links the abstract requirements of aesthetic universality to the experience of sensual embodiment. The "Sachem" may not yet be able to render universal aesthetic judgments, but neither can Kant's preferences determine without his assent what such judgments will reveal. The metaphor of taste thus contains a paradox since it confirms the autonomy of every body's sense perceptions while evoking, at the same time, what Kant refers to as a *sensus communis*—a socio-aesthetic consensus that transcends without violating individual sensibilities.[73] Kant's negotiation of this fine line between autonomy and heteronomy requires a delicate balance between identification and projection. Playing a role analogous to that of the circus performers in *The Coquette*, the "Sachem" must be othered within the *Critique* without becoming alien to it. His aesthetic judgments may vary from those of enlightened Europeans, but Kant warns that such variations ought not lead to skeptical or relativistic conclusions. The metaphor of taste prevents this (multicultural) outcome by mapping a route from bodily sensation to universal aesthetics, from the "Sachem's" actual preference for Parisian "cook shops" to his theoretical inclusion in the "collective reason of humanity."[74]

As the ideological antithesis of the universal judgment of taste, Lucy's expression of disgust negotiates a similarly fine line between autonomy and heteronomy, between identification and projection. The circus performers share Lucy's sexual identity as "women," while their deviation from middle-class gender norms (their adoption of "the masculine habit and attitudes") provokes her critical judgment of them. "Ladies," Lucy warns, ought not to "countenance" "women" who "depart from the female character." This complicated prescription could lead to debate concerning the "habit and attitudes" of the "female character," but Lucy's disgust forecloses that possibility. Like the tears that secure gender norms elsewhere in this and other sentimental novels, disgust refers questions of gender normativity to the presumably unmediated experience of bodily sensation. This response echoes Rush's biological determinism, but with a difference. Lucy agrees with Rush that gender norms emerge from the body, but the body to which she refers gains a gender identity on sentimental rather than anatomical grounds. Where Rush conceives of the feminine virtues of "modesty" and "delicacy" as a reflex of a sexually dimorphic anatomy, Lucy views them as (natural) resources available through an aesthetic education of the senses.[75] The resulting gap between sex ("women") and gender ("ladies") frees the circus performers from the strictures of Rush's anatomical destiny, but it also deprives them of the social and political benefits accrued by subjects whose bodies are trained to the normalizing code of sentimental gender aesthetics. "Like sensibility," Barker-Benfield observes, "'taste' expressed distinction, not only from 'the world' but above the 'vulgar.'"[76] Paired with Eliza's dismissal of Miss Lawrence as "soulless," Lucy's disgust at the circus performers allows Foster to construct a specifically middle-class femininity—a *sen-*

sus communis—that is both theoretically universal (authorized by the sensations of any body) and practically exclusive (limited to bodies trained in the
codes of sentimentality).

That *The Coquette* ends with Eliza's death marks her individual failure to
make the transition from *lumpen* to "true" womanhood, from sentiment to
sentimentality. But it also does little to disrupt the hegemony of middle-class
gender norms. Pictured in the novel's concluding letter, Eliza's gravestone
redeems her by transforming her failure into a lesson: "Let candor throw a
veil over her frailties, / For great was her charity to others. / She sustained
the last / Painful scene, far from every friend; / And exhibited an example /Of
calm resignation" (169). Where the "open graves" of tragic dramas like
Romeo and Juliet "distress" "sensibility" by "rack[ing] the soul with grief,"
the closing of Eliza's grave stages her death as an exhibit which pacifies and
contains the bodily sensations that it relies upon and provokes (112–13).
This conclusion ought to be neither surprising nor fully satisfying. As
Barker-Benfield points out (and any reader of *Uncle Tom's Cabin* knows),
deathbed and graveyard scenes mark a critical tension within the culture of
sensibility.[77] *The Coquette* begins by evoking sentimentalism's generic commitment to the authenticity of individual sensibility as a bulwark against
heteronomous authority. And Eliza enacts this ideal in her opening letters
when she relegates social conventions concerning her subjective experience
of grief to the realm of the "fashionable": "To have our enjoyments arrested
by the empty compliments of unthinking persons, for no other reason than
a compliance with fashion is to be treated in a manner, which the laws of
humanity forbid" (9). By the end of the novel, however, sentimentalism's
ideological commitment to the collective management of sensation prevails:
grief harnesses the autonomy of any aleatory sensibility to the middle-class
code of sentimental femininity. Like the "refined amusement" of Mr.
Bowen's museum, the "example" of Eliza's "calm resignation" teaches a lesson that passes "without palling the taste" from exhibitor to spectator, from
Eliza's "weeping friends" to the "strangers" whose tears "watered her grave"
(169).

The Ends of the Epistolary

The reduction of sentiment to sentimentality ultimately secured by Eliza's
death has more than one effect in sentimental novels like *The Coquette*. At
times, it anchors a conservative idealization of conjugal domesticity as
women's natural vocation. Boyer, for example, reconciles Eliza's subjective
"enjoyment" with the objective requirements of what would become the
"woman's sphere" when he describes her as the type of "cheerful wife . . .
necessary to a person of a studious and sedentary life" (11). Mrs. Richman

echoes Boyer when she informs Eliza that "[i]t is the glory of the marriage state . . . to refine, by circumscribing our enjoyments. Here we can repose in safety" (24). At other points, the same reduction opens onto less restrictive possibilities. Not only does Eliza imagine a divergence from the marriage plot when she "recoil[s] at the thought of immediately forming a connection, which must confine [her] to the duties of domestic life" (29), but she and Mrs. Richman also reject the belief of Miss Laurence and her mother that the public world of "politics" does not "belong to the ladies." Presented in her drawing room, Mrs. Richman's response aligns her with Eliza. "Miss Wharton and I," she retorts, "beg leave to differ":

> We think ourselves interested in the welfare and prosperity of our country; and, consequently, claim the right of inquiring into those affairs, which may conduce to, or interfere with the common weal. We shall not be called to the senate or the field to assert its privileges, and defend its rights, but we shall feel for the honor and safety of our friends and connections. . . . Why then should the love of country be a masculine passion only? Why should government . . . be wholly excluded from our observation. (44)

Applauded by her "gentlemen" auditors as "truly Roman" and "truly republican," Mrs. Richman's speech drives a wedge between sex and citizenship, between the "masculine passion" of patriotism and a republican interest in the "common weal." Along with Eliza, Mrs. Richman may be excluded as a woman from the official functions of the "senate" and "field," but her appeal argues for and from within the theoretically ungendered and democratic space of the literary public sphere.

The staging of this speech in the Richman's drawing room highlights its structural implications. As Habermas and others have argued, the historical significance of the eighteenth-century salon lay in its status as an unofficial public space of literary and political debate. Like other such spaces (the male-dominated coffeehouse, for example), the salon both secured and bridged the boundary dividing private and public life. "The line between private and public spheres," Habermas observes, "extended right through the home. The privatized individuals stepped out of the intimacy of their living rooms into the public sphere of the *salon*."[78] What is "republican" about Mrs. Richman's appeal is that it exploits this structural interpenetration of private and public spheres in order to critique the ideological separation of those spheres along gender lines. Her appeal assumes that citizens' actions in the unofficial public sphere of the literary salon bear only a contingent relation to the (gendered) attributes of their (sexed) bodies. Such an appeal suggests, in turn, a central contradiction within sentimental novels like *The Coquette*. Drawing on the sensationalist and materialist psychology of the early Enlightenment, such novels deploy a conception of sentiment that both grounds subjectivity in the experience of the body and dissociates

that experience from any socially sanctioned forms of embodiment.[79] Sentiment consequently refers to an array of bodily sensations that provide both
the site and the ground of debate concerning the relations (or nonrelations)
among sex, gender, and citizenship. The tension between these two uses of
sentiment—as site and as ground of debate—produces an ambiguous model
of identification in *The Coquette* since it interpellates individuals like Eliza
and Mrs. Richman into the public space of the literary salon both as citizens
capable of debating the political effects of sex and gender, and as subjects
whose (gender) politics are determined by their (sexual) identity. This dual
interpellation allows (and even requires) Mrs. Richman to speak as an
ungendered citizen of the republic (one who "feels" for her country), even
when the content of that speech prescribes the gender norms central to the
conservative attack on (re)public(an) women.

Speeches like Mrs. Richman's thus point to a fissure within the genre of
sentimentalism between its structural commitment to the unfettered publication of bodily and intimate sensations on the one hand, and its ideological
commitment to policing the boundaries of the public sphere along gender
lines on the other. Outside of the novel, the same fissure reappears in Foster's signature. As "a Lady of Massachusetts" or, later, "Mrs. Hannah Foster," Foster participates in the literary public sphere, even as she grounds
her participation in her status as a married woman, a "feme covert" in the
eyes of the state. While the speech and the signature assume a sexed and
gendered body, they also reveal the structural contradictions within a sentimental code of (sexual) embodiment that can be secured only through a
disavowal of the (gender) politics of its own public construction. This contradiction is replayed in Eliza's own comments on public entertainments. In
response to Lucy's letter, Eliza suggests that public stages like the circus
and theater need better supervision. "I think it a pity," she writes, "they have
not female managers for the theater. I believe it would be under much better
regulations, than at present" (124). Eliza's recourse to specifically "female"
managers as a safeguard against ideological misrepresentation expands,
without betraying the aesthetics of sexual dimorphism upon which the sentimental discourse of womanhood rests. In this sense, her suggestion foreshadows what Paula Baker has referred to as the "domestication of America
politics"—the metaphorical extension of the duties of wives and mothers to
the public and political spheres.[80] But her language also contains more subversive implications. Where Lucy's judgment of (dis)taste figures bodily sensation as expressively linked to sentimental gender norms, Eliza's reliance
on "managers" to enforce those norms highlights their strategic and regula-
tory nature.[81] If one assumes that "female managers" invariably adhere to
the middle-class norms of the "female character," Eliza's prescription averts
the scandal provoked by the circus performers' adoption of the "masculine

habit and attitudes." Without this assumption, however, Eliza's prescription merely repeats that scandal.[82]

Foster's thematization of this contradiction through a characterization of the unmarried and childless Eliza is no coincidence, of course. In their response to Miss Laurence and her mother, Mrs. Richman and Eliza together argue against the belief that a "passion" for national politics betrays the "female character." Though never explicitly attacked in *The Coquette*, this defense of female citizenship is vulnerable to a counter-argument central to later revisions of republicanism. Nineteenth-century sentimental reformers and domestic ideologues typically worried that virtually any form of civic activity would repeat the transgressive conflation of the "female character" with the "masculine habits and attitudes" that Lucy and Eliza elsewhere attribute to the circus performers. For Mrs. Richman, this counter-argument holds little force since she shares with many of those reformers a (gendered and nonpolitical) identity as mother and wife that provides her with a private life acceptable for publication. For Eliza, however, the same argument maintains its force since Foster constructs her identity around the poles of fancy and sensation, not public (gender) and private (sex). Eliza begins the novel by discovering the "unusual sensation" of "pleasure" upon leaving her "parental roof" (5). A few pages later, she generalizes from this singular experience: "[T]he mind, after being confined at home for a while, sends the imagination abroad in quest of new treasures, and the body may as well accompany it, for ought I can see" (15). In each case, the conjugal home Mrs. Richman idealizes becomes a space of confinement. "Marriage," Eliza tells Mrs. Richman, "is the tomb of friendship. It appears to me a very selfish state" (24). Like the "protean" Sanford, Eliza refuses marriage in order to act upon a libertarian potential common to democratic political theory and sentimental aesthetics. "But whether the fancy ought not to be consulted in our settlement in life," Eliza writes in a statement that nicely defines her character, "is with me the question" (88).

Eliza's opening letters provide one answer to this question. In the republic she begins by imagining, political virtue involves the right to the public pursuit of what Thomas Jefferson referred to twenty years earlier as "happiness." In this context, Olympe de Gouges (the author of the French "Declaration of the Rights of Woman and Citizen") provides a transnational analogue for Foster's "coquette." As Joan Scott argues, the critical and revolutionary potential of the imagination served as the battleground upon which feminists like de Gouges confronted their critics. "She likened herself to the great thinkers of the age," Scott writes, "not in her command of philosophy and political theory, but in her ability to dream: 'But don't expect me to discuss these matters in political and philosophical discourses; only in dreams have I been able to pursue them.'" As in the journalistic accounts of

Elizabeth Whitman's death, this admission of fancy as a source of social and political autonomy could be marshaled in retrospect as evidence of an inevitably tragic fate. Hence, *La feuille du salut public* eulogized de Gouges as follows: "Olympe de Gouges, born with an exalted imagination, mistook her delirium for an inspiration of nature. She wanted to be a man of state. She took up the projects of the perfidious people who want to divide France. It seems the law has punished this conspirator for having forgotten the virtues that belong to her sex."[83] Eliza's mother, for one, agrees with this intertwining of sex, gender, and citizenship. "With regard to [Boyer's] being a dependent situation," Mrs. Wharton asks, "what is not so? Are we not all links in the great chain of society, some more, some less important; but each upheld by others, throughout the confederated whole?" (41). Merging Renaissance social theory (the "great chain of society") with the language of contemporary Federalism (the "confederated whole"), Mrs. Wharton envisions society as an indivisible space of positive identities. Within this republic, fancy plays no part. Virtue involves knowing and maintaining one's divinely ordained place since, as John Winthrop puts it in "A Modell of Christian Charity," the "glory of [God's] power" is revealed in his "ordering all these differences for the preservation and good of the whole."[84]

Echoing Lucy's response to the circus performers, Eliza's correspondents agree with Mrs. Richman's advice, but for different reasons. Concerned that Eliza's "fancy will mislead [her]," Lucy responds to her declaration of independence by reconciling the freedom that imagination provides with the constraints of middle-class gender norms: "Act then with that modest freedom, that dignified unreserve which bespeaks conscious rectitude and sincerity of heart" (26–27). One letter later, Lucy refines this advice: "You are very tenacious of your freedom, as you call it; but it is a play on words. A man of Mr. Boyer's honor and good sense will never abridge any privileges which virtue can claim" (31). In contrast to Mrs. Wharton, whose emphasis on social (inter)dependence neglects the values of sentimental autonomy, Lucy urges Eliza to follow her "heart." But she also assumes that its "modest" passions will remain within the institutional bounds of marriage and family. "Slight not the opinion of the world," she writes, "We are dependent beings; and while the smallest traces of virtuous sensibility remain, we must feel the force of that dependence" (133). This emphasis on "dependence" echoes Mrs. Wharton's earlier letter. But the form of dependence Lucy imagines is grounded neither in divine law (Mrs. Wharton), nor in secular law (*La feuille du salut public*). It relies instead on the concept of "virtuous sensibility." The paradox of a "dignified unreserve" captures the tension within this attempt to wed virtue and sensation, "conscious rectitude" and the "sincerity of the heart." Like Harriet Beecher Stowe's demand that the reader "feel right" at the end of *Uncle Tom's Cabin*, Lucy merges a sentimental faith in the authenticity of sensation with a moral authority that gains its force from—to use Stowe's terms—the "strength," "health," and "justice" of those sensations.[85] The authority of the law, in other words, relies not on the heteronomous power of either God or the state, but on the sentimental body's autonomous expression of (moral) sensation.

This exchange of opinions between Eliza and her correspondents reflects pressing ideological differences between competing models of republicanism during the 1790s.[86] Read structurally, though, the same exchange reveals an important similarity among those ideologies. As in all epistolary novels, differences of opinion are mediated through the publication and exchange of personal letters.[87] This insistence on literary correspondence as a means of ideological synthesis relies, in turn, on a fundamental opposition between ideology and publication, between the conclusions of public opinion and the structures of the public sphere. "Politics," to paraphase Mrs. Richman, "belongs to the ladies" because the literary ideal of the public sphere is universal, neither male nor female, masculine nor feminine. This intersection of ideology and structure pinpoints the crux of the novel's (feminist) politics, as well as Baym's and Davidson's readings of the novel. What is at stake in both contexts is the relation between an aesthetics of sentimental embodiment and its public mediation and, in this sense, it is appropriate that Butler's structural critique of essentialist feminism illuminates both the novel and its critical reception. Writing against feminist advocates for state censorship of pornographic representations, Butler argues that the anti-pornography position relies on an internally contradictory understanding of the relation between fantasy and identity: "The fixed subject-position of 'women' functions within the feminist discourse in favor of censorship as a phantasm that suppresses multiple and open possibilities for identification, a phantasm, in other words, that refuses its own possibilities as fantasy through its self-stabilization as the real." Opposed to the regulation of publication by any state (even a "feminist" state), Butler argues instead for a structural expansion of unofficial public spaces of ideological production: a "proliferation of representations and sites of discursive production." "The task," she concludes, "must be to safeguard the open production of [identity] categories, whatever the risk."[88]

Butler's argument resonates with *The Coquette* because Foster attributes Eliza's seduction and death to her adoption of a parallel strategy in relation to both her male suitors and her female correspondents. Throughout the first half of the novel, Eliza's personal letters maintain an expressive relation to her body that blocks the one-way path from sentiment to sentimentality, from subjective experience to social norm. As Michel Foucault writes of the nineteenth-century hermaphrodite Herculine Barbin, she allows one to "imagine that all that counted was the reality of the body and the intensity of its pleasures."[89] Like Eliza herself at the beginning of the novel, these diverse bodily sensations are loosed without reserve in the literary public sphere. "I must write to you the impulses of my mind," Eliza tells Lucy, "or I must not write at all" (8). By the second half of the novel, though, the relation between Eliza's "impulses" and her letters changes. Her sensational publications are privatized (relegated to a "clandestine intercourse" with Sanford that the reader never sees), while her public letters lose their counter-hegemonic force and, eventually, vanish altogether (87). The first indication of this shift appears when Eliza reflects upon Boyer's marriage to Maria Selby: "This theme carries away my pen, if I but touch upon it. And no wonder; for it is the sole exercise of my thoughts" (109). A subsequent letter to Julia reveals the degree of Eliza's alienation from all epistolary models of sentimental publication. "Writing," she explains, "is an employment which suits me not at the present. It was pleasing formerly, and therefore, by recalling the idea of circumstances and events which frequently occupied my pen in happier days, it now gives me pain" (134). This rejection of writing deprives Eliza of publication as a means of expressive self-determination by confirming a separation of public and private spheres. Having eschewed marriage, she lacks the conjugal home that generates and shelters the audience-oriented subjectivities of her middle-class correspondents. The corrosive effects of this lack are confirmed by Foster's narrative: childbirth (out of wedlock) and death (in a public tavern) collapse the writing and the sexed body by "disclos[ing]" the involuntary effects of Eliza's "intercourse" with Sanford (146).

This shift in Eliza's letters could be explained thematically. Like Abigail Adams, Eliza arguably acts as a strategist, opting to censor her letters due to the critical judgments they would inevitably provoke. The problem with this explanation is that it assumes a liberal separation of personal motivations and public opinion without accounting for it. It overlooks, in other words, the structural significance of the displacement of Eliza's initial understanding of personal and public life as internally linked through sentimental publication. Foster validates Eliza's faith in expressive letters in her advice to young writers published, a year after *The Coquette*, in *The Boarding School*. In a chapter on "Writing and Arithmetic," Foster's fictional preceptress (Mrs. Williams) advocates "the epistolary" as a method of "exchanging sentiments." "Ease, frankness, simplicity, and sincerity," she explains, "should be its leading traits."[90] Eliza adheres to this advice when she writes the "impulses of [her] mind" in her early letters, but she never manages to follow the contradictory advice Mrs. Williams provides on the following page:

> Your characters during life, and even when you shall sleep in the dust, may rest on the efforts of your pens. Beware then how you employ them. Let not the merits of your attainments in this noble art be degraded by improper subjects for its exer-

cise. Suffer not the expectation of secrecy to induce you to indulge your pens upon
subjects, which you would blush to have exposed. In this way your characters may
be injured, and your happiness destroyed.[91]

The "characters" such letters construct are divided between two demands.
Mrs. Williams advocates the "ease, frankness, simplicity, and sincerity" typical of Eliza's early letters, while she simultaneously requires a strategic self-
management of all literary "subjects," proper or improper. Like other sentimental reflexes (tears, taste, disgust), the "blush" of the letter writer ideally
links bodily sensation and sentimental norm. But as Eliza quickly learns,
even blushes may expose a secret no more authentic than the "tear of sensibility" that Sanford feigns (29).

Foster never reconciles these two demands. The pens that write in *The
Boarding School* are both strategically and expressively linked to the hands
that hold them, while Eliza's will to maintain the sort of expressive relation
between personality and publicity conventionally valued in eighteenth-century letters dooms her to silence in *The Coquette*.[92] Indeed, the alienation
from her pen that Eliza experiences toward the end of the novel can be read
as the Janus face of the strategic use of the pen that Mrs. Williams advocates
in *The Boarding School*. Like Miss Laurence and the circus performers,
Eliza lacks the desire (and the structures) that would enable her to differentiate personal (sexual or gender) identity from publication. As a result, she
remains unable to use her pen to construct an identity around the poles of
sex and gender—to position herself within what is referred to in the vocabu-
lary of late-twentieth-century liberalism as an identity politics. Within most
varieties of republican political discourse, this resistance to an identitarian
and strategic use of publication would be understood as a form of political
virtue; within the novel, the same resistance introduces a threat of corruption into an otherwise virtuous society. Eliza's ungendered sensations may
free her from the constraints of middle-class gender norms, but her fate
marks the cost of that freedom. Her seduction, her withdrawal from the
literary public sphere and, finally, her death narrate the future of a republican citizen who fails to act, in public *and* private, as a properly gendered
subject. Any more democratic conception of virtue as grounded in citizens'
autonomous civic activity is, in *The Coquette*, an inevitable failure due to the
vulnerability of any woman outside of the home. This inevitability explains
the sudden introduction of Eliza's brother at the end of the novel to confirm
her death and retrieve her belongings (162). Foster's deferral to fraternal
authority is necessary because, she insists, Sanford's "snares" are "too deeply
laid for any one to escape who had the least warmth in her constitution, or
affection in her heart" (158). Sanford's (masculine) control of public space
provides narrative confirmation of Mrs. Richman's liberal defense of the
"marriage state": "Here we can repose in safety."

There is one exception to this general rule. As the novel concludes, Julia Granby remains publicly active and unmarried. Sanford himself provides a gloss of this exception. "She is a most alluring object," he assures the reader, "But the dignity of her manners forbid all assaults upon her virtue" (140). Julia escapes from the threat of (hetero)sexual seduction because her "manners" exclude passion from public life. This exception becomes the rule of much nineteenth-century sentimentalism. In *Uncle Tom's Cabin*, for instance, Rachel Halliday provides Stowe with an emblem of the sexed *and* desexualized heroine: "Bards have written of the cestus of Venus, that turned the heads of all the world in successive generations. We had rather, for our part, have the cestus of Rachel Halliday, that kept heads from being turned, and made everything go on harmoniously."[93] For Eliza, Therese, and other passionate heroines, the tactic of marginalizing sexuality as an "improper subject" within the genre of sentimentalism holds little promise. Not only does the "sensation" of (sexual) "pleasure" lead to seduction that leads to pregnancy that leads to death, but death enables the publication of a narrative that censors the activities of sexed and (hetero)sexualized citizens in public. According to Mrs. Williams, of course, Eliza's historical predecessor Elizabeth Whitman should have known that her life and letters would be used to such posthumous ends. "Your characters during life," Mrs. Williams warns, "and even when you shall sleep in the dust, may rest on the efforts of your pens." Foster exploits this inevitability by penning letters for Whitman, but she also marks the alienation involved in such posthumous forms of citizenship. "I know not what to say," Eliza writes in one of the orthodox letters Whitman never wrote, "my brain is on fire. . . . These letters have almost distracted me; but they are written, and I am comparatively easy" (150). No longer easily linking sensation and publication, such letters become sites of nervous disorder. For Eliza, death lies at the end of the epistolary, if only because she fancied that by taking pleasure in epistles as ends in themselves she could reconcile the autonomy of bodily sensation to the heteronomous demands of the sentimental code.

Sentiment and the Public Sphere

Partly an elegiac response to Elizabeth Whitman's death, *The Coquette* is equally and more importantly a pedagogical response which capitalizes on that death in order to publicize a fantasy of sexual identity—of a sexed body—unmediated by the (gender) politics of (sexual) identification. While many of the ideological effects of this fantasy are historically specific to the 1790s, the structures that condition it have a longer and more varied existence. As Elizabeth Grosz points out, modern identity-based political movements (liberal feminism, in this case) rely upon a similarly paradoxical understanding of embodiment. "The body," Grosz writes, "provides a point of mediation between what is perceived as purely internal and accessible only to the subject and what is external and publicly observable, a point from which to rethink the opposition between the inside and the outside, the private and the public, the self and other."[94] By installing the body as both a ground and a site of political contestation, sentimental novels like *The Coquette* provide a prehistory of this paradox *and* require an analogous rethinking. The sentimental (non)distinction between sensation and norm—between sentiment and sentimentality—transects the body by locating, within it, the political (non)distinction between citizenship and subjection. This paradox produces a contradictory model of identification in *The Coquette* since the novel interpellates readers, first, as republican citizens of the literary public sphere and, only second, as gendered subjects of the nation-state. Foster attempts to resolve this ideological contradiction by reducing the bodily sensations Eliza experiences and inspires to a sentimental aesthetics of sexual embodiment, but such a reduction remains structurally impossible as long as it can be secured only through publication. Foster's letters, in other words, advocate the sort of sentimental identity politics typical of later liberalisms, yet they do so only within and against a republican understanding of all subjectivity as audience-oriented and publicly mediated.

The significance of this paradox emerges with particular clarity in the sentimental seduction narrative that Mary Wollstonecraft left unfinished at her death in 1797. The story of a woman unjustly imprisoned by her husband, *Maria* concludes with notes in which the heroine (Maria) defends her lover against the legal charge of seduction brought against him by her husband. In those fragments, Maria pleads guilty to adultery, but argues that the charge of seduction cannot be justified since it deprives her of any sense of autonomy by positioning her between the competing, but equally heteronomous authority of her husband and her lover. "To force me to give my fortune," she explains, "I was imprisoned. . . . I met the man charged with seducing me. We became attached—I deemed and shall ever deem myself free. The death of my babe dissolved the only tie which subsisted between me and my, what is termed, lawful husband."[95] Maria's argument participates in the emerging ideology of republican womanhood: only the death of her child frees her from what she refers to elsewhere as the "duties of a wife and mother."[96] Yet Wollstonecraft frames that argument so that duty remains both responsive to Maria's sensations and inseparable from her abstract principles. "The sarcasms of society, and the condemnations of a mistaken world," writes Wollstonecraft, "were nothing to her, compared with acting contrary to those feelings which were the foundation of her principles."[97] The revolutionary implications of this recourse to sensation as a source of political autonomy are not lost on Maria's paternalistic judge.

Echoing her earlier description of marriage as having "bastilled [her] for life," the court rules against Maria's introduction of "French principles in public and private life."[98] Because it allows a woman to "plead her feelings, as an excuse or palliation of infidelity," Maria's defense threatens to open "a flood-gate for immorality."[99] Following a similarly sentimental logic, Federalist judges in the United States acted throughout the 1790s to "protect" both "seducible" women and the "virtue" of the social order by restricting, if not eliminating more democratic divorce, property, rape, and inheritance laws passed during the 1770s and 1780s.[100]

Nor are the implications of Wollstonecraft's recourse to sensation lost on later sentimental writers. Accepting the reduction of sensation to sex, authors ranging from Fanny Fern to Harriet Jacobs articulated what Foucault refers to in *The History of Sexuality* as a "reverse-discourse."[101] By adopting the dimorphic logic of the modern sex-gender system as the foundation upon which demands for social and political equality rest, these authors rely upon their identification of and with the category of "woman" in order to transform the legal and political status of both properly and, at times, improperly gendered subjects of the republic. "O, ye happy women, whose purity has been sheltered from childhood," Jacobs writes in *Incidents in the Life of a Slave Girl*, "whose homes are protected by law, do not judge the poor desolate slave girl too severely."[102] Itself an abolitionist refiguring of the conventions of the seduction narrative, *Incidents* maintains a complicated relation to the genre of sentimentalism. This relation will be the subject of the sixth chapter of this book. In the immediate context, what is significant is that *Incidents* both appeals to and challenges its readers' affective identification with a now deracialized and deregionalized category, "woman." Like Stowe, who condemns the slave system for producing "women who were not women," Jacobs deploys naturalized gender conventions in order to denaturalize relations between masters and slaves.[103] Reversing and radicalizing the dimorphic logic of the sex-gender system, Jacobs relies on the stability of the category "woman" in order to construct a public site of affective identification for readers otherwise divided along alternative lines of identification—race, class, and region, to name three. To the degree that Jacobs succeeds not only in reflecting, but also in transforming her readers' identifications, however, her reliance on the stability of the category "woman" is itself threatened by her inevitable foregrounding of the constructedness and, hence, the potential incoherence of that category.

As in *The Coquette*, what is at stake in Jacobs's narrative is the wedding of sentimental autonomy and social normativity through the construction of the category "woman" as the public site of readers' affective identification. Since sociality in this case involves a progressive abolitionist politics, Mrs. Flint, the slave-holding mistress, replaces Miss Lawrence and the circus performers as the figure which marks the boundary between sex and gender,

between "women" and "ladies." While this substitution is undoubtedly crucial to any appraisal of the ideological significance of Jacobs's narrative, the
very interchangeability of the figures highlights a structural contradiction
central to the affective power of sentimentalism as a genre. Both narratives
negotiate political questions by constructing public sites of affective identification with a form of embodiment that is seen, itself, as sentimental and
private. If it is in this sense that, as Shirley Samuels suggests, "sentimentality is literally at the heart of nineteenth-century American culture," then I
would further suggest that both of these metaphors need to be taken literally.[104] If, in other words, sentimental letters are "literally at the heart" of the
culture, then those same letters foreground the figurativeness, the literar-
iness and, ultimately, the public mediation of the body itself. Even novels
like *The Coquette* that move narratively toward the stabilization of the sort
of sentimental identity politics typical of later liberalisms still rely structurally on a democratized literary public sphere as the space in which those
identity politics are constructed and reconstructed. The public sphere thus
names the space of the political within any politics of identification, the
space that renders identification political in the first place. This is the structural lesson that *The Coquette* teaches. At the "heart" of nineteenth-century
culture lies not only a privatized sentiment, but also a republican model of
the literary public sphere without which any sentimental politics of identification would be impossible.

5

Masochism and Male Sentimentalism: Charles Brockden Brown's *Clara Howard*

> Depend upon it, We know better than to repeal our
> Masculine systems. Altho they are in full Force, you
> know they are little more than Theory. We dare
> not exert our power in its full Latitude. We are
> obliged to go fair, and softly, and in Practice you
> know We are the subjects. We have only the Name
> of Masters, and rather than give up this, which
> would compleatly subject us to the despotism of
> the Peticoat, I hope General Washington, and all
> our brave Heroes would fight.
> 	*(John to Abigail Adams, 1776)*[1]

> The moral is that woman, as nature created her and
> as man up to now has found her attractive, is man's
> enemy; she can be his slave or his mistress but
> never his companion. This can only be when she has
> the same rights as he and is his equal in education
> and work. For the time being there is only one
> alternative; to be the hammer or the anvil. I was fool
> enough to let a woman make a slave of me, do you
> understand? Hence the moral of the tale: whoever
> allows himself to be whipped deserves to be
> whipped. But as you see, I have taken the blows
> well; the rosy mist of supersensuality has lifted.
> 	*(Leopold von Sacher-Masoch,* Venus in Furs,
> 	*1870)*[2]

The Cultural Problem of Masochism

As a fable addressed to sentimental men, Leopold von Sacher-Masoch's *Venus in Furs* concludes with a simple and misogynist lesson. In the words of Sacher-Masoch's protagonist, Severin, the male masochist must learn to shed his "supersensuality." He must regain what John Adams calls "the Name of Master" by rejecting his sensual and perverse submission to a feminized law. Unlike Adams, Severin does recognize the possibility of more egalitarian relations between women and men. But woman can be man's "companion," he cautions, only "when she has the same rights as he and is his equal in education and work." In the absence of a democratic social contract, in other words, sexual difference produces a master-slave dialectic that renders the possibility of social and political equality strictly utopian: "For the time being there is only one alternative; to be the hammer or the anvil." Echoing this moral, *Venus in Furs* begins as a subversive narrative in which Sacher-Masoch inverts the nineteenth-century marriage contract. "In the contractual relation," Gilles Deleuze observes, "the woman typically figures as an object in the patriarchal system. The contract in masochism reverses this state of affairs by making the woman into the party with whom the contract is entered into."[3] And in *Venus in Furs*, this tension between the two contracts is played out between the novel's main characters, as Wanda, unwilling to marry Severin, consents to a contract that makes him into *her* "slave." But the same narrative concludes by reinstating both the marriage contract and the Victorian gender conventions that accompany it. Psychoanalytic critics may argue that the male masochist resists and fractures the association of law with paternity or, in Kaja Silverman's words, "radiates a negativity inimical to the social order," but Sacher-Masoch's own narrative confirms that order.[4] The previously dominant and cold-hearted Wanda contracts to marry a man whom she "worships" as a "master" (the "Greek"), while the previously submissive and sentimental Severin learns to whip and torture his female attendants. "The treatment was cruel but radical," Severin concludes, "but the main thing is that I am cured."[5]

Like the story of Elizabeth Whitman, the details of Severin's narrative may be singular but the lesson it teaches is not. From Nathaniel Hawthorne's infamous lament that "America is now given over to a d——d mob of scribbling women" to William Dean Howells's reluctant submission to the literary judgments of the "court of women," from Leslie Fiedler's *Love and Death in the American Novel* to Ann Douglas's *The Feminization of American Culture*, warnings that male sentimentality leads to male masochism echo through the U.S. literary and literary critical canons.[6] Most famously, Fiedler complains that a "robust masculine sentimentality, turned out, oddly enough, to have no relevance to the American scene." Rather, male sentimentalism takes the form of what Fiedler calls, in another context, "an abyssal male masochism."[7] As its title suggests, Douglas's study of New England sentimental literary culture bemoans a similar reversal of what she refers to as "masculine" and "feminine" values (though Douglas also suggests that sentimentalism fails because it disavows "matriarchal values" or, in other words, never affirms its own masochistic subtext).[8] "The liberal minister," Douglas argues, "was pushed into a position increasingly resembling the evolving feminine one. Who else was barred with him from the larger world of masculine concerns, who else was confined with him to a claustrophobic private world of over-responsive sensibility, who else but the American lady?"[9] For such writers and critics, the pathology of male sentimentalism results from (and in) its tendency to confound the homosocial worlds of (public) "masculinity" and (private) "femininity." Like Richard von Kraft-Ebbing's original sentimental masochist Jean-Jacques Rousseau, the "essential element" for the "over-responsive" male is the irrationality and intensity of the "feelings" that dictate his "subjection to the woman."[10]

The writings of Charles Brockden Brown occupy a privileged position within this literary and literary critical diagnosis of male sentimentalism as male masochism. Brown, critics suggest, "capitulated" to the demands of his allegedly female audience in 1800 when he shifted from his early gothic novels (*Wieland, Ormond, Edgar Huntly, Arthur Mervyn*) to his late sentimental novels (*Clara Howard, Jane Talbot*). Evidence of this "capitulation" appears in a letter written by Brown to his brother James in April 1800. Hoping to appeal to the large (and lucrative) audience for sentimental novels like *Charlotte Temple* and *The Coquette*, Brown pledged to "[drop] the doleful tone and assum[e] a cheerful one."[11] According to his critics, Brown's decision enacts the masochist's surrender to a feminized law by contracting with his public to produce less "experimental" and "radical" fictions. "Like Edgar [Huntly]," Bill Christophersen suggests in a recent book-length study of Brown's career, "Brown may have come to fear his [psychological] discoveries and their possible repercussions."[12] Fiedler is less oblique: Brown "fails in his direct attempt to recapture passion from the 'female scribblers.'"[13] For the same critics, this failure is heroic rather than pathetic, however. Brown becomes the antetype of nineteenth- and twentieth-century male authors whose (masculine) art resists (feminine) sentimentality, even as it eventually falls prey to the demands of the mass market and the unenlightened taste of a female reading public. The story of Brown's career thus becomes a fable that warns the male reader (and critic) against the perils of sentimental publication—public displays of male affect—in an increasingly gendered literary public sphere. *Clara Howard* and *Jane Talbot* are, Norman Grabo concludes, "trivial and silly."[14]

Of course, many of the critics I have alluded to have never given half as much thought to either *Clara Howard* or *Jane Talbot*, as they have to Brown's earlier works. Critical convention seems to require a summary dismissal. The only significant exception to this generalization is Sidney Krause's 1981 article, "*Clara Howard* and *Jane Talbot*: Godwin on Trial."[15] Referring to Clara Howard as the "original iron maiden of American literature" (a phrase he takes from Fiedler), Krause reads the novel as a battle between the Godwinian rationalism of Brown's female protagonist (Clara Howard) and the Rousseauist sentimentalism of his male protagonist (Edward Hartley).[16] Brown's irony, Krause concludes, is aimed at the inflexibility and "coldness" of Clara's law: "Just as Brown had shown the limits of Reason in the breakdown of Ormond, his most obviously Godwinian character, so in *Clara Howard* was he revealing what it would be like to write the Enlightenment's courtesy book, with a Godwinite Iron Maiden as instructress in love."[17] Krause's reading is instructive, especially in its insight into the republican intertexts that inform Brown's novel. More interesting, however, is Krause's unreflective repetition of the masochistic figures that inform other critical accounts of the novel. Edward Hartley is, according to Krause, "put on the rack" by the "hard-core Godwinism" of the "Prussian" Clara Howard.[18] The novel includes no scene of torture; its erotics are softcore at best; Clara Howard is of British origin. Like other critics, Krause draws on a set of rhetorical conventions that not only mislead the reader, but also leave unanswered the central question raised by the novel. Why does Brown flout Godwinian and, more generally, Enlightenment conventions by gendering reason female and sentiment male? Why does he place his male character's "over-responsive sensibility" under the rational authority of his female character's abstract law?

An answer to this question requires a rethinking of the relations among sex, gender, and sentiment that many critics take for granted. In the last chapter, I argued that the genre of female sentimentalism both contributes to and resists an emerging liberal political culture intent on separating masculinity from femininity along the lines of public and private spheres, of political and social relations. In this chapter, I pursue this argument further by focusing on the paradoxical figure of the sentimental male in a cultural context that increasingly provides those spheres with a gendered content: masculine rationality and feminine sentimentality. *Clara Howard*, in this context, both marks and adds to a contemporary ideological shift in the national understanding of the relation between gender and polity, sentiment and reason. Using the shorthand of intellectual history, this shift can be described as a transition from a theoretically ungendered eighteenth-century republic of letters to a theoretically gendered nineteenth-century empire of the mother.[19] Under the former regime, the existence of a sentimental male or, in Henry MacKenzie's words, a "man of feeling" like Edward Hartley, remains unproblematic since sentiment is, ideally, ungendered.[20] In a 1775 bookplate from Bell's Circulating Library, for example, potential subscribers are hailed as "sentimentalists, whether ladies or gentlemen."[21] Under the latter regime, Edward Hartley's sentimentalism marks his gender cross-identification. Like his literary progeny Natty Bumpo and Huck Finn, Brown's hero is left with only two options: either submission to Clara's feminized law *or* escape from the law altogether. Much to the critics' dismay, Edward submits. No Edgar Huntly, Edward Hartley remains, in Grabo's words, "a very domesticated pussycat."[22] By substituting Hartley for Huntly, Brown produces an early version of what would become a persistent reaction to the post-revolutionary alignment of sentimental authority with femininity in novels like *The Coquette*—the melodrama of sentimental manhood.

Sentimental Authorship in the Republic of Letters

An epistolary novel, *Clara Howard* consists of a series of letters concerning the relations between three main characters: Clara Howard, Edward Hartley, and Mary Wilmot. As the novel opens, Edward is in love with Clara, but engaged to Mary whom he "esteems" but does not "love."[23] In the letters that pass between Edward and Clara, Clara refuses marriage out of respect for Mary. "You know," Clara writes to Edward, "what it is that reason prescribes to you with regard to Miss Wilmot. If you cannot ardently and sincerely seek her presence, and find in the happiness which she will derive from union with you, sufficient motives to make you zealously solicit that union, you are unworthy not merely of my love, but of my esteem" (20). In the letters that pass between Edward and Mary, Mary similarly refuses out of respect for Clara. "This Clara will be yours," Mary writes, " . . . She will offer you happiness, and wealth, and honor, and you will accept them at her hands" (15–16). Toward the middle of the novel, Edward tires of this romantic double bind and vows to escape civilization altogether. Remembering a map of North America that hung in his uncle's parlor, he decides to pursue his "juvenile reveries" of traveling west by canoe to the Spanish territories of California (115). This experience promises to be curative since it will free him of all social (and human) demands. "I shall be dead," he tells Clara, "to all the offices and pleasures of civilized existence. I shall hasten to embrute all my faculties. I shall make myself akin to savages and tygers, and forget I was once a man" (134). Interrupted at the outset of this geographically and psychically improbable journey by the chastening summons of both Clara and Mary, Edward returns east. The entire predicament is resolved only in the final pages of the novel when a wealthy suitor (Mr. Sedley) appears for Mary, thus dissolving their troubled threesome into respectable, heterosexual dyads.

These already vexed intimate relations are further complicated by the characters' respective class positions. Clara is the daughter of a wealthy Englishman who befriends and educates Edward, while Mary is both poor and orphaned. Mr. Howard wants to marry Clara to Edward in order to cement the latter's position in the family, while Mary and Edward lack the financial means of supporting a middle-class marriage and home. In a plot that Brown adopts from *Edgar Huntly*, Mary's brother dies midway through the novel, leaving five thousand dollars in a previously unknown bank account. This windfall appears to solve Mary and Edward's problem, but only until a stranger recently held captive in Algeria (Morton) returns to the United States and claims the money as his own. This plot twist leads Mary to abandon Edward to Clara. Clara, in turn, insists that Edward pursue Mary despite her poverty. Again, this predicament is resolved by the appearance of Mr. Sedley. The money, as it turns out, does not belong to Morton; rather, Sedley gave the money to Mary's brother with the intention of enabling her to marry Edward. The supreme disinterestedness of this gesture produces the opposite effect, however. It ensures that Sedley is himself an appropriate suitor for Mary, who obediently vows to "devote her life to Sedley's happiness" (130). Thus restored to her rightful class and marital status (yet another subplot reveals Mary to be a lost relative of Clara), Mary's decision frees Clara and Edward to become engaged as well. The novel's final letter from Clara to Mary promises that, if Mary add "one more week of probation to the four already decreed, it is, by no means impossible, that the same day may witness the happiness of both" Clara and Mary (148).

This happy ending would seem to bear out the plot summary that Edward provides in his introduction to the packet of letters that makes up *Clara Howard*. Addressed to an anonymous reader, that introduction promises that the letters will explain Edward's social ascent from the position of a "simple lad . . . sprung from obscurity, destitute of property, of parents, of paternal friends" to that of a wealthy man, "crowned with every terrestrial felicity, in possession of that most exquisite of all blessings, a wife, endowed with youth, grace, dignity, discretion" (3). Read in this fashion, *Clara Howard* becomes a male bildungsroman in which what Fritz Fleischmann refers to as the "patronage model" of Brown's earlier novels reaches a positive resolution.[24] In contrast to the failed patriarchs of those novels, Mr. Howard provides both a narrative means for Edward's assent to full masculine subjectivity, and a political argument for benevolent paternalism within the early republic. What this reading (and Edward's introductory gloss) misses, however, are the gaps that emerge in the otherwise happy ending. Most important, *Clara Howard* concludes with the promise of a dual marriage, but not with the marriages themselves. The penultimate letter from Clara to Edward obsessively pictures the physical obstacles that still stand in the way of their marriage (a "boisterous river," "wind and rain," roads "kneedeep in mire," stagecoach wheels that "groan and totter" [146–47]), while the final letter from Clara to Mary encourages Mary not to perform, but to defer her marriage in the service of Clara and Mary's mutual happiness. "May that day," Clara writes, "whenever it shall come, prove the beginning of joy to Mary, and to her who, in every state, will be [her] affectionate Clara" (148). The ceremony that will allow Mr. Howard to "give" Clara to Edward as a "possession" is simply not performed. Clara maintains her primary attachment to Mary, as well as the power that she enjoys throughout the novel as a wealthy, lettered, and unmarried woman.

Unlike the seduced and abandoned heroines of contemporary sentimental novels, Clara thus remains both publicly powerful and, to use an only somewhat anachronistic phrase, woman-identified. This combination led the nineteenth-century feminist Margaret Fuller to applaud Brown's characterization for proving conclusively that "the term *feminine* is not a synonym for *weak*," while the same combination elicits approval from the early critic Lillie Demming Loshe who portrays Clara as "the resolute and reasonable woman directing the gentle and irresolute boy."[25] Yet, it thoroughly disempowers Edward who responds by criticizing Clara on both counts. From the beginning to the end of the novel, the sentimental Edward accuses the rational Clara of being "inhumane and insensible" (9), of possessing a "narrow" or "cold" heart (74, 136) and, in a letter that later critics cite as evidence of Brown's own attitude toward Clara, of "reap[ing] the fruits of disinterested virtue" by using her power to make Edward, Mary, and herself miserable (112). At other points, Edward accuses Clara of ignoring the desires of the male suitors in the novel (Sedley and himself) by siding unfairly with Mary. "With regard to us," Edward writes immediately before threatening to "embrute" himself by going west, "you have neither consideration nor humanity. They are all absorbed in the cause of one, whose merits, whose claim to your sympathy and aid, if it be not less, is far from being greater than Sedley's or mine" (113). Forced to account for Mary's own compliance with Clara's presumably homosocial reasoning, Edward adopts the explanation Basil Ransom would repeat some eighty years later in *The Bostonians*. Mary, he suggests, found Clara more seductive than himself: "She was too blind an admirer, and assiduous a follower of Clara Howard, to accept my proffers. I abruptly withdrew" (118). Where Basil responds to a similar situation with an act of "muscular force" (hurrying the tearful Verena away from Olive), Edward defers to Mary's desires.[26] Here and throughout the novel, Edward's admittedly passionate appeals to his audience's sentiments fail either to balance or to refute Clara's dispassionate appeals to their reason.

Mapped elsewhere in the novel as a geographic opposition between East and West, or as an ethnographic opposition between civilization and "embrutement," this battle between Clara's reason and Edward's passion appears in the opening letter as a sexual opposition between women and men. In sharp contrast to the self-assurance of Edward's introduction, that letter begins with radical self-doubt. "Why do I write?" Edward asks, "For whose use do I pass my time thus? There is no one living who cares a jot for me. There was a time, when a throbbing heart, a trembling hand, and eager eyes were always prepared to read, and ruminate on the scantiest and poorest scribble that dropped from my pen, but she has disappeared. The veil between us is like death" (5). Addressed to Clara, the anonymous reader and the general public, this letter both establishes Edward's subjection to Clara's judgment and suggests an affinity between the author and his male protagonist. Both Brown and Edward begin the novel in search of a sympathetic audience for their letters; both despair that those letters will fail to reach their destination; both explain that failure by gendering their audience female. In a subsequent letter, Brown not only repeats this authorial *mise-en-abyme*, but does so in terms that echo his epistolary pledge to his brother James. "What are you doing now?" Edward asks Clara, "Busy, I suppose, turning over the leaves of some book. Some painter of manners or of nature is before you" (88). Having dropped the "doleful tone" of his earlier "gothic" novels, Brown self-consciously aligns the reader of his first "sentimental" novel with Clara Howard—Brown's figure for the virtuous, female audience that he now represents himself as soliciting. The problem with male sentimentalism, both Brown and Edward suggest, is that any publication of those sentiments subjects their male authors to the moral judgments of a literary public sphere that is worse than anonymous—one that is dominated by women like Clara.

In one sense, then, Brown's critics are right. Clara is one of the "original iron maiden[s] of American literature," and the novel clearly encodes both Edward's and Brown's discomfort with their status as male sentimentalists as a discomfort with the masochistic potential inscribed therein. But those same critics are less convincing when they portray the sentimental bonds that tie both Edward to Clara and Brown to his audience as resulting from a "capitulation," as unselfconscious or, in Edward's case at least, as undesired. Far from acting on his threat to escape from Clara's power, Edward becomes the assiduous follower of Clara Howard that he accuses Mary of being. "I who know my own frailty," Edward writes to Clara, "am therefore undesirous of power: So far from wishing to rule others, it is my glory and my boast to submit to one whom I deem unerring and divine. Clara's will is my law: her pleasure the science that I study; her smiles the reward that, next to an approving God, my soul prizes most dearly" (90). Aware of his own imperfections, Edward divorces desire from power by transforming himself from a master into a slave. And this act of submission to Clara's "will" and "law" promises to survive even the prospective marriages to which the conclusion of the novel points. In her final letter to Edward, Clara responds to his offer of "hand and heart" with a promise not of love, but of moral education (145). "In moral discernment," Clara writes, "much art thou still deficient. Here I claim to be more than equal, but the difference shall not subsist long. Our modes of judging and our maxims, shall be the same" (147). Precisely the qualities that Edward criticizes in Clara (her coldness, her impersonality, her abhorrence of mere sentiment and sensuality) are the qualities that ensure her continued power over his sentiments and desires.

Nor are the critics convincing in their portrayal of Clara's power as necessarily damaging, her reasoning as necessarily flawed. Edward does rebel against Clara's power and criticize her rationalism, yet Brown himself provides Clara with an impressive intellectual pedigree. Educated in accordance with her father's enlightened and republican principles, Clara judges others not by the "specious but delusive considerations of fortune or birth, but by the intrinsic qualities of heart and head" (51). Having learned to eschew all arbitrary, anti-democratic markers of personal worth, Clara enacts a purely republican ethic. Her "esteem" can be won only through "just and disinterested conduct," while her "love" has nothing in common with "sensuality and selfishness" (20). Indeed, all of her criticisms of Edward concern his inability to abstract his selfish interests from his moral conduct, to act with proper disinterest in relation to his own sentiments and desires. Ironically, then, the very persistence of Edward's confessions of love for Clara evince the inadequacy of that love. "It shews," Clara writes, "you unable to comprehend that the welfare of another may demand self-denial from us, and that in bestowing benefits on others, there is a purer delight than in gratifications merely selfish and exclusive" (24). As an author of sentimental letters, Edward necessarily fails in the self-abstracting ethics that the republican Clara teaches. Yet the precision of Clara's ethical pedagogy generates a paradox within the ideal of republican citizenship that she upholds. As self-abstracting, disinterested, rational judges of others' sentiments and interests, Clara and Edward must bracket their own sentiments and interests. But if they succeed in this process of self-abstraction, then they are left with no subjective motivation for rendering any judgment. It is this self-abstracting rationalism which informs both Clara's ethical practice *and* her (ungendered) resistance to Edward's (gendered) desires.

Embodiment and Self-Abstraction

While Brown's investigations of the paradox generated by Clara's republican ethics are influenced directly by Godwin, they resonate perhaps even more fully with those of his Enlightenment contemporary Immanuel Kant.[27] As I have suggested in earlier chapters, the central antinomies of Kant's critical philosophy oppose reason and sentiment, duty and interest, morality and legality. These antinomies themselves result from Kant's (and Clara's) republican assumption that acts of moral judgment must begin by bracketing all sentiments and interests as subjective. "The moral law," Kant writes in *The Critique of Practical Reason*, "which alone is truly . . . objective, completely excludes the influence of self-love from the highest practical principle and forever checks self-conceit."[28] Again, the very rigor of this theoretical demand for self-abstraction generates a paradox when Kant poses the question of what sentiments and interests motivate moral practice. At times, the answer to this question seems obvious. The "moral interest," Kant argues in a related passage, "must be the pure nonsensuous interest of the practical reason alone."[29] Yet, Kant also recognizes that the ideal of the "moral interest" as "nonsensuous" remains a paradox: "Complete fitness of the will to the moral law is holiness, which is a perfection of which no rational being in the world of sense is at any time capable."[30] The result of this limitation is that the paradox of the moral interest can be resolved only negatively. Since a truly moral interest can never be realized, the effect of the moral law on the sentimental or "feeling" subject is not fulfillment, but "humiliation" due to that subject's recognition of its inadequacy.[31] Neither "spontaneous goodness of heart" nor "sympathy" ensures moral practice. Rather, in the words of the Prussian Immanuel Kant, "spur," "bridle" and "command" are required.[32]

Edward Hartley would reluctantly but undoubtedly agree. "If reason be inadequate to my deliverance," Edward writes to Clara, "pride should hinder me from disclosing my humiliation; from confessing my voluntary servitude" (117). Despite these hints of hesitation, the self-conceit of pride does nothing to hinder Edward from subjecting himself to Clara's lessons in republican citizenship. Dedicated to reassuring Clara that she wrongs him in calling his "passion by the odious name sensual," Edward spends the majority of the novel in acts of personal confession and public disclosure (23). Indeed, Edward's climactic decision in the novel involves an act of publication. Caught between the contradictory demands of Clara and Mary, Edward chooses to provide Mary with all of the letters that have passed between Clara and himself. "She shall judge," Edward writes to Clara, "with all the materials of a right judgment before her. I am prepared to devote myself to her will" (113). With regard to the disciplining of his sentiments, Edward is, to use his own analogy, "like one set loose upon a perilous sea, without rudder or sail" (115). And Edward's motivational crisis results directly from his successful education in the art of self-abstraction. Having bracketed any interest in who commands him, Edward's search for a judicious captain becomes strictly arbitrary. Either Clara or Mary will suffice. While this act of disinterested submission to the moral law marks Edward's emergence as a self-abstracting, republican citizen, it also reveals an important difference between the moral practice of Edward and that required by Kant. The "duty" to which Kant advises submission remains perfectly abstract, disembodied, and unrealizable; the "duty" to which Edward submits is not abstract, but embodied. It can be realized only through his submission to either (or both) of the novel's two female characters, Clara and Mary.

In part, this difference between Brown's and Kant's analyses of the practice of republican self-abstraction is a difference between two understandings of the relations among sex, gender, and citizenship. While a dimorphic logic of sexual difference operates throughout *Clara Howard*, a similar logic figures in *The Critique of Practical Reason* at only two points. Both occur late in the *Critique*, and both appear as part of Kant's counter-argument to any potential criticism that the ideal of the moral law is either heteronomous or, in Kant's words, an "empty fantasy." "If we attend to the course of conversation in mixed companies consisting not merely of scholars and subtle reasoners but also of business people and women," Kant writes, "we notice that besides storytelling and jesting they have another entertainment, namely, arguing." For Kant, this interest in moral argumentation demonstrates a subjective "receptivity" to "the objectively practical laws of pure reason."[33] The opposition of "scholars and subtle reasoners" to "business people and women" may be less than enlightened, but Kant's point here is not to exclude such private persons from the public forums within which moral argumentation takes place. Rather, Kant suggests that their interest in such argumentation indicates an ability and desire to participate in public processes of moral decision making. Kant's moral philosophy remains, in this sense, both republican and progressive. Due to its very abstraction, its disembodiment, the requirements of the moral law militate against any exclusive claims to superior judgment grounded in forms of embodiment such as sexual dimorphism. Though the art of republican self-abstraction could become, in Michael Warner's words, a "differential resource" that "provides a privilege for unmarked identities: the white, the male, the middle class, the normal," the reverse is also true.[34] Kant's resistance to the restriction of moral judgment through any form of embodiment could equally enable counter-hegemonic claims to republican citizenship by those subjects otherwise marked as "non-white," "non-male," "non-middle class," "abnormal."

Kant's second reference to gender is more complicated and revealing. Faced again with a widening gap between the objectivity of the moral law and the subjectivity of the moral interest, Kant bridges that gap through the metaphor of the "stepmother." *The Critique of Pure Reason*, Kant reminds his reader, "demonstrates the utter insufficiency of speculative reason to solve the most weighty problems which are presented to it in a way satisfactory to its end." "[B]ut," Kant continues, "that critique did not ignore the natural and unmistakable hints of the same reason or the great steps that it can take in approaching this great goal which is set before it but which it can never of itself reach even with the aid of the greatest knowledge of nature. This nature here seems to have provided us only in a stepmotherly fashion with a faculty needed for our end."[35] By grounding the potentially heteronomous authority of the moral law in a "stepmotherly" nature, Kant in this passage draws on the canon of natural law theorists to which his own rationalist moral philosophy is generally opposed. From Rousseau to Sacher-Masoch, this canon employs maternity (often in opposition to paternity) as a figure for embodiment and nonabstraction. In his essay on Sacher-Masoch's influential contemporary Johann Bachofen, Ernst Bloch confirms this generalization: "'Mother nature' was always a powerful ingredient in different phases of natural law. . . . [I]t is through maternal law that this element was transmitted and brought back to natural law."[36] "Mother nature," in other words, provides a romantic antidote to the coldness of Enlightenment reason. It is, Bloch writes later in the same essay, "a warm harmony, which in the midst of the history of law of the romantic origin, unexpectedly reminds one of Rousseau's return to nature, of natural law without artificiality."[37]

That Kant draws on this natural law tradition reveals the degree to which the association of maternity with embodiment and nonabstraction lies at the heart not only of the nineteenth-century culture of sentiment, but also of the most rational of eighteenth-century republicanisms. That Kant refers to a nature that operates in a specifically "stepmotherly fashion," however, indicates his rationalist critique of that tradition. In Sacher-Masoch's novelizations of Bachofen's gynocentric legal philosophy, the male masochist both betrays the gender to which his sex has assigned him (through his alignment with paternity) *and* becomes fulfilled as a subject through that betrayal. As Deleuze observes, the "masochist experiences the symbolic order as an intermaternal order in which the mother represents the law. . . . she generates the symbolism through which the masochist expresses himself."[38] In contrast, Kant's rigorous opposition between rationality and embodiment disables both the gendering of reason (as either maternal or paternal) *and* the experience of an undivided subjectivity. Kant's figure of a nature that operates in a "stepmotherly fashion" indicates a nature that is not natural but legally sanctioned, a mother who rules over her children not by natural but by contractual right. A "stepmotherly" nature is, in other words, a nature that supplements, not one that negates Enlightenment rationality and republican self-abstraction. Both of Kant's references to gender point toward forms of embodiment that potentially restrict claims to rationality; yet, neither reference pursues that argument to the point of sanctioning such restrictions. Despite Freud's assertion that Kant's categorical imperative is "a direct inheritance of the Oedipus-complex," *The Critique of Practical Reason* pursues an ideal of rationality that remains both ungendered and, in psychoanalytic terms, anti-Oedipal.[39] Its authority is grounded not in the symbolic function of paternity (or maternity), but in the institutions of literary publication and critical debate central to eighteenth-century republicanism.

Feminism and Male Masochism

Kant is alone neither in his republican insistence on maintaining an opposition between rationality and embodiment nor in his recognition of its political implications. The same opposition pervades the writings of the Enlightenment feminists who were Kant's contemporaries. As Nina Baym has suggested, such writers are distinguishable by their "refusal to see mind as

affected by its connection with a gendered body."[40] While this opposition of
mind and body would be attacked by later feminists who mobilized a dimorphic logic in order to mark and privilege women's difference from men, the
same opposition was defended by Enlightenment feminists who sought access to public discourse by deploying a universalist ideal of rationality. Such
authors continued to write, in Baym's words, "as women, but like men,
thereby implicitly claiming language and rationality as constituents of their
humanity."[41] While often understood as historically consecutive "waves" of
feminism, these two strategies are better interpreted as mutually constitutive tendencies within a single movement. As Joan Scott has argued, they
together produce one of the central paradoxes of modern feminism:

> Feminism was a protest against women's political exclusion; its goal was to elimi-
> nate "sexual difference" in politics, but it had to make its claims on behalf of
> 'women' (who were discursively produced through "sexual difference"). To the
> extent that it acted for "women," feminism produced the "sexual difference" it
> sought to eliminate. This paradox—the need both to accept *and* to refuse "sexual
> difference"—was the constitutive condition of feminism as a political movement
> over its long history.[42]

Scott's insight echoes other accounts of what Martha Minow refers to as the
"difference dilemma" within modern feminism.[43] The advantage of Scott's
account is that it locates the origins of this dilemma in the theoretical tension
between embodiment and rationality central to the political discourse of
early republicanism. Reason could secure its claims to nonheteronomous
universality only by anchoring those claims in the bodily and, in this case,
gendered sensations that it ultimately sought to transcend.

At its extreme, this tension within the self-abstracting demands of republican rationality could structure the career of a writer like Brown's contemporary Judith Sargent Murray. In the concluding essay of *The Gleaner* series
("The Gleaner Unmasked"), Murray explains that her use of a gender-neutral pseudonym ("The Gleaner") was necessitated by her ambition of "being
considered *independent as a writer*."[44] In the *Story of Margaretta* (a novel
published serially in *The Gleaner*), Murray thematizes this idea by criticizing those readers who search for the "real author" behind the Gleaner's
mask: "I cannot help regarding this *hunting after names*, as descriptive of the
frivolity of the human mind. . . . The business of the reader is to scan the
intrinsic value and *general tendency* of the composition; if that is considerable, if that is laudable, he ought to leave the author to announce himself
under what auspices he shall judge proper."[45] The Gleaner's admonishment
plays on the enabling conventions of a literary public sphere understood as
a space of rational-critical debate. Well aware that many would argue, like
Rousseau, that a woman could only "*ostensibly* wield the pen," Murray dons
a public "mask" analogous to those of the *Tatler* and *Spectator* earlier in the

century.[46] Though identified within the narrative with Margaretta's male guardian, the Gleaner thus exploits a gap between the impersonal values of the "composition" on the one hand (its *"intrinsic value* and *general tendency"*), and the identity of the composer on the other (the author who may or may not "announce himself"). Murray's mask then operates as both a defensive strategy and a theoretical counter-argument to masculinist versions of republicanism. Only after ensuring her reputation as an "author" does Murray reveal her identity as a "woman." By disembodying reason through a logic of self-abstraction, this type of argument does more than simply privatize sexual difference in order to access a still masculine public discourse. It also theorizes a republicanism in which such access would not rely on any logic of embodiment, sexual or otherwise.

At times in his career, Brown pens a similar argument. In *Alcuin*, a feminist dialogue published three years before *Clara Howard*, Brown's female interlocutor (Mrs. Carter) echoes Murray when she demands social and political equality due to the sexes' shared rationality: "Men and women are partakers of the same nature. They are rational beings, and, as such, the same principles of truth and equity must be applicable to both."[47] Throughout the first half of the dialogue, Brown's male interlocutor (Alcuin) grants Mrs. Carter's rationalist premise, but questions her radical dissociation of mind and body, of reason and sex. "Suppose," he asks, "an anatomist should open his school to pupils of both sexes, and solicit equally their attendance, would you comply?"[48] This hypothetical is clearly tendentious. It conjures a scene in which reason and bodies necessarily intersect, while it also alludes to the theater in which contemporary medical experts were responding to feminist arguments like Mrs. Carter's by moving from a one-sex to a two-sex model of the human body. As my previous chapter argued, this paradigm shift responded to Enlightenment critiques of gender hierarchy by locating sexual dimorphism as the corporeal gounding of civil and political relations. "Whatever the political agenda," Thomas Laqueur concludes, "the strategy is the same. . . . sex is everywhere precisely because the authority of gender has collapsed."[49] Still, Mrs. Carter remains firm in her initial position. To segregate any type of public space on the grounds of "delicacy" would be "obviating an imaginary evil at the price of a real one." "Nothing," she insists, "has been more injurious than the separation of the sexes."[50] Thwarted by this response, Alcuin pulls out his trump card. "We all know," he insists, "in what the sexual distinction consists, and what is the final cause of this distinction. It is easier to conceive than describe that species of attraction which sex annexes to persons."[51] An interruption by a third guest at the salon prevents Mrs. Carter from answering, and the first half of the dialogue ends on this point.

Published posthumously in 1815, the second half of *Alcuin* inverts the rhetorical positioning of the first half. The previously skeptical Alcuin begins by telling Mrs. Carter of his conversion to her principles—a conversion that results from his journey, between the two halves of the dialogue, to a utopian "paradise of women."[52] Alcuin's account of that journey begins as he reports his native guide's confusion when asked about his country's social and political principles with regard to sexual difference. Himself a political philosopher, Alcuin's guide pleads ignorance, referring him to the "anatomist, or to the hall where he publicly communicates his doctrines."[53] Like Mrs. Carter, the guide divorces sex from gender, biology from culture, in order to marginalize the former and denaturalize the latter. When Alcuin later repeats his query, his guide grows irritable. He admits that "a species of conduct is incumbent on men and women towards each other on certain occcassions, that cannot take place between man and man; or between women and women." But his example is trivial: "I may properly supply my son with a razor to remove superfluous hairs from his chin, but I may with no less propriety forbear to furnish my daughter with this implement, because nature has denied her a beard."[54] By the end of the dialogue, all of Alcuin's beliefs in sexual difference as a form of embodiment that determines social and political principles have been exploded. Neither dress, nor education, nor employment can be rationally linked to sex.[55] "One would imagine that among you," Alcuin's guide tells him, "one sex had more arms, or legs, or senses than the other."[56] Even marriage, Alcuin informs the now skeptical Mrs. Carter, is nothing more than a formal term "descriptive of that mode of sexual intercourse, whatever it may be, which custom or law has established in any country."[57]

This last point proves problematic. As an unmarried teacher, Alcuin is as poor as Edward Hartley. As a result, he hesitates to broach the question of marriage with a wealthy widow like Mrs. Carter who, in turn, takes exception to the "devious tract" mapped by Alcuin's guide (37). This critique of marriage, she asserts, places Alcuin among that "class of reasoners" who "aim at the deepest foundation of civil society" (52). Two points are notable here. First, Mrs. Carter is right. Alcuin's argument does align him with libertine critics of marriage like Peter Sanford in *The Coquette* or Murray's own "Mr. Sinisterus Courtland," the villain of *The Story of Margaretta*.[58] "What conduct is incumbent upon me," Alcuin asks, "when the species of marriage established among my countrymen, does not conform to my notions of duty."[59] As Michael Grossberg and Nancy Cott have argued, nineteenth-century legal reformers reacted against this disestablishment of the marriage contract by allowing the state to regulate the terms of that contract, as well as the number and identity of the persons involved.[60] Second, Mrs. Carter's objection results narratively from the possibility that Alcuin's argument is itself a strategy for seduction. This possibility cuts short their mutual investigation of social and political institutions by assuming that sexual difference inevitably produces an erotic charge or, in eighteenth-century terms, that sexuality *is* sensuality.[61] In the presence of Mrs. Carter, Alcuin finds it impossible to "reason dispassionately."[62] Since it is possible for him to reason dispassionately with his male guide, this impossibility suggests that the dialogue replaces the institution of marriage with a naturalized heterosensuality as the means of "regulat[ing] sexual intercourse." Combined, the disruptive appearance of the third guest at the end of the first half of the dialogue and the specter of seduction at the end of the second provide two of the axioms that police the modern sex-gender system: "Opposites attract" and "Three's a crowd."

Brown's endorsement of this policing may be indicated by the fact that he locates his alternative to it—Alcuin's "paradise of women"—in a clearly utopian space.[63] As several critics have suggested, the dialogue itself can be read as a satire, a reductio ad absurdum of Enlightenment feminist arguments which model, in Wollstonecraft's words, a "world *where there is neither marrying*, nor giving in marriage."[64] And this satire may expand to include the literary salon in which the dialogue takes place as a public space where poor schoolteachers like Alcuin become, in Mrs. Carter's words, "dissolute by theory . . . modelling voluptuousness into a speculative system."[65] Read in this fashion, *Alcuin* parallels *Venus in Furs* in its rendering of social and political equality as strictly utopian due to the reality of sexual difference.[66] This interpretation wins further support from Brown's tendency in his later novels to equate utopian speculation with sexual seduction. Taken seriously, however, *Alcuin* suggests that Brown's initial understanding of the relation between sex or, more precisely, between embodiment, and citizenship is as progressive as those of his Enlightenment contemporaries. At the very least, *Alcuin* evinces Brown's awareness of the democratic potential inscribed within the disembodying logic of republican self-abstraction. In contrast, *Clara Howard* reconfigures the relations among sex, embodiment, and citizenship. Faced with the possibility of a republic governed without regard to sexual difference, Brown reacts by mobilizing a logic of embodiment that assumes the centrality of sexual difference to any republic. In *The Coquette*, this reaction relies on a grounding of gender norms in the sensations of the (sexed) body; in *Clara Howard*, the same reaction draws on a now sexualized opposition between rationality and sentimentality. No longer gender-neutral terms, reason and sentiment are embodied in the figures of Clara and Edward.

That this arrangement inverts the emerging normative association of reason with masculinity and sentiment with femininity makes little difference in the context. Confronted with either logic of embodiment, Enlightenment principles produce a battle of the sexes. Clara's reason disciplines Edward's sentiments. The republican attack on "Masculine systems" leads, in John Adams's words, to a "Despotism of the Peticoat" against which "General Washington and all our brave heroes would fight." And there is an element of truth in Adams's hyperbole. The logic of republican self-abstraction does open the possibility that women among others will ascend to positions of political and civil power. Even in domestic affairs, Wollstonecraft reasons in her *Vindication of the Rights of Woman*, "many individuals have more sense than their male relatives; and . . . some women govern their husbands without degrading themselves, because intellect will always govern."[67] As indicated by the displacement of the gendered referent "women" by the abstract referent "individuals," Wollstonecraft's insistence in this passage that "intellect" ought to govern suggests that the governing individuals may be women as well as men. In a scenario familiar from the ERA battles of the 1970s, both Adams and Brown react to this possibility by mobilizing a logic of embodiment that transforms a democratic call for social and political equality into a masochistic contract for sexual domination. What is most radical and threatening about the rational Clara is, in this sense, neither her characterization as a woman, nor her homosocial identification with Mary, but her penchant for rendering moral judgments without regard to any logic of embodiment, including sex. Like Murray, whose "mask" ensures her "independence as a writer," Clara mobilizes a disembodying logic of self-abstraction in order to ensure her independence as a moral subject and judge. Clara's reason remains as sexually indifferent as the republican polity it ideally regulates.

At the level of plot, Clara's mobilization of this logic places her in direct opposition to the men in the novel not simply as men, but as individuals who threaten her independence. Throughout *Clara Howard*, Edward searches for a strategy that will allow him to fulfill his introductory pledge to narrate the story of his acquisition of both wealth and "that most exquisite of all blessings, a wife." Initially, this narrative of Edward's ascent to full masculine subjectivity seems realizable through the agency of Mr. Howard who, despite his republican principles, offers Clara to Edward. "This heiress of opulence and splendor," Edward exclaims, "this child of fortune, and appropriator of elegance and grace, and beauty, was proffered to me as a wife!" (54). That Clara resists her father's positioning of her as an object of exogamous exchange is predictable. In her marriage choice, Mr. Howard acknowledges, Clara "will forget ancestry and patrimony, and think only of the morals and understanding of the object" (51). Forced to abandon Mr. Howard's increasingly anachronistic logic of patriarchal exchange, Edward's second recourse is to what could be referred to as an emerging erotics of heterosexual embodiment. As Niklas Luhmann suggests in *Love as Passion*, this erotics is typical of a liberalism in which "love could no longer be connected to a theory of state or economics; rather the concept corresponded precisely to what was to be expected in terms of the other's love."[68] While Mary inspires in Edward a "sentiment, very different from love," Clara provides him with an experience of "passion." Divorced from all social and political logics except gender, this passion takes the form not of a "boundless esteem," but of an unmediatable and, Edward hopes, fully reciprocal relation between (male) self and (female) other (43). For Edward, in short, sex ideally expresses itself in that form of sensuality that many modern readers would recognize (and naturalize) as heterosexuality.[69]

It is Clara's resistance to this second, specifically heterosexual (or heterosensual) strategy that draws the harshest criticism from both Edward and the critics who align themselves with him. Unwilling to differentiate "passion" from the civil and political codes within which it operates, Clara applies the same republican logic to Edward's liberalism as she does to her father's paternalism. "Perhaps esteem is not the only requisite to marriage," Clara writes in her first letter to Edward, "Of that I am not certain; but I know that it is an indispensable requisite to love. I cannot love in you anything but excellence" (20). Later, Clara reaffirms this logic: "I love you, Edward, as I ought to love you. I love your happiness; your virtue" (109). Clara's insistence on linking passionate love to moral rationality may mark her as cold, but it is crucial to recognize the source of that coldness. Despite her father's benevolence, his offer of Clara to Edward positions her as an object of exchange in a plot hatched between two men. Despite Edward's willingness to give her control of any marriage gift from her father, his very need to make this concession indicates an economic asymmetry inscribed within the institution of marriage (89). In either case, the completion of Edward's bildungsroman plot entails the loss of Clara's independence—her translation in legal terminology from a *feme sole* to a *feme covert*. In relation to both her father and Edward, Clara resists engendering logics of embodiment that mediate her relation to Edward by transforming her, as a woman, into the "possession" of either a husband or a father. Clara affirms and reaffirms what could be called, for lack of a better term, a hetero-critical republicanism—a republicanism that resists the engendering logics common to the hetero-normative plots of both Edward and Mr. Howard.[70]

In its very extremity, then, Brown's characterization of Clara's republicanism reveals not only the overt gender asymmetry inscribed in Mr. Howard's benevolent paternalism, but also the covert asymmetry inscribed in Edward's romantic liberalism. The logic of self-abstraction that empowers Clara is the same logic that undermines each of Edward's (contradictory) beliefs concerning romantic love: that love consists of a reciprocal passion between selves and others that are implicitly gendered male and female; that such a passion ought to be unmediated by any such impersonal concerns. At times, Clara seems to agree with Edward's romantic belief in unmediated passion. Fearful that her rigorous adherence to her "duty" has led Edward to abandon her, Clara envisions a post-Enlightenment world in which "conscience" and "heart"—reason and sentiment—are in perfect accord. "Has it come to this!" she asks Edward, "now, that the impediment has vanished, that my feelings may be indulged at the cost of no one's peace; now that the duty which once so sternly forbad me to be yours, not only permits, but enjoins me to link together out fates; that the sweet voice of an approving conscience is ready to sanction and applaud every impulse of my heart, and make the offices of tenderness not only free from guilt, but coincident with every duty; that now . . . " (141). This passage's concluding ellipses point toward the romantic fulfillment of both Edward and Clara as complementary subjects, but it is important to note that even here Clara justifies her love for Edward through reference to an abstract and impersonal duty—both its absence in relation to Mary and its presence in relation to Edward. Since duty continues to mediate desire, Clara's reason continues to regulate Edward's sentiments. What this injection of an impersonal logic into interpersonal relations implies is that the antinomy of rationality and sentimentality that dominates the novel remains unresolvable. More important, it remains unresolvable not because a logic of embodiment results in a sexual difference that is itself unresolvable, but because a logic of self-abstraction insists on the rational mediation of even the most sentimental of personalities. The first logic promises to transform Clara into Edward's "possession." Only the second legitimates her political, moral, and erotic independence as a citizen of the republic.

The Male Complaint

To the end, the Enlightenment feminism of Clara Howard, the character, prevents the romantic completion of *Clara Howard*, the novel. Because it remains separate from her heart, Clara's hand remains that of a writer, not that of a wife. Historically, of course, the logic of self-abstraction that structures the eighteenth-century republic of letters gave way to the logic of embodiment that structures the nineteenth-century empire of the mother. As social historian Mary Ryan points out, the very stability of this logic of embodiment produced a tension within the seat of women's supposed power—the conjugal home: "The cult of domesticity celebrated a logical and practical impossibility. It bred male and female into dichotomous roles and temperaments, then venerated their union and required their independence within an isolated home. The heterosexual tension was lodged at the very center of the domestic mode of social reproduction, and it casts a shadow over the empire of the mother." [71] One resolution of this tension—this "difference dilemma"—lay in the ideological coding of social and political space as itself gendered. As in the writings of Ann Douglas, the public sphere of disinterested rationality could be figured as male, while the private sphere of interested sentimentality could be figured as female. Or, as in *Clara Howard*, the "wilderness" of the West could be male, while the "civilization" of the East could be female. Even as astute a critic of liberal gender relations as Margaret Fuller could reproduce this heterosexist ideology. Though she claims in "The Great Lawsuit" that there is "no wholly masculine man, no purely feminine woman," her rhetoric nevertheless divides society into male and female as "the two sides of the great radical dualism."[72] "The Great Lawsuit" may begin by linking feminism and abolitionism through a critique of both engendering and racializing logics of embodiment, yet it concludes by collapsing all difference into sexual difference through the figure of the Virgin Mother.[73]

The reductiveness of the engendering hermeneutic produced by this logic of embodiment is surpassed only by its persistence. As Nina Baym pointed out in 1981, the U.S. literary and literary critical canons are themselves constituted through a logic of embodiment that engenders both the content and the form of those canons. "Melodramas of beset manhood," Baym argues, contrast an androcentric form of literary innovation—narratives that focus on "exploring and taming the wilderness"—to a gynocentric form of literary conventionality—narratives that focus on domestic and social concerns. By privileging the former over the later, these "melodramas" leave, in Baym's words, "no place for women . . . she is either to be silent, like nature, or she is the creator of conventional works, the spokeswoman of society."[74] Since 1981, Baym's argument has been extended in two directions. On the one hand, critics like Jane Tompkins have inverted the androcentric literary canon by celebrating sentimental writings by women as powerful critiques of prevailing conventions; on the other hand, critics like Gillian Brown have questioned the presumed unconventionality of the same canon by suggesting that male anti-sentimentalism is merely the ideological antithesis of female sentimentalism.[75] Both of these approaches yield insights into sentimentalism as a cultural project focused, in Shirley Samuels's words, on the "problem of the body and what it embodies," yet neither moves beyond either the sexual dimorphism of the late eighteenth century, or the nineteenth-century logics of embodiment that associate femininity with sentimentality.[76] In accordance with these critical axioms, sentimental literature remains (as it was for Baym in *Woman's Fiction*) a literature written "by," if not exclusively "about" women.[77] U.S. literary history continues to be written as if the author of *Edgar Huntly* either never wrote *Clara Howard*, or did so only reluctantly.

By focusing on *Clara Howard* as the novel in which Brown investigates the relation between sentimentality and masculinity, I have extended Baym's argument in a third direction. An androcentric canon focused on anti-sentimental writings may afford little space for women, yet Baym's own reasoning implies that it affords no greater space to male sentimentalism. The literary feminization of sentiment renders the figure of the male sentimentalist paradoxical, while literary criticism that assumes this feminization renders the male sentimentalist invisible. *Clara Howard* is an exception to this generalization, but I do not mean to suggest that Brown escapes the engendering logic that feminizes sentiment. It would be more accurate to read his inversion of that logic as producing a "male" version of the rhetorical form that Lauren Berlant refers to as the "female complaint." The "female complaint," as Berlant defines it, originated in the late eighteenth century as a "mode of public discourse that demonstrates women's contested value in the patriarchal public sphere by providing commentary from a generically 'feminine' point of view."[78] As such, the complaint's criticisms of social and political relations are circumscribed in two ways. First, they reduce all difference to sexual difference. By the end of *Clara Howard*, for example, the class (Clara/Mary) and ethnic (European/Native American) antagonisms that structure the novel's opening letters are resolved through the (contested) ideal of (hetero)sexual complementarity. Second, they are also circumscribed by a rhetorical commitment to the emerging ideology of sexual dimorphism—the "heterosexual matrix," to use Judith Butler's term—which divides both the body and the body politic into male and female.[79] By inverting male and female, Brown's masochistic "male complaint" both resists and reinscribes that logic of embodiment. If, to paraphrase Barbara Stanwyck in *The Lady Eve*, Clara needs Edward like the axe needs the turkey, then Edward needs Clara like the turkey needs the axe.

Nor do I mean to construct a symmetry between the genres of the female and the male complaint. Fanny Fern's parody of generic masculinity in *Ruth Hall* does parallel Mark Twain's parody of generic femininity in *The Adventures of Huckleberry Finn*.[80] But a criticism unable to distinguish between the rhetorical strategies and political motivations of, say, the women's and the men's movement would be impoverished at best. As elsewhere within the letters of the republic, the false symmetry produced by the ideology of sexual difference masks power asymmetries. Edward's narrative ascent (and assent) to full masculine subjectivity promises to secure for him social and political privilege, while Clara's complementary descent (and dissent) within that same narrative results from her prospective loss of that privilege. What I do mean to suggest is that a critique of the logic of embodiment that underpins both the female and the male complaint is inscribed within Brown's masochistic melodrama of Edward's sentimental manhood. In the figure of Clara Howard, Brown encodes an Enlightenment feminist attack on the engendering logics of embodiment which, as Monique Wittig succinctly puts it, "systematically heterosexualize that personal dimension which suddenly emerged . . . almost two centuries ago."[81] Wittig's dates may be off by a century or so, but her allusion to a "personal dimension" that became politically significant at the end of the eighteenth century accurately locates the prehistory of (hetero and homo) sexuality within the discourse of sentimentalism. What fades from view in both Edward's engendering narrative and the critical responses to *Clara Howard* that focus on that narrative is the eighteenth-century counter-possibility of ungendered sentimental citizenship—a counter-possibility that appears, within *Clara Howard*, in Clara's republican letters. As such an understanding of citizenship reappears today in the fields of feminist and queer theory, it is doing so only by drawing (unintentionally) upon the less rigorously gendered and, at times, ungendered conceptions of mind and body out of which both male and female sentimentalism emerged.[82]

Part Three

SENTIMENT AND SEXUALITY

6

Obscene Publics: Jesse Sharpless and Harriet Jacobs

Why be afraid to write useful truths for the good of
society? Well, my dear benefactor, I will resist no
longer: I'll write; my ingenuity will make up for my
lack of a polished style—at least for thinking men,
and I care little for fools. No, you'll be denied
nothing by your dear Therese, you'll know all the
secret places of her heart from her earliest days. Her
soul will be completely revealed through the little
adventures which have led her, despite herself, step
by step, to the heights of sensual pleasure.

    Jean-Baptiste de Boyer, Therese Philosophe,
    1748)[1]

You may believe what I say; for I write only that
whereof I know. I was twenty-one years in that cage
of obscene birds.

    Harriet Jacobs, Incidents in the Life of a Slave
    Girl, *1861)*[2]

Publicity, Obscenity, Privacy

The central chapter of Harriet Jacobs's *Incidents in the Life of a Slave Girl*
records the imprint that the liberal idealization of privacy leaves on the bodies of U.S. citizens and subjects. Entitled "A Loophole of Retreat," the chapter describes the nine-by-seven-by-three-foot garret in which Jacobs (Linda
Brent) lived for seven years as a fugitive slave while pursuing freedom for
herself and her children. As a "loophole" within the antebellum slave economy, this "retreat" provides Jacobs with "privacy" in each of the two senses
of the term. It serves as a space of both privation and privilege. While Jacobs
later writes that her "body still suffers from the effects of that long imprisonment, to say nothing of [her] soul," she also allows the garret to prefigure the
"home made sacred by protecting laws" for which she longs throughout *Incidents* (144, 114). Confinement in the garret leaves its mark on Jacobs as
surely as the slaveholder's whip, but it also holds out the promise of privacy

as a source of personal autonomy unavailable to her in either a slaveholding or a capitalist economy. In one critic's reading of *Incidents*, the garret becomes a metaphor for Jacobs's difficulties in finding textual and architectural shelter in the antebellum United States, while another treats it as a metaphor for the ways in which "feminist agency" must work within and against systems of racial and sexual oppression.[3] In either case, the military resonances of the phrase "loophole of retreat" alert the reader that the boundary between public and private is a battleground that transects Jacobs's body. The garret becomes a strategic position in her struggle to publicize the structural asymmetries that both underlie *and* belie nineteenth-century liberalism as a political ideology.

Nowhere are the stakes in this battle over and between publicity and privacy higher than in Jacobs's narration of her sexual relations. When she describes categorically nonsexual forms of racial exploitation, Jacobs draws on the publicist conventions of antebellum moral reform movements—including those of the abolitionist slave narrative. Testifying from her own experience, Jacobs opposes her firsthand knowledge of the physical brutality of master-slave relations to Southern, pro-slavery accounts of the "patriarchal institution."[4] When she moves to specifically sexual forms of exploitation, Jacobs's faith in publicity wavers, and with good reason. She knows that any frank discussion of her sexual subjection threatens to alienate her largely Northern, white, middle-class, female audience—an audience for whom slave testimony is one thing, but sexual testimony quite another. "The experiences of this intelligent and much-injured woman," writes Jacobs's editor Lydia Maria Child, "belong to a class which some will call delicate subjects, and others indelicate" (4). Jacobs responds to this (in)delicate situation by shifting from the generic conventions of the slave narrative to those of the sentimental novel.[5] Originally a literary form concerned with the construction, analysis, and regulation of bodily and intimate relations, the sentimental novel provides Jacobs with a means of publicizing sexual relations elsewhere coded as private and rendered opaque to political critique. Playing Clarissa to Flint's Lovelace (Eliza to his Sanford), Jacobs places onstage and in-public incidents that both she and Child fear her audience will reject as obscene. *Incidents* thus becomes, in Lauren Berlant's apt phrase, a "counterpornography of citizenship"—a form of political obscenity that breaks the "silences of sexual privacy in order to create national publics trained to think, and thus to think differently, about the corporeal conditions of citizenship."[6]

Still, Jacobs does not tell all. While she confesses to choosing a "white unmarried gentleman" (Mr. Sands) as a lover to protect her from Flint, she places offstage the details of that relationship and, in particular, its duration (54). This reserve may result from Jacobs's negotiations with her audience's sense of propriety, but it also reveals a deeper suspicion of publicity as a vehicle for (abolitionist) moral and political reform. Having spent a good portion of the first twenty years of her life fending off Flint's invasions of her sexual privacy, Jacobs uses the same defensive tactics in relation to her reader. Like her audience, Jacobs expects to be treated chastely as a woman; unlike her audience, she experiences a series of legally sanctioned sexual violations as a slave. Caught between her status as woman and as slave (as a "delicate" and "indelicate" subject), Jacobs intentionally limits the publication of her sexual history in order to access the privileges of privacy enjoyed by her reader.[7] "Young slave girls," she writes, "hear such talk as should never meet youthful ears, or any ears" (52). As receiver and transmitter of obscene talk, Jacobs positions herself as both victim and pornographer. She remains torn between her belief that (sexual) privacy ought to be a right accessible to all and her realization that, without acts of publication like *Incidents*, privacy will remain a source of privation for sexually, racially, and economically exploited subjects like herself. "It would have been more pleasant to me," she writes in her preface, "to have been silent about my own history." Jacobs identifies and sympathizes with her audience's desire not to hear her history, but she writes it nonetheless in order to publicize the "condition of two millions of women at the South, still in bondage, suffering what I suffered, and most of them far worse" (1).

The tension between Jacobs's desire for sexual privacy and her need to publicize her sexual history remains unresolved. In contrast to many domestic anti-slavery narratives, *Incidents* concludes with the nonrealization of Jacobs's desire for a secure space of privacy. "The dream of my life is not yet realized," she writes, "I do not sit with my children in a home of my own" (201). Lacking a home as a resource for personal autonomy, Jacobs opts to address to the public the story of her not yet private life.[8] As such, the narrative non-resolution of *Incidents* results from Jacobs's biographical and historical circumstances. But it also reflects a more general contradiction between moral and obscene publication within the sentimental sub-genre David Reynolds refers to as "immoral reform": "This overlapping . . . was nowhere more clearly visible than in the fierce wars that raged between the reformers and the popular newspaper editors, who regularly charged each other with obscenity and false sensationalism."[9] In his attempt to synthesize this opposition, Reynolds suggests that the "immoral-reform apologia" typical of the sub-genre operate for both groups as little more than marketing devices.[10] A pornographic novel published a year before *Incidents*, for example, also contains a preface justifying descriptions of the "worst horrors of Slave Trading" as "calling attention to the Crimes of the Slave Trade."[11] By collapsing the distinction between moral and immoral reform (between *Incidents in the Life of a Slave Girl* and *Revelations of a Slave Trader*), Reynolds both pinpoints a central anxiety within narratives like *Incidents*, and serves

as a modern example of the sort of prurient reader Jacobs and Child fear.
Wary of such readers (those for whom *Incidents*'s sexual descriptions may
elicit sensations that diverge from any abolitionist intent), Jacobs heeds
warnings against publicity like the one offered by her Northern patron, Mr
Durham. After listening to Jacobs's story, Durham advises her to be cautious
with its publication: "Your straightforward answers do you credit, but don't
answer everyone so openly. It might give some heartless people a pretext for
treating you with contempt" (160). Even at age ten, Jacobs seems aware of
this double bind. Worried about her grandmother's response, she resists
publicizing Flint's sexual suggestions: "I was very young, and felt shame-
faced about telling her such impure things, especially as I knew her to be
very strict on such subjects" (29).

Yet obscene publication remains a necessary evil for Jacobs, as it does for
other antebellum reformers committed to the public critique of privatized
relations. It is the immoral means to the moral end of shifting the boundary
between public virtue and private vice. In an argument parallel to my own,
Carla Kaplan has noted that Jacobs's vexed relation to her audience mirrors
her ambivalent assessment of liberal social contract theory: "Not only do
[contracts] represent power, or at least the possibility of it, but they also
represent an ideal of equal and equalizing social relations."[12] My argument
expands on this ambivalence: Jacobs's reliance on the generic conventions of
sentimentalism leads her simultaneously to uphold *and* to challenge the
norms of decency that were transforming the structure of the public sphere
within which the terms of the social contract are negotiated. As both an
advocate and a critic of this liberal transformation, Jacobs speaks obscenely
in order to shift *and* to stabilize the boundary between publicity and privacy.
Obscenity, to modify Walter Kendrick's well-known description of pornography, thus names both an argument *and* a thing within the nineteenth-
century culture of sentimental reform.[13] For Jacobs, as for her audience, that
argument concerns the location of sexuality within the mutually constitutive
relation between public and private life. My contribution to that (ongoing)
argument leads through an investigation of contemporary changes in the
legal category of obscenity before returning to Jacobs's sentimental use of
that category in *Incidents*. I follow this path for two reasons. First, the juxtaposition of the legal deployment of obscenity by the state and the sentimental redeployment of obscenity by reformers like Jacobs and Child fore-
grounds their shared contribution to the liberal construction of the public
sphere as a space constituted by its exclusion of either sexual acts or sexual
politics. Second, the same juxtaposition also indicates potential dissonances
between state and civil authority as the locus of moral and political judgment
shifts from the nation's courtrooms to those private spaces that are ideally,
though never fully opaque to the critical gaze of the public at large.

The Democratic Origins of Obscenity

The legal understanding of obscenity that informs narratives like *Incidents* emerges only at the beginning of the nineteenth century. Prior to the democratic revolutions of the late eighteenth century, obscenity tended to be grouped with blasphemy and sedition as crimes of libel against the church and state. *Therese Philosophe*, for example, was banned—along with other works of Enlightenment philosophy—as a political tract attacking the clergy.[14] Only after the revolutions did libel for obscenity take on its modern significance as a nonpolitical crime concerned with offenses against public morality and decency. As the victims of obscenity became more speculative, attempts on the part of the state to prosecute obscene-libel began to focus away from the actual representation of political and religious figures within texts, and toward the hypothetical effects that such representations would have on the public outside of those texts. One structural explanation for this historical shift traces its cause to contemporary legal and economic transformations in the relations among publicity, privacy, and state authority. The revolutionary disestablishment of religion and constitutional guarantee of free speech in secular republics like France and the United States combined with the capitalist expansion of print technology to produce a seemingly anarchic public sphere. Under this new regime, the task of regulating publication fell not to the state, but to the market. As Lynn Hunt, Beverley Brown, and Walter Kendrick have all argued, obscenity and pornography surfaced at this moment as categories that enabled the modern state to respond to this loss of authority. Figures like the French jurist who coined the term "pornography" in 1806 grappled, Hunt explains, with "the problem of print in modern society; books should not be suppressed just because religious and political authorities do not like them but because they offend some basic shared sense of the social order."[15] Relinking secular market relations and public morality, the first federal anti-obscenity statute in the United States appeared in the Customs Act of 1842, sandwiched between regulations concerning tariff duties and the meaning of the term "ton."[16]

What is new about this modern redeployment of the category of the obscene is not that it relies upon a distinction between public and private spheres. As indicated by the Latin etymology of the term (*obscaena*, or "not for stage"), the category of the obscene is structurally necessary to any (ancient *or* modern) political regime founded upon an antithesis between public and private life.[17] What is new about the category is that it relies on the idea of public morality or decency as the means of regulating the relationship between the terms of that antithesis. In doing so, it renders the boundary between public and private simultaneously foundational and debatable.

The modern category of obscenity thus contains a paradox since, to modify Kendrick's argument once again, it names both a thing *and* an argument. Obscenity names a thing because the republican ideal of a democratic public space for moral and political debate requires an antithetical private space as a resource enabling equal participation in public. This structural requirement of a boundary separating public and private is an historical constant. Obscenity names an argument because the location of that boundary is determinable only through critical debate in the public arena. Since the outcome of that debate varies over time, the ideological content or "thing-ness" of obscenity is historically contingent. Anti-obscenity polemicists ranging from Anthony Comstock to Edwin Meese tend to resolve this paradox in favor of an understanding of obscenity as inhering in an object or act. Anti-censorship advocates ranging from Comstock's nemesis, Victoria Woodhull, to Susie Bright ("Susie Sexpert") resolve the same paradox by assuming that judgments of obscenity are subjective contributions to an ongoing struggle over the objective parameters of public debate.

Nearly thirty years prior to the Customs Act of 1842, the first successful conviction for obscene-libel in the United States illustrates the tension between these anti-obscenity and anti-censorship positions. Tried in the Pennsylvania Supreme Court in 1815, the case of *Commonwealth v. Sharpless* involved the prosecution of six "evil-disposed persons" charged with exhibiting "for money . . . a certain lewd, wicked, scandalous, infamous and obscene painting, representing a man in an obscene, impudent and indecent posture with a woman."[18] The defendants plead guilty to this charge: they did own and exhibit the painting. But their attorney then moves to arrest judgment for three reasons. First, temporal courts in Pennsylvania lack any statutory authority or common law precedent to establish jurisdiction over the alleged crime. While the defendants may be punishable in English ecclesiastical courts, they deserve only extra-legal censure—what Sharpless's attorney refers to as the "frowns of society"—in a state regulated by temporal courts (92–93). Second, the indictment does not specify that the painting was exhibited in public, even though "publicity is the essence of the crime" in this case. Indictments for "open and *gross* lewdness," the defense reminds the court, cannot be supported by evidence of a "private act of lewdness, which an individual saw without the knowledge of the parties" (93–94). Third, the indictment fails to describe the painting with sufficient detail to determine whether or not its content is obscene. "In every public exhibition," the defense reminds the court, "there are pictures which are viewed with pleasure and approbation, by many respectable and pure-minded persons . . . while others, more fastidious, consider them improper to be exhibited to the public eye" (94–97).

The defense's three anti-censorship arguments revolve around the structural requirements of any democratic political regime. The first draws on the constitutional disestablishment clause to divest the state of any authority over moral judgment, public or private. The second draws on liberalism's understanding of the right to privacy to establish a space of bodily and intimate relations unsupervised by the state. The third draws on republicanism's understanding of the right to publicity to establish a space of public debate similarly free from state intervention. In response, the prosecution begins by establishing jurisdiction through the straightforward counter-assertion that the court is the moral custodian of the public: "It is necessarily invested with the power to punish, not only open violations of decency and morality, but also whatever secretly tends to undermine the principles of society" (97). Since this necessity applies not only to manifestly public offenses, but also to those "secret" crimes whose "effect is to injure the public," the defense's second argument concerning the right to privacy is moot. The fact that the painting was exhibited for money and, indeed, the fact that it was exhibited at all is sufficient proof that the offense was public (97–98). As to the final objection that the painting is not adequately described in the indictment, the prosecution simply accepts the characterization of it as "obscene," adding that "the courts are not to be polluted by obscene and indecent language" (98).

In rendering a verdict for the prosecution, the judges in *Sharpless* support and elaborate on these three anti-obscenity arguments. In addition to agreeing with the prosecution that "actions of public decency were always indictable as tending to the corruption of public morals," Justice Tilghman's majority opinion establishes jurisdiction by citing an English common law precedent for *Sharpless* in the case of *Sir Charles Sedley*. Tried in 1663, Sedley was charged for appearing drunk and naked on a balcony above Covent Garden where he preached blasphemy and excreted on a plebeian crowd below. As Peter Stallybrass and Allon White point out, Sedley's actions transgressed the norms of decency that were beginning to carve out a space of unofficial public debate located between the court on the one hand, and the street or tavern on the other.[19] Like Sharpless's attorney, the defense in *Sedley* disputes the Crown's right to police that space (to render it official), arguing that moral crimes fall under the jurisdiction of ecclesiastical, not temporal courts. For Justice Tilghman, the significance of *Sedley* lies in the Crown's response that offenses against "public morality" are prosecutable in temporal courts. "What tends to corrupt society," Tilghman writes, "was held to be a breach of the peace and punishable by indictment. The courts are the guardians of public morals, and therefore, have jurisdiction in such cases" (100–101). In *Sedley*, the phrase "public morals" allows the Crown to wrest authority from the ecclesiastical courts. In *Sharpless*, the same phrase enables the democratic state to regain authority in the absence of those courts.

Having established jurisdiction, Tilghman's opinion turns to the defense's second argument that its clients are not indictable because the painting was never exhibited in public. Here again, the phrase "public morals" works in the prosecution's favor since the subversion of those morals can result from either public or private causes. Dismissing the structural distinction between public and private acts, Tilghman argues that "the law is not to be evaded by an artiface of that kind." To illustrate the importance of his point, Tilghman conjures a fantasy familiar to any reader of eighteenth-century pornography—public subversion effected through private means: "[I]f the privacy of the room was a protection, all the youths of the city might be corrupted, by taking them, one by one, into a chamber, and there inflaming their passions by the exhibition of lascivious pictures. In the eye of the law, this would be a *publication*, and a most pernicious one" (101). As attractive as this fantasy may be to some, it allows Tilghman to argue that virtually any act is public, any "exhibition" a "publication." An ideological opposition between law and society thus supercedes the structural distinction between public and private spheres. By concentrating on the social effect of "lascivious pictures," Tilghman authorizes the "eye of the law" not only to regulate both public and private morality, but also to collapse any distinction between the two. While this line of reasoning is moderated by Tilghman's subsequent assertion that Sharpless made his exhibition public by charging money for it, Justice Yeates's concurring opinion foregoes even this modification. The liberal distinction between the market economy and the conjugal home is as suspect as that between publicity and privacy. "No man," Yeates writes, "is permitted to corrupt the morals of the people; secret poison cannot be thus disseminated" (101, 104). In the face of such a threat, all rights to privacy vanish for the simple reason that the law recognizes no private sphere (economic *or* domestic) within which such rights could be safely exercised.

Rights to publicity suffer a similar fate in the judges' assent to the prosecution's third argument. The defense assumes that opinions concerning the obscenity of any given object are subjective, and therefore adjudicatable only through public debate. This assumption leads to the provocative insight that the terms with which the indictment refers to the painting ("lewd, wicked, scandalous, infamous and obscene") are "descriptive of desires and qualities belonging to animated beings, and are incorrectly applied to an inanimate object" (96). The indictment, in other words, fails to recognize that the obscene thing to which it refers is also a site of argumentation. To judge the painting properly, the court ought to exhibit it before the scrutiny of what the defense refers to as the "public eye." Tilghman and Yeates evince little interest in this republican defense of the public sphere as a space of moral and political debate free from state supervision. Confronted with the uncanny possibility that a future courtroom may resemble those "chambers" within which the "youth of the city might be corrupted," they are quick to protect what Tilghman refers to as the "chastity of our records"

(103). Yeates agrees with the defense that "some immodest paintings . . . may carry grosser features than others," but he dismisses the necessity of anyone either seeing Sharpless's painting or hearing a full description of it: "If the painting . . . tended to the manifest corruption of youth and other citizens, and was of public evil example to others, I think it sufficiently described" (104). The representational content of Sharpless's painting is irrelevant since its offensiveness lies in its hypothetical effect, not its content. By preempting public debate or disagreement over that content (or its effect), the judges legitimate the state's ability to regulate any publication offensive to its own, as yet unspecified standards of decency.

As a legal precedent, *Sharpless* provides an understanding of obscene-libel as a nonpolitical offense against public or, in later cases, community morality. In doing so, it equips the democratic state with three weapons in the struggle to define and police the relation between publicity and privacy: an expansive jurisdiction, a justification for violating privacy rights, an ability to avoid public debate. By substituting the "eye of the law" for the "public eye," the judges position the state as the moral guardian of what Yeates refers to as "our eyes and ears" (103). The interpellative effect of this "our" is potentially infinite. It refers to the "eyes and ears" of the judges, the population of the courtroom, the reader of the judicial record, and anyone identified with the state. Each of these overlapping audiences may have different senses, but they share a common sensibility. Like the category of the "American fair" in *The Coquette*, the concept of "public morality" in *Sharpless* weds individual sensation to a uniform (and nonheteronomous) sentimental code. The fact that Sharpless's painting never appears in court reveals the institutional power behind this act of interpellation. Because the painting is neither displayed nor fully described, the court's role in positing a common sensibility that it then defends remains unchallenged. Unlike the "public eye" whose unity emerges only in and through debate, the "eye of the law" asserts its coherence by eliminating the occasion of that debate. The public may wage a war on the category of obscenity, but the state defines which acts and objects are obscene. By locating Sharpless's painting offstage, the court positions it as the structuring absence in the case. In the "eye of the law," the painting serves as an obscene point of focus for a "public eye" whose moral vision necessarily coincides with that of the democratic state.

The Liberal Origins of Obscenity

The classical liberal response to an anti-obscenity decision like *Sharpless* tends to maintain and strengthen the structural antithesis between publicity and privacy. Jacobs's allusion to her "loophole of retreat" echoes this re-

sponse if one hears it as reconstructing that antithesis as an opposition between the state and the market on the one hand, and the bourgeois home on
the other. For those capable of accessing the privileges of domestic privacy,
such "retreats" provide spaces of moral freedom conceived in Isaiah Berlin's
terms as a negative freedom from political surveillance and economic control.[20] Because the term political here refers equally to state and civil forms
of power, this liberal response conflicts with the republican defense of the
public sphere as an arena of politically significant moral debate free from
state censorship. As in the defense's second argument, the promise of moral
freedom is preserved, but only within a depoliticized private sphere (Sharpless's "chamber," for example) rendered opaque to both the "public eye" and
the "eye of the law." As Jürgen Habermas argues, this strategic recoding of
(im)moral dissent as politically insignificant was (and is) reactionary: "The
right to the free expression of opinion was no longer called on to protect the
public's rational-critical debate against the reach of the police but to protect
the nonconformists from the grip of the public itself."[21] This exchange of the
positive liberty to participate in public debate for the negative liberty to
withdraw from that debate results in an ambivalent assessment of decisions
like Sharpless. Classical liberalism opposes the state's deployment of obscenity as a legal category to abridge privacy rights, while it simultaneously
redeploys obscenity as an ideological category to place (im)moral acts and
objects off the public stage. Though committed to protecting privacy and
publicity rights as legal entitlements guarded by the state, this liberalism
allows the category of obscenity to curtail public debate concerning the
(im)moral foundations of the public order.

Viewed from this perspective, the problem with Sharpless lies in its tendency to blur the opposition between public and private life, not in its reduction of the likelihood of meaningful moral and political debate in public.
While Habermas's republicanism counters this liberal reaction by holding to
an ideal of unrestricted public debate, recent social histories have tended to
reinscribe the liberal opposition between (public) politics and (private) morality. In her two contributions to an important collection of essays on the
"invention of pornography," for example, Lynn Hunt charts and uncritically
repeats liberalism's narrow definition of political (as opposed to moral) criticism by contrasting the "political pornography" of eighteenth-century writers like the Marquis de Sade to the "modern, apolitical genre of porn."[22]
Where the former uses sexual description as a means of attacking the church
and state, the latter isolates and focuses on sexuality as an end in itself. Other
contributors in the volume agree with this historical generalization. According to Randolph Trumbach, John Cleland's Memoirs of a Woman of Pleasure
inaugurates the "modern pornographic genre" because "its purpose does not
seem, in any marked way, to have been political."[23] As in contemporary
obscenity law, these generic arguments overlook the disciplinary tactics of a

regime intent on policing the boundaries that divide public from private life by legitimating the "moral" censorship of indecent publications, while also protecting all forms of "political" speech. As Cleland's own protagonist notes, this very distinction has both political effects and moral implications. "The greatest men," Fanny Hill writes in her prefatory remarks, "those of the first and most leading taste, will not scruple adorning their private closets with nudities, though, in compliance with vulgar prejudices, they may not think them decent decorations of the staircase or saloon."[24] Hunt elsewhere acknowledges that the post-revolutionary transition in the ideological justification of censorship militated against pornography which "continued to test social and moral taboos without targeting political figures," but she also insists on the generic argument that "politics occupies a tiny place" in those writings.[25]

For republicanism, the same acts and objects liberalism codes as obscene remain politically significant precisely for moral reasons. Those acts and objects remain significant in both a broad sense due to the structural challenge they pose to the existing boundary between publicity and privacy, and in a narrow sense due to the ideological challenge they pose to the moral judgments invoked by the state in order to police that boundary. Read from this perspective genre-based histories like those in *The Invention of Pornography* repeat liberalism's use of the category of the obscene to establish the political insignificance of what Hunt calls "social and moral taboos." The effects of this complicity reappear in Hunt's suggestive but cursory allusions to the contemporary origins of the pornographic and the sentimental novel. Both genres evolve out of the sensationalist psychology of the early eighteenth century, both concern the publication of bodily and intimate experience, and both draw on a republican model of the literary public sphere as an unrestricted space of moral and political debate. Yet, Hunt notes these parallels only to reaffirm the eventual separation between the two genres.[26] While this analysis accurately locates the construction and disavowal of the pornographic at the ideological core of nineteenth-century sentimentalism, it ignores the two genres' structural affinity. For republican pornographers like Sade, this oversight is critical. In an essay lauding Richardson and Fielding, Sade highlights the genres' shared commitment to a principle of public disclosure: "The profound study of man's heart—Nature's veritable labyrinth—alone must inspire the novelist. . . . Therefore we must know them all, we must employ every passion and vice, if we wish to labor in this field."[27] By leaving little or nothing offstage, Sade pursues the republican logic of sentimental publication to a conclusion liberalism labels pornographic and polices as obscene.

The legal and historical reception of writers like Sade attests to the power of this post-revolutionary transformation of the term "political obscenity" into an oxymoron. From Walt Whitman's *Leaves of Grass* to Bill T. Jones's

"Last Supper at Uncle Tom's Cabin/The Promised Land," the categories of obscenity and pornography work to erase the political significance of radical reimaginings of the relation between sensation and citizenship, between bodies and publication.[28] Writing a half century after Sade, Jacobs is fully aware that her abolitionist sentiments are similarly vulnerable to the political invisibility that accompanies the charge of obscenity. When she threatens to publish the "secret memoirs" of Congress, Jacobs intentionally draws on the generic conventions of pre-revolutionary political pornography (144). Just as eighteenth-century writers like Thomas Paine and Mary Wollstonecraft exploited descriptions of the British court's moral corruption, Jacobs threatens to tarnish the moral reputation of the modern nation-state by revealing the private vices of public representatives such as her ex-lover Congressman Sands. When she publishes the private conversations that she overhears in her garret retreat, Jacobs updates those conventions to include civil relations. "Southerners," she writes, "have the habit of stopping and talking in the streets, and I heard many conversations not intended to meet my ears" (117). While these Southerners assume the privileges of privacy even in public, Jacobs responds by reporting within an abolitionist public sphere what she hears from her "loophole of retreat." From the perspective of Southern slaveholding culture, Jacobs's disclosures are obscene in a structural sense since they cross the official boundary between publicity and privacy upon which the moral code (and political institutions) of that culture depends.[29]

Obscene Sentiments

Were *Incidents* obscene only in this structural sense, its critique would be limited to the moral code and political institutions of Southern chattel slavery. But *Incidents* is also obscene in an ideological sense more familiar and threatening to its Northern audience. Just as the painting in *Sharpless* remains offstage due to the hypothetical effect of its alleged sexual content, explicit descriptions of sexual relations form the structuring absence of *Incidents*. I have already suggested that Jacobs's reticence in describing her sexual experience can be read either as evidence of her vexed engagement with her Northern audience or as a means of accessing the privileges of privacy theoretically enjoyed by that audience. In relation to both Flint and the abolitionist public sphere, Jacobs's struggle to control the circulation of her letters parallels her struggle to control her sexual relations. But neither of these readings accounts for the reappearance of the conventions of modern anti-obscenity discourse elsewhere in *Incidents*. In a chapter that investigates the contaminating effects of slavery on Northern society, for example, Jacobs tells the story of Luke, a slave owned by a "degraded wreck of manhood" who stripped and whipped his servant, forcing him to submit to the "strangest freaks of despotism." Despite her resolution a paragraph earlier that "knowledge should be increased," Jacobs concludes with a vivid nondescription of Luke's fate. "Some of these freaks," she writes, "were of a nature too filthy to be repeated. When I fled from the house of bondage, I left poor Luke still chained to the bedside of this cruel and disgusting wretch" (192). Luke's experience of sexual enslavement mirrors Jacobs's own, as does the rhetorical strategy Jacobs employs when she publicizes that experience. Echoing the prurient circumlocutions of anti-obscenity tracts and legal prosecutions (as well as anti-sodomy discourse), Jacobs grants her audience what Eve Sedgwick refers to as the "privilege of unknowing."[30] *Incidents* provides its readers with sexual knowledge, even as it assures them that their eyes and ears remain chaste.[31]

Jacobs may fear that a full description of Luke's experience would alienate her audience, or she may intend her conspicuous silence to spare him any unwanted publicity. But the effect of her circumlocution is to position sexuality as a field of knowledge both central to the liberal public sphere and invisible within it. Such knowledge is central because sexuality names the type (or types) of bodily and intimate relations that provide the content of liberal privacy; it is invisible because the stability of the boundary between the publicizable and the private requires that those relations remain off the public stage. Sexuality consequently becomes, in Michel Foucault's terms, not an "intractable element within power relations," but a "point of support" or "linchpin" in the liberal attempt to transform the relation between publicity and privacy into an opposition that pits one against the other.[32] Foucault's analysis is, in this sense, an important corrective to liberal theorists of obscenity who simply assume that sexuality inevitably marks the boundary between public and private. In *The New Politics of Pornography*, for example, Donald Downs writes that "the search for boundaries may incline individuals to grasp at absolutes and certitude in the face of complexity and uncertainty. Sexual issues are prime candidates for this talismanic quest because sex is central to personality, mysteriously powerful, and inherently complex."[33] Downs draws up short of an older and more extreme liberal argument that, as Harry Clor puts it, "a people devoted exclusively to the satisfaction of sensual appetites is not, strictly speaking, a citizen body at all. It is a collection of private individuals, each concerned with private gratification."[34] Despite their differences, both writers locate sexuality at the heart of liberal subjectivity.[35] Like the generic category "sex life," sexuality names something all citizens share in common as long as no one begins to publicize the uncommon practices that enable their "private gratification[s]."

Since the publication of specific sexual practices is the source of both Jacobs's authenticity as a testifying slave and her inauthenticity as a sentimental heroine, *Incidents* maintains a contradictory assessment of this liberal deployment of sexuality. As a sentimental heroine (a "delicate subject"), Jacobs shares with her audience a normative equation of sexuality with privacy as the basis of liberal subjectivity. As a testifying slave (an "indelicate subject"), her experience as Flint's sexual property betrays that equation. The significance of this betrayal emerges in Jacobs's second encounter with Luke. When the two meet again in the North, Luke tells her that he escaped after stealing his master's money by placing it in the pockets of an old pair of pants, and then asking for the pants. "You see," he concludes, "I didn't *steal* it; dey *gub* it to me." Luke's faulty reasoning mirrors his imperfect grammar by evincing for both Jacobs and her audience the corruption of the "moral sense" occasioned by the economics of slavery.[36] Like the Fugitive Slave Law, which provides the title for the chapter, Luke's presence in the North reveals that such corruption may cross the Mason-Dixon line. But while Luke purifies the North by continuing his flight into Canada, Jacobs remains south of the border. Her subsequent "confession" that she "agrees with poor, ignorant, much-abused Luke, in thinking he had a *right* to the money" thus positions her alongside him as both a victim *and* a potential contaminant. Jacobs's Northern education may have left her "somewhat enlightened," at least to a point where she agrees with her audience in condemning Luke's disrespect for private property (193). The problem with slavery, she assures them earlier, is that "a slave, *being* property, can *hold* no property" (6). Yet Jacobs's "confession" also reveals that she differs from her audience in remaining tainted by her experience of enslavement. The sexual nature of that enslavement only intensifies this problem since it associates Jacobs with the conventional figure of the libidinous and seductive mulatta slave. Just as Luke's experiences of sodomy bar him from access to "true manhood," Jacobs's enslavement threatens to undercut the claims to "true womanhood" that mediate her relation to her Northern audience.[37]

One corrective to this widening gap between Jacobs and her audience appears within *Incidents* when Flint proposes to make her into a "lady" by giving her a "home of her own" (53). Quick to recognize the trap laid beneath Flint's adherence to sentimental conventions, Jacobs rejects his offer of sexual privacy with a republican demand for more publicity. Like the "remote plantations" where the "secrets of slavery are concealed like those of the Inquisition," Flint's home promises Jacobs privacy only as a means of shielding his sexual violence from any public scrutiny (35). Here and elsewhere in *Incidents*, publication provides a defense against private abuses of power, both sexual and economic.[38] A second corrective appears in Child's introduction. After acknowledging potential objections to *Incidents*'s indecent subject matter, Child justifies her publication of it: "I do this for the sake of my sisters in bondage who are suffering wrongs so foul, that our ears are too delicate to listen to them" (4). In her attempt to bridge the gap between her "sisters" like Jacobs and the delicate "ears" of Jacobs's audience, Child applies the publicist conventions of antebellum moral reform movements to the sentimental novel. She publishes the narrative in order to persuade "conscientious and reflecting women at the North to a sense of their duty in the exersion of moral influence on the question of Slavery" (4). By justifying *Incidents*'s obscenity through its hypothetical effect on public morality, Child employs and inverts the logic of anti-obscenity verdicts like *Sharpless*. And while this justification may be persuasive to an abolitionist audience accustomed to the conventions of the slave narrative, it is also reversible since a less sympathetic (or more "delicate") audience might hypothesize that *Incidents*'s descriptions of (sexual) immorality will effect a subversion of public morality. Alert to this threat, Jacobs meets Child's offer of sexual publication with liberal tactics that ensure her privacy.

These two antithetical responses to Flint and Child indicate Jacobs's implication within sentimentalism's ambivalent assessment of the norms of decency that structure the liberal public sphere. And it is no coincidence that this ambivalence reaches a climax in *Incidents*'s most sexually explicit and rhetorically complicated chapter, "A Perilous Passage in the Slave Girl's Life." In that chapter, Jacobs explains that she chose with "deliberate calculation" to frustrate Flint's advances by becoming Sands's mistress (54). Flint responds to news of the pregnancy that effectively publicizes that relationship by acting exactly as Jacobs had planned. The fact of Jacobs's sexual relation with another man deprives Flint of access to her *and* to her grandmother's home—at least for the moment. "He stood," she writes, "and looked at me with dumb amazement, and left the house without a word" (56). Aware that this strategic use and publication of her sexual activities may offend her audience's sense of decency, Jacobs begins by aligning herself with them: "It pains me to tell you of it; but I have promised to tell you the truth, and I will do it honestly, let it cost me what it may" (53–54). She then counters that reaction with a structural analysis of the economic and legal privilege assumed by the liberal equation of sexuality with privacy. "O virtuous reader!" Jacobs admonishes, "You never knew what it is like to be a slave; to be entirely unprotected by law or custom; to have the laws reduce you to the condition of a chattel, entirely subject to the will of another" (55). Jacobs overestimates the security of Northern homes, but her point is to link moral judgments to the unequal social and political structures that inform them. "The slave woman," she concludes, "ought not to be judged by the same standards as others" (56).[39]

What *Incidents* gives its audience with one hand, it takes away with the other. Like the justices in *Sharpless*, Jacobs asserts a common moral sense. But she also insists that any criticism of her sexual relations come from one who shares her uncommon sensibility. "I know I did wrong," she writes, "No one can feel it more sensibly than I do" (55). This claim positions her as a sentimental heroine by linking moral judgment to bodily sensation, while it also modifies sentimental conventions by allowing the idiosyncratic nature of those sensations to justify that heroine's sexual calculations. Jacobs's foregrounding of her difference from her audience thus works to her advantage since it enables her to expand the boundaries of the liberal public sphere by blurring the generic distinction between the sentimental and the obscene. But it also contains liabilities. One troubling response to *Incidents* is represented by the wife of Jacobs's early patron, Mr. Durham. When her husband repeats Jacobs's history to her, Mrs. Durham reacts with what Jacobs refers to as the "delicate silence of womanly sympathy" (162). This response both fulfills Jacobs's desire for sexual privacy, and constructs an unspoken link between herself and Mrs. Durham as "women." But it also relocates any discussion of Jacobs's sexual enslavement beyond the liberal norms of decency that constitute the objective parameters of public debate. A second, more damning response is represented by Jacobs's grandmother who reacts to the news of her pregnancy by uttering the greatest of all sentimental curses ("You are a disgrace to your dead mother"), and then banishing Jacobs from her home (56–57). Deprived of both access to the public sphere by her alliance with Mrs. Durham and domestic security by her confession to her grandmother, Jacobs turns to an anonymous friend of her mother, who advises her to reapproach her grandmother. Like Mrs. Durham, Jacobs's grandmother reacts this time by "listen[ing] in silence" and, unlike Mrs. Durham, responding with overt compassion: "She laid her old hand gently on my head, and murmured, 'Poor child! Poor child!'" (57).

The two opposed responses of Jacobs's grandmother highlight the dilemma Jacobs shares with other radical sentimental writers of the antebellum period. Her sexual testimony enables her to avoid the home Flint offers as a "retreat" from slavery, while it also threatens to deprive her of the home that later provides a "loophole" in her battle against slavery. By positing her grandmother's second reaction as a model for the reader, *Incidents* attempts to avoid the literal and metaphorical homelessness produced by this double bind. Jacobs assumes that the social privilege enjoyed by her readers will lead them to a liberal understanding of sexuality as marking a stable opposition between publicity and privacy. And she recognizes that the conventions of the sentimental novel contribute to that understanding by distinguishing between publicizable and obscene sentiments, between sentimentality and sexuality. In response, Jacobs both critiques and redeploys this understanding of the relations among sexuality, publication, and privacy. Her critique suggests that anti-obscenity discourse works to limit public debate concerning structural inequalities in individuals' access to privacy. Like other "immoral reformers," she challenges her reader to react to *Incidents* as her grandmother does when she welcomes Jacobs into her home as both a sentimental heroine *and* a testifying slave. Her redeployment suggests that anti-obscenity discourse can also work to provide a textual simulacrum of the

architectural privacy denied to slaves (and servants) like herself.[40] By mim-
ing the silences that structure anti-obscenity discourse, Jacobs stages a private life that serves as an unspoken (and unspeakable) point of identification
between herself and readers like Mrs. Durham. As indicated by the conspic-
uousness of those silences, it is not what Jacobs says that enables her to
construct that point of identification. Rather, it is the precision with which
she isolates and names sexuality as the unspoken (and unspeakable) content
of her private life that secures the "womanly sympathy" of her audience.

Sexual Subjects

At various points a forger, a cross-dressed sailor in blackface, and a married
woman returning to her husband, Jacobs is nothing if not a master of dis-
guise (137, 112–13, 156). It would be a mistake, however, to read her simply
as a trickster figure uncommitted to any of the masks she wears. As Karen
Halttunen has argued, a dialectic between strategic publication and personal authenticity is central to nineteenth-century sentimental culture.[41]
And Jacobs's implication within that culture is indicated by her simultaneous critique and deployment of anti-obscenity discourse. Committed in
principle to the uncensored publication of bodily and intimate sensations as
the means of linking publicity and privacy, sentimentalism betrays that commitment in practice when it secures the opposition between sentimentality
and sexuality central to the liberal transformation of the public sphere. By
locating sexuality as the (private) *thing* excluded from any (public) *argument*,
sentimentalism works in conjunction with legal arguments that resolve the
paradox of obscenity at the heart of the liberal separation of public and private space. And it worked. Faced with emergent cultures committed to sexual education and critique, thirty states had enacted an anti-obscenity statute by 1900. All fifty had enacted one by 1970.[42] As a cultural analogue to
political liberalism, sentimentalism supports such statutes by positing an
imaginary point of identification for a public whose anarchic sensibilities
otherwise threaten to diverge. Where legal prosecutions like *Sharpless* deploy the category of the obscene to shift the locus of moral and political
authority from the public sphere to the state, sentimental narratives like
Incidents redeploy the category to shift that locus from the state to the domestic sphere. And while both react against the republican principle of publication, only the latter figures sexual silence and domestic privacy as privileged forms of citizenship.

This ideological alliance between liberalism and sentimentalism locates
obscenity as the liberal discourse of sexuality not in a repressive, but in a
productive sense. Obscenity produces a privileged site of liberal subject
formation by naming sexuality as the content of private life. But the same

alliance also masks a structural contradiction within the liberal equation of sexuality with privacy. As Foucault observes and Jacobs demonstrates, the era of modern anti-obscenity discourse is characterized not by sexual silence, but by an incitement to sexual speech. This incitement is central to both liberalism and sentimentalism because the category of the obscene can serve as a means of regulating the structural antithesis between public and private only if the ideological content of that category remains malleable. Campaigns to exclude sexuality from the public sphere never end because their point is not to stabilize the boundary between public and private, but to mobilize the discourse of sexuality (and the sexualized body that discourse constructs) in order to gain control over it. Sexuality, in other words, becomes useful either to the state (*Sharpless*) or to associations within civil society (*Incidents*) only if it refers to a (private) *thing* that is also a (public) *argument*, only if it names both a ground and a site of public debate. As a *thing*, sexuality thus transforms the distinction between publicizable and obscene sentiments into an opposition which sexuality, as an *argument*, destabilizes. Sentimentalism's structural investment in the publication of bodily and intimate relations ensures the continuation of that argument, even as it threatens to collapse the ideological distinction between sentimentality and sexuality upon which that argument depends. Sentimentalism may investigate sexual silences and, as in *Incidents*, may open critical debate concerning privatized forms of violence rendered invisible within the liberal public sphere. But it also assures its audience that, in the end, the ideological foundations and objective parameters of that debate will remain structurally obscene.

7

Afterword: Closeted Sentiments

I mind how we lay in June, such a transparent summer
  morning;
You settled your head athwart my hips and gently
  turned over upon me,
And parted the shirt from my bosom-bone, and
  plunged your tongue to my barestript heart,
And reached till you felt my beard, and reached till you
  held my feet.
  (*Walt Whitman,* Song of Myself, *1855*)[1]

Certain regions of the body, such as the mucous
membrane of the mouth and anus, which are constantly
appearing in these practices, seem, as it were, to be
claiming that they should themselves be regarded and
treated as genitals.
  (*Sigmund Freud,* Three Essays on the Theory of Sexuality, *1905*)[2]

I BEGIN this brief afterword with two epigraphs that summarize this study's major themes, while also gesturing beyond them. In the first, Whitman tweaks his antebellum readership by figuring the transcendental union of body and soul—of me and myself, of author and audience—as a specifically sexual act. By substituting the poet's "barestript heart" for his aroused genitalia, this joke cuts in two directions. On the one hand, it lampoons the circumlocutions of the mid-nineteenth-century sentimental code since the reader clearly knows that the poet's "heart" is, in truth, his "sex." On the other hand, it also questions the basis of that knowledge by making the poet's sensations available to the reader only through the same code. How, Whitman seems to ask, have we come to localize the truth of the body in either the heart or the genitals? How have we come to believe that either is the organ that joins the body and the body politic? In the second epigraph, Freud writes more seriously of a similar problem. Having earlier transformed the entire surface of the body into a field of "polymorphous perverse" pleasure, he worries that the very category of the genitals may lose its local significance. Demanding, but undeserving organs like the "mouth" and "anus" call for scientific recognition. Like other early sexologists, Freud produces a response that is both anxious and final. In hysteria, he notes, "repression affects most of all the actual genital zones and these transmit their susceptibility to stimulation to other erotogenic zones (normally neglected in adult life), which then behave exactly like genitals."[3] Freud's parenthesis (his simultaneous bracketing and assertion of the normal) mark both his uncertainty and his resolution. He imagines a body whose sensations are (normally) "polymorphous," just as surely as they are codified as (sexually) "perverse." The category of "adult life" marks the unrealizable dissolution of this psychoanalytic double bind. Maturity, Freud insists, requires a disavowal of "other erotogenic zones." This disavowal ensures that the "actual genitals" will take their rightful position as the seat of Freud's early-twentieth-century bodily norm.

These two epigraphs conclude this study because they locate the emerging discourse of sexuality within the contours of the sentimentalizing process that began in the early eighteenth century to divide and organize both the body and the body politic. As I have argued in relation to Jacobs, the contradictions within this process are highlighted by the intensification in the mid-nineteenth century of a distinction between sexual and nonsexual sensations. The utopian promise of sentimentalism relies upon its structural commitment to the publication of all bodily sensations—sexual and nonsexual—as a non-heteronomous means of linking the body and body politic. Its ideological realization betrays that commitment by privatizing those (sexual) sensations that threaten to disrupt the equivilence between "code" and "feeling" upon which sentimentalism depends. The significance of this contradiction between the structure and the ideology of sentimentalism— between what I have referred to as a republican and a liberal body politics— emerges at the intersection of cultural and political criticism. Because this contradiction cannot be resolved within the generic conventions of sentimentalism, writers committed to stabilizing the corporeal boundaries of public life are forced to encode the genre itself as obscene. And it is no coincidence that two of the most powerful of those writers conclude their histories of (anti-)sentmentalism by turning to Herman Melville's *Billy Budd*. Hannah Arendt and Ann Douglas agree that sentimentalism finds its proper telos in a private space that collapses sentimentality with the love that, at the turn of the century, dared not speak its name—the space of the closet in which Billy shares a "passionate" interview with Captain Vere.[4] For Arendt, Vere's closeting of his sentiments for Billy is laudable because it respects (and enforces) the crucial opposition between "compassion" and "politics": "Because compassion abolishes the distance, the worldly space between men where political matters . . . are located, it remains, politically speaking, irrelevant and without consequence."[5] Douglas agrees. "In *Billy Budd*," she assures her reader, "genuine communication does occur although—and this is the significance—only off-stage."[6]

The epigraphs from Whitman and Freud also gesture beyond the scope of this study because they mark the transition from sentimentality to sexuality—from the "heart" to the "genitals"—that shapes body politics in the twentieth century. One reason that sentimentalism looks so silly to many modern readers is that it speaks against Freud's axiom that "sexuality" names and delimits the "sensations" that link the body to the body politic. Like "sentiment," "sexuality" performs this function in both repressive and liberationist polemics, but only after it has been isolated from other forms of social, political, and corporeal practice.[7] The ruse that lies behind this isolation of "sex" as the truth of the body is most familiar from Foucault's *History of Sexuality* and the interviews that followed its publication in 1976. In perhaps the best known of those interviews, Foucault repeats his earlier criticism of sexual taxonomies and identity categories, then concludes with a rallying cry. "I am," he announces, "for the decentralization, the regionalization of all pleasures."[8] What is striking about this hyperbolic assertion is its rhetorical commitment to the language of revolutionary republicanism. As indicated by the interview's title ("Down with the Dictatorship of Sex"), Foucault's metaphor constructs a now familiar analogy between the body and the body politic. Just as the "state" nationalizes its citizens' economic and intimate relations, "sex" centralizes the body's corporeal relations. As such, the "deployment of sexuality" Foucault maps repeats the contradictions that I have located at the heart of the culture of sentiment. "Sex" replaces "sentiment" as the name for the utopian possibility of bodily liberation from state power at the same time as "sex" begins to act as the conduit through which the state gains access to those bodies. Critical of both the repressive and the liberatory sides of this dialectic, Foucault's slogan aligns him with neither Freud nor Whitman. It calls for the politicization of the study of "sexuality," while also questioning the role that "sex" plays in organizing the pleasures and the politics of the body.

So, to return to the question that Arendt and Douglas place at the center of *Billy Budd*, what is the political significance of the sentimental body? Both critics respond by endorsing Vere's anti-sentimental moral: the "heart," the "conscience," and the "feminine in man" are all "ruled out" of public life.[9] What this endorsement overlooks is the strategic function of the categories upon which it depends. Like Jacobs's garret retreat, Vere's closet is a space of political power operating under the guise of privacy. Positioned in opposition to the galley where Claggart publicly reveals his (homo)sexual desire for Billy, *and* the cabin where Vere persuades his drumhead court to judge Billy without regard to their "warm hearts," the closet allows Vere to stage a private affect that is both powerful and sentimental—one that quells the paired threats of homosexuality and mutiny aboard the *Bellipotent*.[10] In keeping with this don't-ask-don't-tell policy, Vere's disciplinary tactics consistently forbid public displays of affect—sentimental or sexual—either in official spaces controlled by the state (the courtroom) or unofficial spaces outside of state control (the galley). And even the exception to this generalization proves Vere's rule. At the moment of Billy's hanging, his unexpected utterance ("God Bless Captain Vere") invokes a "sympathetic echo" from the "ship's populace."[11] This substitution of a sentimental loyalty oath for the ejaculation of semen that normally coincides with a death by hanging is, in the words of the ship's surgeon, "phenomenal."[12] Yet Billy's transcendence of the (sexual) demands of his body combines with the crew's involuntary repetition of his oath to secure the rule of law that anchors Vere's authority. Standing as "rigid as a musket in the ship-armorer's rack," Vere watches as the crew's "echo" waxes into a "clamor" that is met by a "strategic command": "Shrill as the shriek of the sea hawk, the silver whistles of the boatswain and his mates pierced the ominous low sound, dissipating it."[13] Evoked *and* contained within the architecture of martial law, the sensations of the crew's bodies shore up the very discipline that they momentarily threaten to disrupt.

Both Arendt and Douglas garner support for their arguments by aligning Vere with the author of *Billy Budd*. Yet Melville's own criticism of this brand of anti-sentimental liberalism becomes explicit at (at least) two points. The most obvious appears at the moment of Billy's impressment. In his first act of spontaneous insubordination, Billy stands upright in the boat transferring him to the *Bellipotent* and returns his former shipmates' salutes by shouting a politically loaded farewell: "And good-bye to you too, old *Rights-of-Man*."[14] Billy's parting shot may be free from what the narrator refers to as "satire" or "double meaning" (he seems loyal to virtually any legislated authority), but Melville's clearly is not.[15] As Eve Sedgwick points out, it would be inaccurate (and quixotic) to construct a simple opposition between military and civil forms of discipline, between the *Bellipotent* and the *Rights-of-Man*.[16] But a conflation of the two is equally problematic: it not only mutes Melville's objection to Vere's reliance on military discipline as the ground of his liberalism, but also forecloses any attempt to investigate the connections among republicanism, liberalism, and sentiment at the turn of the century. The second criticism reopens this investigation. "In the time before steamships," Melville writes at the start of *Billy Budd*, "or then more frequently than now, a stroller along the docks of any considerable seaport would occasionally have his attention arrested by a group of bronzed mariners, man-of-war's men or merchant sailors in holiday attire, ashore on liberty."[17] This initial focus on the spectacle of bodies moving freely through public space is prophetic, though not in the ways Arendt and Douglas suggest. Set amid the battles of the French and American Revolutions, the story of Billy's impressment from the *Rights-of-Man* to the *Bellipotent* provides an allegory of liberalism's historical *and* contemporary disciplining of the erotics of republican liberty. Melville's merging of past and present in his opening line indicates his belief that these battles over the liberatory promise of republicanism will continue into the future, while his assumption that the reader's gaze will be "arrested" by the mariners' "bronzed" bodies points to (homo)sexuality as one of the (obscene) sites where, at the turn of the century, those battles would be waged.

Notes

Chapter 1
Body Politics

1. J. G. Ballard, "Project for a Glossary of the Twentieth Century," in *Incorporations*, ed. Jonathan Crary and Sanford Kwinter (New York: Urzone, 1992), 269.

2. Mary Wollstonecraft, *An Historical and Moral View of the Origin and Progress of the French Revolution and the Effect It Has Produced in Europe*, in *A Wollstonecraft Anthology*, ed. Janet M. Todd (Bloomington, Ind.: Indiana University Press, 1977), 141.

3. Ibid., 140–41.

4. Ibid., 135.

5. Ibid., 126.

6. Ibid., 133.

7. Ibid., 138.

8. Ibid. A similar differentiation and displacement of sympathy occurs throughout Wollstonecraft's writings. In *Maria; or The Wrongs of Woman*, for example, the protagonist (Maria) is imprisoned unjustly in an asylum by a tyrannical husband. In that prison, she listens and begins to identify with the sane and melodious laments of a woman in the next cell, only to be repelled upon subsequently hearing her insane "fits of laughter" and "unconnected exclamations." Quickly, however, Wollstonecraft translates Maria's disgust at the madwoman into a meditation on the "wrongs of woman" as a class: "'Woman, fragile flower! why were you suffered to adorn a world exposed to the inroad of such stormy elements?' thought Maria, while the poor maniac's strain was still breathing on her ear, and sinking into her very soul." Repulsed by her unconscious sympathy with the cries of a madwoman, Maria nevertheless salvages her initial response by shifting the site of her identification to the category "woman": "woman" becomes the abstraction that structures the relation between individuals like Maria and the "wrongs" that their experiences exemplify. "Woman," in this sense, is a political category with which neither Maria nor the madwoman are identical. Mary Wollstonecraft, *Maria; or The Wrongs of Woman* (New York: New American Library, 1983), 144. For a reading of Wollstonecraft along these lines, see Claudia Johnson, *Equivocal Beings: Politics, Gender, and Sentimentality in the 1790s* (Chicago: University of Chicago Press, 1995).

9. Mary Wollstonecraft, *An Historical and Moral View* (London: J. Johnson, 1795), 401.

10. Quoted in Philip S. Foner, "The Democratic-Republican Societies: An Introduction," *The Democratic-Republican Societies, 1790–1800: A Documentary Sourcebook of Constitutions, Declarations, Addresses, Resolutions, and Toasts* (Westport, Conn.: Greenwood Press, 1976), 17–18.

11. Alexis de Tocqueville, *Democracy in America*, trans. George Lawrence (New York: Doubleday, 1969), 72.

12. Hannah Arendt, *On Revolution* (New York: Viking Penguin, 1963), 94–95.

13. Ibid., 76.

14. Karl Marx, "On the Jewish Question," *The Marx-Engels Reader*, ed. Robert Tucker (New York: W. W. Norton, 1978), 31. Engels is quoted in Michael Denning's "Marxism and American Studies," *American Quarterly* 38 (1986); 356.

15. Karl Marx, *The Eighteenth Brumaire of Louis Napoleon* (New York: International Publishers, 1963), 75.

16. Karl Marx, "Theses on Feuerbach," *The Marx-Engels Reader*, 143.

17. Marx, "On the Jewish Question," 146.

18. Claude Lefort, "The Question of Democracy," in *Democracy and Political Theory*, trans. David Macey (Minneapolis: University of Minnesota Press, 1988), 16, 17–18.

19. Ibid.

20. Without this provision, Lefort's analysis would fall prey to the totalizing and teleological conception of immanence which, as Phillipe Lacoue-Labarthe and Jean-Luc Nancy convincingly argue, promises in totalitarian fashion to realize the political through the social (or visa versa): "In immanentism it is the community itself, the people or the nation, that is the work (*oeuvre*) following the conception acknowledged by Romanticism of the work as subject and the subject as work: the 'living artwork' indeed, though this in no way prevents it from working lethally." Phillipe Lacoue-Labarthe, *Heidegger, Art and Politics*, trans. Chris Turner (Cambridge: Basil Blackwell, 1990), 71. Jacques Derrida makes a similar argument in relation to Marx's "exorcism" of the "specter" of mediation in *Specters of Marx: The State of Debt, the Work of Mourning, & the New International*, trans. Peggy Kamuf (New York: Routledge, 1994).

21. Claude Lefort, "Reversibility: Political Freedom and the Freedom of the Individual," in *Democracy and Political Theory*, 178.

22. Claude Lefort, "Hannah Arendt and the Political," in *Democracy and Political Theory*, 53.

23. Ibid., 43.

24. This distinction is marked more explicitly in the original French, as Nancy Fraser points out. *Le politique* refers to the narrow sense of the term "politics" as an isolated (and protected) space of public opinion formation; *la politique* refers to the broad sense of the term as coextensive with virtually any action or judgment—"public" or "private." Nancy Fraser, *Unruly Practices: Power, Discourse and Gender in Contemporary Social Theory* (Minneapolis: University of Minnesota Press, 1989), 69–92.

25. Ernesto Laclau and Chantal Mouffe, *Hegemony and Socialist Strategy: Towards a Radical Democratic Politics*, trans. Paul Cammack and Winston Moore (London: Verso, 1985), 156.

26. Chantal Mouffe, "Hegemony and New Political Subjects: Toward a New Concept of Democracy," in *Marxism and the Interpretation of Culture*, trans. Stanley Gray (Chicago: University of Illinois Press, 1988), 89. This emphasis on the political nature of the "new democratic movements" also seems to me to belie the central argument of Dick Howard's sustained critique of Laclau and Mouffe in *Defining the Political*: "Just as Gramsci's theory of hegemony remained caught in the implications of his economism, Laclau and Mouffe's contemporary reconstruction of that theory for explicitly modern societies is the victim of an unexamined premise: the priority

of 'the social.' They know that they need an explicitly *political* theory 'as the space for the game which eludes the concept.' Yet their hegemonic politics remains caught in the social." From Laclau and Mouffe's perspective, it is precisely Howard's critique that remains "caught up" in an ontologically stable division of the political from the social. Dick Howard, *Defining the Political* (Minneapolis: University of Minnesota Press, 1989), 96.

27. In the case of feminism, for example, this critique bypasses the antinomies developed in the debate over essentialism and anti-essentialism—political action based on a pre-political identity versus political indecision due to the lack of such an identity—by triangulating the otherwise oppositional relation between the corporeal and political referents of that debate, between sex and gender. At the same time, it also bypasses the current difficulties of a feminism that calls for attention to an endless catalogue of "differences" other than gender (race, class, ethnicity, sexual orientation, etc.), neither by ignoring those differences nor by seeking a closure to that catalog, but by articulating them through an anti-essentialist democratic politics. In *Gender Trouble*, Judith Butler suggests such a politics when she argues that gender "ought not to be constructed as a stable identity or locus of agency from which various acts follow." Butler concludes by calling for a politics "no longer understood as a set of practices derived from the alleged interests that belong to a set of ready-made subjects." While this argument may lack specificity, it remains significant in its opening of feminism onto questions concerning political subjectivity. See Judith Butler, *Gender Trouble: Feminism and the Subversion of Identity* (New York: Routledge, 1990), 140, 149. For a critique of essentialism that links democratic political philosophy and anti-essentialist feminism, see Mary Dietz, "Context Is All: Feminism and Theories of Citizenship," *Daedalus* 116, no. 4 (Fall 1987): 1–24. For two essay collections that sample these critical debates, see Judith Butler and Joan W. Scott, eds., *Feminists Theorize the Political* (New York: Routledge, 1992), and Selya Benhabib, ed., *Democracy and Difference: Contesting the Boundaries of the Political* (Princeton, N.J.: Princeton University Press, 1996).

28. Jürgen Habermas, "The New Obscurity: The Crisis of the Welfare State and the Exhaustion of Utopian Energies," in *The New Conservativism: Cultural Criticism and the Historians' Debate*, trans. Shierry Weber Nicholsen (Cambridge: MIT Press, 1989), 54.

29. Ibid., 59.

30. Ibid., 63.

31. Andrew Arato and Jean Cohen, "Civil Society and Social Theory," *Thesis 11* 21 (1988): 60, 54. For the extended version of Arato and Cohen's argument, see *Civil Society and Political Theory* (Cambridge: MIT Press, 1992).

32. Gordon Wood, *The Creation of the American Republic, 1776–1787* (New York: W. W. Norton, 1969), 47–48. Bernard Bailyn, *The Ideological Origins of the American Revolution* (Cambridge: Harvard University Press, 1967).

33. Wood, *The Creation of the American Republic*, 58, 65–70, 91–124.

34. Ibid., 418–19.

35. "Our pursuit," Pocock writes, "of the Machiavellian consequences of the republican principle of virtue is active and has led us through realms of consciousness in which deference was not passive and the republic was not a hierarchy." See J. G. A. Pocock, *The Machiavellian Moment: Florentine Political Thought and the*

Atlantic Republican Tradition (Princeton, N.J.: Princeton University Press, 1975), 524. One might also invoke Tocqueville in this context. Though he tends throughout *Democracy in America* to view freedom substantively as something jeopardized by demands for democratic equality, Tocqueville also suggests that "voluntary associations" may act to preserve more egalitarian forms of freedom: "I am firmly convinced that one cannot found an aristocracy anew in this world, but I think that associations of plain citizens can compose very rich, influential, and powerful bodies, in other words, aristocratic bodies. . . . An association, be it political, industrial, commercial, or even literary cannot be twisted to any man's will or quietly trodden down, and by defending its private interests against the encroachments of power, it saves the common liberties." Tocqueville, *Democracy in America*, 697. Notable here in addition to Tocqueville's defense of associations are his distinction between power and common liberties and his articulation of private interests and those liberties, both of which fit more closely with a republican than a liberal political theory. What Tocqueville misses is the possibility emphasized by Lefort, and Laclau and Mouffe of associations not only "saving," but also constructing common liberties. See Claude Lefort, "From Equality to Freedom: Fragments of an Interpretation of *Democracy in America*," in *Democracy and Political Theory*, 183–209, and Laclau and Mouffe, *Hegemony and Socialist Strategy*, 149–94. For an incisive defense of the principle of political virtue, see Bonnie Honig, *Political Theory and the Displacement of Politics* (Ithaca, N.Y.: Cornell University Press, 1993).

36. J. G. A. Pocock, "The American Founding in Early Modern Perspective," in *Conceptual Change and the Constitution*, eds. Terence Ball and J. G. A. Pocock (Lawrence, Kans.: University of Kansas Press, 1988), 65.

37. Ibid., 567–92. Thomas Paine, "Agrarian Justice," in *The Thomas Paine Reader*, eds. Michael Foot and Isaac Kramnick (New York: Viking Penguin, 1987), 471–89. Harriet Jacobs, *Incidents in the Life of a Slave Girl*, ed. Jean Fagan Yellin (Cambridge: Harvard University Press, 1987). For analyses of laboring men's and women's republicanism respectively, see Sean Wilentz, *Chants Democratic: New York City & the Rise of the American Working Class, 1788–1850* (Oxford: Oxford University Press, 1984), and Christine Stansell, *City of Women: Sex and Class in New York, 1789–1860* (Urbana, Ill.: University of Illinois Press, 1987). The Seneca Falls Declaration is included in *The Feminist Papers: From Adams to de Beauvoir*, ed. Alice S. Rossi (Boston: Northeastern University Press, 1988), 413–21.

38. Jay Fliegelman, *Declaring Independence: Jefferson, Natural Language, and the Culture of Performance* (Stanford, Calif.: Stanford University Press, 1993); Christopher Looby, *Voicing America: Language, Literary Form, and the Origins of the United States* (Chicago: University of Chicago Press, 1996); Michael Warner, *The Letters of the Republic: Publication and the Public Sphere in Eighteenth-Century America* (Cambridge: Harvard University Press, 1990); Larzar Ziff, *Writing in the New Nation: Prose, Print, and Politics in the United States* (New Haven, Conn.: Yale University Press, 1991).

39. Warner, *The Letters of the Republic*, ix.

40. Ibid., xi.

41. Ibid.

42. Robert Shallope, "Toward a Republican Synthesis: The Emergence of an Understanding of Republicanism in American Historiography," *William and Mary*

Quarterly 29 (January 1972): 49–80. For two critical responses, see Isaac Kramnick, "Republican Revisionism Revisited," *American Historical Review* 87 (June 1982): 629–64, and Linda Kerber, "The Republican Ideology of the Revolutionary Generation," *American Quarterly* 37, no. 4 (Fall 1985): 474–95.

43. This literature is now quite extensive. I will limit myself to citing only the two books that initiated the debate in 1980: Linda Kerber, *Women of the Republic: Intellect & Ideology in Revolutionary America* (New York: W. W. Norton, 1980), and Mary Beth Norton, *Liberty's Daughters: The Revolutionary Experience of American Women, 1750–1800* (Boston: Little, Brown, 1980).

44. For a useful sampling of the positions in this debate, see Craig Calhoun, ed., *Habermas and the Public Sphere* (Cambridge: MIT Press, 1992).

45. Warner, *The Letters of the Republic*, 42.

46. Ibid., 174.

47. Shirley Samuels, "Introduction," in *The Culture of Sentiment: Race, Gender, and Sentimentality in Nineteenth-Century American Culture* (New York: Oxford University Press, 1992), 3.

48. Karen Sanchez-Eppler, *Touching Liberty: Abolition, Feminism, and the Politics of the Body* (Berkeley, Calif.: University of California Press, 1993), 1.

49. Jonathan Elmer, *Reading at the Social Limit: Affect, Mass Culture, and Edgar Allan Poe* (Stanford, Calif.: Stanford University Press, 1995), 103.

50. The reasons for this oversight are complicated. They reflect relatively minor factors such as the academic division of examination fields between the eighteenth and nineteenth centuries and the institutional segregation of literary from political theory, as well as more significant ones like the historically overdetermined distinction between republicanism and liberalism. If the discourse of sentimentalism is categorically liberal, then it cannot have any deep roots in an eighteenth-century culture that is categorically republican. While there are exceptions to this generalization, the best studies of U.S. sentimental culture differ from their British counterparts in their tendency to isolate sentimentalism as a nineteenth-century phenomenon.

51. Janet Todd, *Sensibility: An Introduction* (New York: Methuen, 1986); G. J. Barker-Benfield, *The Culture of Sensibility: Sex and Society in Eighteenth-Century Britain* (Chicago: University of Chicago Press, 1992); Ann Van Sant, *Eighteenth-Century Sensibility and the Novel: The Senses in Social Context* (Cambridge: Cambridge University Press, 1993).

52. Thomas Laqueur, *Making Sex: Body and Gender from the Greeks to Freud* (Cambridge: Harvard University Press, 1990), 157.

53. Robyn Wiegman, *American Anatomies: Theorizing Race and Gender* (Durham, N.C.: Duke University Press, 1995). Londa Schiebinger, *The Mind Has No Sex?: Women in the Origins of Modern Science* (Cambridge: Harvard University Press, 1989). See also Laqueur, *Making Sex.*

54. Lauren Berlant, *The Queen of America Goes to Washington City: Essays on Sex and Citizenship* (Durham, N.C.: Duke University Press, 1997), 36.

55. Barker-Benfield, *The Culture of Sensibility*, xxviii, 301.

56. While the isolation of civil from state power leads to what Václav Havel has recently dubbed the "anti-political politics" of modern social movements, the isolation of the body from society produces what Claudia Johnson refers to as the "politics made intimate" typical of sentimental literary and reform cultures. See Václav Havel,

"Anti-Political Politics," in *Civil Society and the State*, ed. John Keane (New York: Verso, 1988), 381–98, and Johnson, *Equivocal Beings*.

57. In *Rabelais and His World*, Mikhail Bakhtin encodes this transition to the modern "realistic" understanding of the body as a shift from a "grotesque" to a "classical bodily canon": "[T]he new concept of realism . . . cuts the body in two and separates the objects of grotesque and folklore realism that were merged within the body. The new concept seeks to complete each individual outside the link with the ultimate whole—the whole that has lost the old image and has not yet found a new one." Bakhtin elsewhere notes the persistence of the "grotesque bodily canon"—the (sentimental) theme of the mother nursing the child, for example. But his analysis nevertheless emphasizes the eclipse of intersubjective (and intercorporeal) images of the "body in the act of becoming" within the modern world. Mikhail Bakhtin, *Rabelais and his World*, trans., Helene Iswolsky (Bloomington, Ind.: Indiana University Press, 1994), 53, 322, 317. For a revision of Bakhtin focused on the interdependence of "classical" and "grotesque bodily canons," see Peter Stallybrass and Allon White, *The Politics and Poetics of Transgression* (Ithaca, N.Y.: Cornell University Press, 1986).

58. Walt Whitman, *Song of Myself*, in *Leaves of Grass* (New York: Vintage, 1992), 50–51.

59. Michel Foucault, *The History of Sexuality*, trans. Robert Hurley (New York: Vintage, 1990), 123, 139, 157.

60. Elaine Scarry, *The Body in Pain: The Making and Unmaking of the World* (New York: Oxford University Press, 1985), 14, 6.

61. Judith Butler, *Bodies That Matter: On the Discursive Limits of "Sex"* (New York: Routledge, 1993), 2, 30.

62. Cited in Henry Steele Commanger and Richard B. Morris, eds., *The Spirit of Seventy-Six: The Story as Told by Participants* (New York: Da Capo Press, 1995), 3.

63. Donald M. Lowe, *The Body in Late-Capitalist USA* (Durham, N.C.: Duke University Press, 1995), 5.

64. Claude Lefort, "The Question of Democracy,"*Democracy and Political Theory*, 16.

65. Daniel T. Rodgers, "Republicanism: the Career of a Concept," *The Journal of American History* 79, no. 1 (June 1992): 11–38. See also, Joyce Appleby, *Capitalism and the New Social Order: The Republican Vision of the 1790s* (New York: New York University Press, 1984).

66. Jean-Jacques Rousseau, *Emile; or, On Education*, trans. Allan Bloom (New York: Basic Books, 1979), 365.

67. Ibid., 363.

Chapter 2
United States Liberalism and the Public Sphere

1. Michel Crozier, Samuel P. Huntington, Joki Watanuki, *The Crisis of Democracy: Report on the Governability of Democracies to the Trilateral Commission* (New York: New York University Press, 1975), 115.

2. Similarly, upon his arrival, Klaatu initially alarms the other boarders by standing in a shadowy doorway as they listen to a newscast of the "alien invasion." Klaatu's emergence from the shadows, not as an alien "monster" but as a clean-cut and well-

dressed "visitor," serves to undermine the paranoia of both the newscast and the boarders' collective response to it. Klaatu's alien-ness is then displaced onto Gort who, in a later scene, appears to threaten Helen with (sexual) violence—though only until she repeats the phrase that the again injured Klaatu had taught her: "Klaatu Baradu Necto." On the political paranoia of 1950s films, see Michael Rogin, "Kiss Me Deadly: Communism, Motherhood, and Cold War Movies," *Representations* 6 (Spring 1984): 1–36.

3. H. L. A. Hart, *The Concept of Law* (Oxford: Clarendon, 1961), 97.

4. Ibid., 165, 191.

5. Ibid., 193.

6. Ibid., 202. This narrow understanding of "publicity" as a means to the end of public knowledge of the legal system is common to more recent followers of Hart as well. In his 1979 *The Authority of Law*, for example, Joseph Raz cites F. A. Hayek's definition of the rule of law: "[S]tripped of all technicalities this means that government in all its actions is bound by rules fixed and announced beforehand. . . . rules which make it possible to foresee with fair certainty how the authority will use its coercive powers, and to plan one's individual affairs on the basis of this knowledge." Though Raz's point is to mark the limits of the relevance of the rule of law within political theory, he nevertheless marginalizes broader, political questions concerning "publicity" and public debate (a "free press" versus a "gagged press," for example) as "indirect influences." See Joseph Raz, *The Authority of Law* (Oxford: Clarendon, 1979), 210, 219.

7. Louis Hartz, *The Liberal Tradition in America: An Interpretation of American Political Thought Since the Revolution* (New York: Harcourt, Brace & Co., 1955), 309. Sacvan Bercovitch, "Hawthorne's A-Morality of Compromise," *Representations* 24 (Fall 1988): 12. By portraying Hartz's claim as utopian, I misrepresent it slightly here. It would be perhaps more accurate to describe Hartz as resigned to a neo-liberal acceptance of "American liberalism" as the best of all *possible* political systems. As Klaatu puts it, "we do not pretend to have achieved perfection, but we have a system and it works." Bercovitch's claim, on the other hand, is both dystopian and "quasi-Marxist," not due to any interest in the transformative potential of class antagonism in the United States, but due to its adherence to a long Marxist tradition of viewing the history of the United States as an exception to European narratives of class struggle. On this point, see Michael Denning, "Marxism and American Studies," *American Quarterly*, no. 38 (1986): 356–80. On the 1950s neo-liberals, see Thomas Schaub, *American Fiction in the Cold War* (Madison, Wis.: University of Wisconsin Press, 1991), 3–87.

8. There are, of course, many exceptions to this generalization. What I refer to are the subversion/containment debates within New Historicist cultural criticism, the communitarian/universalism debates within moral and ethical philosophy, and the realism/formalism debates within legal studies. For critical accounts of each of these debates, see Carolyn Porter, "Are We Being Historical Yet," in *The States of "Theory,"* ed. David Carroll (New York: Columbia University Press, 1990); Chantal Mouffe, "rawls: political philosophy without politics," in *Universalism vs. Communitarianism: Contemporary Debates in Ethics*, ed. David Rasmussen (Cambridge: MIT Press, 1990), 217–35; Roberto Unger, *The Critical Legal Studies Movement* (Cambridge: Harvard University Press, 1983).

9. Claude Lefort, *Democracy and Political Theory*, trans. David Macey (Minneapolis: University of Minnesota Press, 1988). See also Ernesto Laclau and Chantal Mouffe, *Hegemony and Socialist Strategy: Towards a Radical Democratic Politics* (London: Verso, 1985), 149–91.

10. J. G. A. Pocock, "Virtues, rights, and manners: A model for historians of political thought," in *Virtue, Commerce, and History* (Cambridge: Cambridge University Press, 1985), 40. See also Quentin Skinner, *The Foundations of Modern Political Thought* (Cambridge: Cambridge University Press, 1978). For a shorter version of Skinner's argument focusing on Machiavelli, see his "The idea of negative liberty: philosophical and historical perspectives," in *Philosophy in History: Essays on the Historiography of Philosophy*, eds. Richard Rorty, J. B. Schneewind, Quentin Skinner (Cambridge: Cambridge University Press, 1984), 194–221. Wendy Brown provides a useful taxonomy of liberalism in *States of Injury: Power and Freedom in Late Modernity* (Princeton, N.J.: Princeton University Press, 1995), esp. 135–65.

11. For polemic summaries of this debate from different perspectives, see Issac Kramnick, "Republican Revisionism Revisited," *American Historical Review* 87 (June 1982): 629–64; J. G. A. Pocock, "The varieties of Whiggism from Exclusion to Reform: A history of ideology and discourse," in *Virtue, Commerce, and History*; Robert Shallope, "Toward a Republican Synthesis: The Emergence of an Understanding of Republicanism in American Historiography," *William and Mary Quarterly* 29 (January 1972): 49–80, and "Republicanism and Early American Historiography," *William and Mary Quarterly* 39 (April 1982): 334–56; Linda Kerber, "The Republican Ideology of the Revolutionary Generation," *American Quarterly* 37 (Fall 1985): 474–95; Joyce Appleby, *Capitalism and a New Social Order: The Republican Vision of the 1790s* (New York: New York University Press, 1984).

12. Hannah Arendt, *The Human Condition* (Chicago: The University of Chicago Press, 1958), 46–47.

13. Ibid., 30–31, 34 and 45, 24, 26, 30–31, 40–41, 41, 51.

14. Ibid., 32.

15. Ibid., 28.

16. Ibid., 28–29.

17. Linda Zerilli, "The Arendtian Body," in *Feminist Interpretations of Hannah Arendt*, ed. Bonnie Honig (University Park, Pa.: Pennsylvania State University Press, 1995), 173. See also Hannah Pitkin's and Bonnie Honig's contributions to the same volume, "Conformism, Housekeeping, and the Attack of the Blob: The Origins of Hannah Arendt's Concept of the Social," 51–81, and "Toward an Agonistic Feminism: Hannah Arendt and the Politics of Identity," 135–66. Honig's essay appears in the context of her larger argument concerning the feminist retrieval of an agonistic (and Machiavellian) concept of political virtue in *Political Theory and the Displacement of Politics* (Ithaca, N.Y.: Cornell University Press, 1993).

18. Arendt, *The Human Condition*, 46.

19. Ibid., 51.

20. Hannah Arendt, *On Revolution* (New York: Viking Penguin, 1963), 125–26.

21. Ibid., 182.

22. Ibid., 68.

23. For an historical critique of *On Revolution*, see Joan Landes, "*Novus Ordo Saeclorum*: Gender and Public Space in Arendt's Revolutionary France," in *Feminist Interpretations of Hannah Arendt*, 195–220.

24. Arendt, *On Revolution*, 94–95.

25. This reduction is evinced most precisely in the otherwise obvious (and abrupt) slippage between "democracy" and "governability" in Huntington's analysis of the effects of the "decline" during and after the Vietnam War of U.S. power abroad: "The turning inward of American attention and the decline in the authority of American governing institutions are closely related, as both cause and effect, to the relative downturn in American power and influence in world affairs. *A decline in the governability of democracy at home means a decline in the influence of democracy abroad*" (my emphasis). "Democracy," in Huntington's analysis, becomes a term interchangeable with "power," while "politics" becomes interchangeable with "governability." As demonstrated by one recent president's patronizing response to a journalist's question concerning the effectiveness of the United States's 1990 military buildup in Saudi Arabia and the Persian Gulf ("Watch, wait, and learn"), Huntington's administrative conception of "politics"—democratic or otherwise—as the ability to manage "power" is hardly exceptional. See Michel Crozier, et al. *The Crisis of Democracy*, 106.

26. Arendt, *On Revolution*, 106.

27. Ibid., 107.

28. Arendt, *The Human Condition*, 63.

29. Arendt, *On Revolution*, 108.

30. Ibid., 136. Arendt's quotes in this passage are taken from James Fenimore Cooper's *The American Democrat* (1838).

31. Ernst Bloch, *Natural Law and Human Dignity*, trans. Dennis J. Schmidt (Cambridge: MIT Press, 1987), 237. In a speech before the Chamber of Deputies on January 27, 1848, Tocqueville foreshadows Arendt in condemning what, for Tocqueville, was the rise of a liberal conception of politics and the public sphere: "What I see, gentlemen, can be put in a word: public mores are changing and have already profoundly changed; . . . common opinions, feelings, and ideas are more and more being replaced by particular interests, particular aims, and points of view carried over from private life and private interests. . . . Whether this new morality, unknown at the great ages of our history and unknown at the beginning of our Revolution, is not spread more and more and daily invading men's minds. This is my question." See Alexis de Tocqueville, *Democracy in America*, trans. George Lawrence (New York: Doubleday, 1969), 751. Richard Sennett echoes this argument in *The Fall of Public Man*—a book with a deep (and unacknowledged) debt to Arendt. "That history," Sennett writes of the development through the eighteenth century of what he calls "intimate tyranny," "is of the erosion of a delicate balance which maintained society in the first flush of its secular and capitalist existence. It was a balance between public and private life." See Richard Sennett, *The Fall of Public Man* (New York: W. W. Norton, 1976), 338.

32. Arendt: "If the ultimate end of revolution was freedom and the constitution of a public space where freedom could appear, the *constitutio libertatis*, then the elementary republics of the wards, the only tangible place where everyone could be free, actually were the end of the great republic whose chief purpose in domestic affairs should have been to provide the people with such places of freedom and to protect them. The basic assumption of the ward system, whether Jefferson knew it or not, was that no one could be called happy without his share in public happiness, that no one could be free without his experience in public freedom, and that no one could

be called either happy or free without participating, and having a share, in public power." Arendt, *On Revolution*, 249, 255.

33. Ibid., 114.

34. President's Committee on Administrative Management, *Administrative Management: Report of the President's Committee* (Washington, D.C.: Government Printing Office, 1937), 47.

35. Arendt, *On Revolution*, 274.

36. Ibid., 131, 274.

37. Jürgen Habermas, *The Structural Transformation of the Public Sphere: An Inquiry into a Category of Bourgeois Society*, trans. Thomas Burger (Cambridge: MIT Press, 1989), 132, 136. For a discussion of the impact of Habermas's book on German cultural and social theory, see Peter Uwe Hohendahl, "Critical Theory, Public Sphere and Culture: Jürgen Habermas and his Critics," *New German Critique*, vol. 16 (1977).

38. Ibid., 117–29.

39. Ibid., 129–40.

40. Ibid., 52, 19.

41. Jürgen Habermas, *Philosophical-Political Profiles*, trans. Frederick G. Lawrence (Cambridge: MIT Press, 1985), 181. For critiques along similar lines, see Hannah Pitkin, "Justice: On Relating Private and Public," *Political Theory*, no. 3 (August 1981): 327–52, and Claude Lefort, "Hannah Arendt and the Question of the Political," in *Democracy and Political Theory*, 45–55.

42. The terms "solidarity," "power," and "money" appear in the central essay of *The New Conservatism: Cultural Criticism and the Historians' Debate*, trans. Shierry Weber Nicholsen (Cambridge: MIT Press, 1990), 48–70. The difference between Habermas's approach and that of liberalism's communitarian critics is that he sees "solidarity" as only one possible steering mechanism, thereby allowing for a differentiation between social logics that communitarianism too hastily groups together. On this point, see Andrew Arato and Jean Cohen, *Civil Society and Political Theory* (Cambridge: MIT Press, 1992), 346–420. In a second collection of essays (*Moral Consciousness and Communicative Action*), Habermas explores this question of the moral basis of a democratic public sphere further by explicitly articulating his discussion of morality to the question of its public and intersubjective adjudication: "In contrast to any philosophy of history, the intersubjectivist approach of discourse ethics breaks with the premises of the philosophy of consciousness. The only higher level intersubjectivity it acknowledges is that of public spheres." Jürgen Habermas, *Moral Consciousness and Communicative Action*, trans. Christian Lenhardt and Shierry Weber Nicholsen (Cambridge: MIT Press, 1990), 209. In other contexts, the same argument takes the form of a polemic against the reduction of critical debate to theories of representation or, following Habermas more closely, the "subject-centered" reason typical of nineteenth- and twentieth-century philosophies of consciousness. On the distinction between "subject-centered" and "communicative" conceptions of rationality, see Jürgen Habermas, *The Philosophical Discourse of Modernity*, trans. Frederick Lawrence (Cambridge: MIT Press, 1987), especially chapters 11 and 12.

43. Arendt, *On Revolution*, 224.

44. Habermas, *The Structural Transformation*, 26.

45. Arendt, *The Human Condition*, 46.

46. Georg Wilhelm Friedrich Hegel, *Philosophy of Right*, trans. T. M. Knox (New York: Oxford University Press, 1967).

47. Habermas, *The Structural Transformation*, 30–31.

48. Hegel, *Philosophy of Right*, 11.

49. The term "principle of publicness" appears in Habermas's encyclopedia article on the public sphere as a means of distinguishing between the practice of publication on the one hand, and the theory that opinions gain authority only through their submission to public debate on the other. See Jürgen Habermas, "The Public Sphere," in *Rethinking Popular Culture*, ed. Chandra Mukarji and Michael Schudson (Berkeley, Calif.: University of California Press, 1991), 399.

50. As this passage indicates, Hegel toys with the Kantian ideal of philosophy as a critical activity oriented toward a public sphere irreducible to the state, but his emphasis on the belatedness of philosophic wisdom forecloses that possibility. Though Hegel does suggest that the "footing of the state itelf is insecure" if "subjective aims are not satisfied," he also insists that his "science of the state" cannot be critical of the state. It is, instead, "nothing other than the endeavour to apprehend and portray the state as something inherently rational." *Philosophy of Right*, 13, 7, 281, 11.

51. Immanuel Kant, "Perpetual Peace," in *On History*, trans. Lewis White Beck, Robert E. Anchor, Emil Fackenheim (New York: Macmillan, 1984), 134.

52. Kant: "We should prove, by observations which anyone can make, that this property of our minds, this receptivity to a pure moral interest and the moving force in the pure thought of virtue when properly commended to the human heart, is the strongest incentive to the good and indeed the only one when it is a question of continual and meticulous obedience to moral maxims." Immanuel Kant, *Critique of Practical Reason*, trans. Lewis White Beck (New York: Macmillan, 1985), 156. For a reading of Kant along these lines, see the first chapter of Philip Lacoue-Labarthe and Jean-Luc Nancy, *The Literary Absolute: The Theory of Literature in German Romanticism*, trans. Philip Barnard and Cheryl Lester (Albany, N.Y.: State University of New York Press, 1988).

53. Arendt, *The Human Condition*, 39.

54. Habermas, *The Structural Transformation*, 48.

55. Oscar Wilde, *The Importance of Being Earnest*, in *The Plays of Oscar Wilde* (New York: Vintage, 1988), 394.

56. Habermas, *The Structural Transformation*, 51. Habermas's observations concerning the early novel parallel those of Ian Watt in *The Rise of the Novel*. Like Habermas, Watt notes the structural grounds of novelistic subjectivity: "we got inside their minds as well as their houses." The difference between the two interpretations is that Habermas locates the public sphere as the final destination of the audience-oriented subjectivity generated within the privacy of the bourgeois home, while Watt sees that subjectivity as essentially private. Like Arendt, Watt thus contrasts the "subjective" forms of narrative typified by the sentimental novel to the "objective" forms prevelant in the classical world: "Richardson's narrative mode, therefore, may also be regarded as a reflection of a much larger change in outlook—the transition from the objective, social and public orientation of the classical world to the subjective, individualist and private orientation of the life and literature of the last two

hundred years." See Ian Watt, *The Rise of the Novel: Studies in Defoe, Richardson and Fielding* (Berkeley, Calif.: University of California Press, 1957), 175, 176.

57. For two readings of the origins of modern social movements in the context of nineteenth-century, public-oriented moral reform, see Henry Abelove, "From Thoreau to Queer Politics," *Yale Journal of Criticism* 6, no. 2 (Fall 1993): 16–27, and Michael Warner, "Whitman Drunk," *Breaking Bounds: Whitman and American Cultural Studies*, eds. Betsy Erkkila and Jay Grossman (New York: Oxford University Press, 1996), 30–43.

58. Habermas, "The New Obscurity," *The New Conservatism*, 63.

59. Ibid., 37. In subsequent writings, Habermas extends this type of argument to his theorization of the "ideal speech situation": "The utopian content of a society based on communication is limited to formal aspects of an undamaged intersubjectivity. To the extent to which it suggests a concrete form of life, even the expression 'the ideal speech situation' is misleading. What can be outlined normatively are the necessary but general conditions for the communicative practice of everyday life and for the procedure of discursive will-formation that would put participants *themselves* in a position to realize concrete possibilities for a better and less threatened life, on *their own* initiative and in accordance with *their own* needs and insights." Ibid., 69.

60. Ibid., 37.

61. Ibid., 55.

62. Habermas thus locates the utopian moment within the idealization of purely consensual familial relations central to the bourgeois ideology of intimacy: "The conception's transcendence of what was immanent was the element of truth that raised bourgeois ideology above ideology itself, most fundamentally in the area where the experience of 'humanity' originated: in the humanity of the intimate relationships between human beings who, under the aegis of the family, were nothing more than human." Ibid., 48.

63. Thomas Paine, "Agrarian Justice," in *The Thomas Paine Reader*, ed. Michael Foot and Issac Kramnick (New York: Viking Penguin, 1987), 487. Paine's argument expands on a commonplace of late eighteenth-century democratic republicanism. In a 1787 letter to *The Independent Gazette* of Philadelphia, for example, "Centinal" opposes the ratification of the Federal Constitution on the grounds that "[a] republican, or free government, can only exist where the body of the people are virtuous, and where property is pretty equally divided." Quoted in Cecelia M. Kenyon, ed., *The Antifederalists* (Boston: Northeastern University Press, 1985), 7.

64. Mary Wollstonecraft, *A Vindication of the Rights of Woman* (New York: Penguin, 1972), 87, 88.

65. Habermas, *The Structural Transformation*, 55–56.

66. Ibid.

67. Ibid., 56.

68. Alexander Hamilton, *Report on Manufactures*, 6. In contrast to Klaatu's (economic) liberalism, which separates the pursuit of "more profitable enterprises" from either politics or law, Hamilton's capitalist republicanism positions "manufactures" as the basis of the republic. As indicated by his inattention to questions concerning citizens' virtue or independence, Hamilton thus marks the boundary between republicanism and liberalism. On Hamilton's republicanism, see Gerald Stourzh, *Alexander Hamilton and the Idea of Republican Government* (Stanford, Calif.: Stanford Uni-

versity Press, 1970). For a similar interpretation of the antagonism between land- and market-based versions of republicanism, see Charles Sellers, *The Market Revolution: Jacksonian America, 1815–1846* (New York: Oxford University Press, 1991), 3–69. I add Paine to the more traditional antithesis of Jeffersonian agrarianism and Hamiltonian capitalism because his emphasis on an egalitarian distribution of capital pursues the agrarian argument without reproducing its (arguably) pre-modern equation of virtue solely with land-ownership.

69. Linda Kerber, *Women of the Republic: Intellect & Ideology in Revolutionary America* (New York: W. W. Norton, 1980), 137–84. For a brief version of Horowitz's argument, see his "The Transformation of the Conception of Property in American Law," in *American Law and the Constitutional Order*, eds. Lawrence M. Friedman and Harry Scheiber (Cambridge: Harvard University Press, 1978), 142–50. For a fuller account of transformations in legal doctrine concerning the family, see Michael Grossberg, *Governing the Hearth: Law and Family in Nineteenth-Century America* (Chapel Hill, N.C.: University of North Carolina Press, 1985).

70. Karl Marx, *The Communist Manifesto*, in *The Marx-Engels Reader*, ed. Robert C. Tucker (New York: W. W. Norton, 1978), 473.

71. As Habermas notes, Marx's terms for the two sides of this dialectic are "human emancipation" and "political emancipation." The difference between Marx and Habermas lies in the latter's resistance to the dangerous collapse of political structures that calls for "human emancipation" tend to require. See Habermas, *The Structural Transformation*, 55, 57, 117–29.

72. Ibid., 88.

73. Ibid., xviiim, and Habermas, "Further Reflections on the Public Sphere," in *Habermas and the Public Sphere*, ed. Craig Calhoun (Cambridge: MIT Press, 1992), 426. For a contrasting analysis of the "plebeian public sphere," see Alexander Kluge and Oscar Negt, *Public Sphere and Experience: Toward an Analysis of the Bourgeois and Proletarian Public Sphere* (Minneapolis: University of Minnesota Press, 1993).

74. Sean Wilentz, *Chants Democratic: New York City & the Rise of the American Working Class, 1788–1850* (Oxford: Oxford University Press, 1984). Christine Stansell, *City of Women: Sex and Class in New York, 1789–1860* (Urbana, Ill.: University of Illinois Press, 1987). For complementary accounts of what Daniel Rodgers refers to as "labor republicanism," see Eric Foner, *Tom Paine and Revolutionary America* (New York: Oxford University Press, 1976); Gary B. Nash, *The Urban Crucible: Social Change Political Consciousness and the Origins of the American Revolution* (Cambridge: Harvard University Press, 1980).

75. Pocock, "Authority and Property: The question of liberal origins," in *Virtue, Commerce, and History*, 71.

76. Habermas, *The Structural Transformation*, 178.

77. Joan Landes, *Women and the Public Sphere in the Age of the French Revolution* (Ithaca, N.Y.: Cornell University Press, 1988).

78. Paine, "Agrarian Justice," 474.

79. Mary P. Ryan, *Women in Public: Between the Banners and the Ballots, 1825–1880* (Baltimore, Md.: Johns Hopkins University Press, 1990).

80. Landes, *Women and the Public Sphere*, 7. In this sense, Landes echoes critics like Geoff Eley ("Nations, Publics, and Political Cultures: Placing Habermas in the Nineteenth Century," in *Habermas and the Public Sphere*, 289–339) and Michael

Schudson ("Was There Ever a Public Sphere? If So, When?: Reflections on the American Case," in *Habermas and the Public Sphere*, 143–63) in using a competing historical account to refute Habermas's theoretical claims. The problem with such arguments is that they radically undertheorize the act of writing history and, in doing so, open themselves to Habermas's often repeated claim that such criticisms lack normative grounding altogether. Landes herself draws on Carole Pateman's influential argument that the model of the social contract central to democratic political theory is itself essentially masculinist. See Carole Pateman, *The Sexual Contract* (Stanford, Calif.: Stanford University Press, 1988). For a critique of Pateman, see Nancy Fraser, "Beyond the Master/Subject Model," *Justice Interruptus: Critical Reflections on the "Postsocialist" Condition* (New York: Routledge, 1997), 225–35.

81. Nancy Fraser, "Rethinking the Public Sphere: A Contribution to the Critique of Actually Existing Democracy," in *Habermas and the Public Sphere*, 117. The phrase "Gramscian moral" is Fraser's, though her primary target here seems to be Foucault, rather than Gramsci. For a critique of Foucault along these lines, see Fraser's "Foucault on Modern Power: Empirical Insights and Normative Confusions," *Praxis International* 1 (October 1981), 272–96. For an expansion of her argument in "Rethinking the Public Sphere," see Fraser's "Sex, Lies, and the Public Sphere: Some Reflections on the Confirmation of Clarence Thomas," *Critical Inquiry* 18 (1992), 595–612.

82. Selya Benhabib, "Models of Public Space: Hannah Arendt, the Liberal Tradition, and Jürgen Habermas," in *Habermas and the Public Sphere*, 94.

83. Ibid., 79.

84. Fraser, "Rethinking the Public Sphere," 137.

85. Habermas, *The Philosophic Discourse of Modernity*. Also see his "Neoconservative Cultural Criticism in the United States and West Germany," in *The New Conservativism*, 22–47.

86. Michel Foucault, *The History of Sexuality*, trans. Robert Hurley (New York: Vintage, 1978), 107, 139–40.

87. Ibid., 144.

88. Fred Glass, "The 'New Bad Future': *RoboCop* and 1980s' Sci-Fi Films," *Science as Culture* 5 (1989), 7–49. *The Day the Earth Stood Still* poses (without thematizing) the same problem. Gort's unbiased enforcement of the law depends on his (its) freedom from human control, just as liberalism's theoretical defense of the rule of law must position itself as politically neutral. Klaatu's later revelation to Helen that he can control Gort's actions undercuts that premise (see note 2 for this chapter). *RoboCop*, in this sense, critiques the earlier film simply by substituting the corrupt and self-interested influence of Dick Jones for the virtuous and disinterested oversight of Klaatu.

89. Habermas, *The Structural Transformation*, 159.

90. Arendt's description of modern intimacy nicely captures the double bind that Murphy-RoboCop experiences in this scene: "[M]ass society not only destroys the public realm but the private as well, deprives men not only of their place in the world but of their private home, where they once felt sheltered against the world and where, at any rate, even those excluded from the world could find a substitute in the warmth of the hearth and the limited reality of family life." Arendt, *The Human*

Condition, 59. As Murphy, RoboCop is incapable of defending his private life from the invasions of the world outside; as "RoboCop," Murphy is unable to return (or retreat) to that life. The film's awareness of this contradition is further established in a later scene when RoboCop's human face is revealed and Ann Louis helps him realign his damaged "targeting system." The realignment works, but the target is the picture of an infant on a jar of baby food. The thematic motivation for this target is complicated. It references an earlier scene in which the "paste" used to feed RoboCop's "organic systems" is referred to as "baby food." The destruction of the jar thus symbolizes RoboCop's liberation from OCP's control (his own infantilization). But it also produces a spectacle rarely seen in Hollywood films: a man and woman teaming up not to produce a baby, but to blow that image away. The scene thus indicates the film's vexed relation to its own idealization of (to adopt Arendt's phrase) the "limited reality" of Murphy's family life. Freed from corporate control, RoboCop now lacks both the means of feeding his "organic systems" and, the film suggests, the motivation for pursuing any extra-legal ends.

91. Habermas, *The Structural Transformation*, 28.

92. Let me clarify this difference through one example. Donna Haraway's now canonical "A Manifesto for Cyborgs" pursues a postmodern critique of modernity through the "ironic political myth" of "cyborg citizenship" (190, 203). Haraway persuasively argues that the figure of the cyborg breaks down many of the oppositions central to modernity, including that of public and private: "No longer structured by the polarity of public and private, the cyborg defines a technological polis based on a revolution of social relations in the *oikos*, the household. Nature and culture are reworked; the one can no longer be the resource for appropriation or incorporation by the other. The relationships for forming wholes from parts, including those of polarity and hierarchical domination, are at issue in the cyborg world" (192). This insight leads to an equally persuasive substitution of a postmodern "alliance politics" (one based in "elective affinities") for a modern "identity politics" (one grounded in "claims for an organic or natural standpoint") (198–99). What Haraway draws up short of theorizing, however, are the (public) institutions and structures within which the exercise of "cyborg citizenship" will be democratic. For Habermas, the latter question is not only crucial to any politics (modern or postmodern), but also requires the re-emergence (and rethinking) of the distinction between public and private, albeit on political rather than natural(ized) grounds. See Donna Haraway, "A Manifesto for Cyborgs: Science, Technology, and Socialist Feminism in the 1980s," in *Feminism/Postmodernism*, ed. Linda J. Nicholson (New York: Routledge, 1990), 190–233.

93. Michael Taussig, *The Nervous System* (New York: Routledge, 1992).

94. Hegel, *The Philosophy of Right*, 281.

Chapter 3
The Patriot's Two Bodies

1. George Washington, letter to Patrick Henry, 9 October 1796, in *George Washington: Writings* (New York: Library of America, 1997), 918.

2. *Debates in Congress*, 22nd Congress, 1st session, Feb. 13, 1832, vol. 8, pt. 2; 1784.

3. Madison's draft is included in Horace Binney, *An Inquiry into the Formation of Washington's Farewell Address* (Philadelphia: Parry & McMillan, 1859).

4. George Washington, "Farewell Address," in *Washington's Farewell Address and Webster's First Bunker Hill Oration*, ed. Charles Robert Gaston (Boston: Ginn, 1906), 2. All further references to the "Farewell Address" will appear as page numbers set off in parentheses.

5. Thomas Jefferson, *The Life and Selected Writings of Thomas Jefferson*, ed. Adrienne Koch and William Peden (New York: Random House, 1944), 127.

6. Horace Binney, *An Inquiry*, 171.

7. Craig Calhoun, "Nationalism and Civil Society: Democracy, Diversity and Self-Determination," in *Social Theory and the Politics of Identity*, ed. Craig Calhoun (Cambridge, U.K.: Blackwell Publishers, 1994), 312.

8. Quoted in Philip S. Foner, ed., *The Democratic-Republican Societies, 1790–1800: A Documentary Sourcebook of Constitutions, Declarations, Addresses, Resolutions, and Toasts* (Westport, Conn.: Greenwood Press, 1976), 354.

9. Jean-Jacques Rousseau, *The Social Contract*, trans. G. D. H. Cole (Buffalo, N.Y.: Prometheus Books, 1988), 94. On Rousseau's significance within the civic republican tradition, see Patrick Riley, *The General Will Before Rousseau: The Transformation of the Divine into the Civic* (Princeton, N.J.: Princeton University Press, 1986). For a general account of debates concerning political representation, see Hannah Pitkin, *The Concept of Representation* (Berkeley, Calif.: University of California Press, 1967).

10. Roger Chartier's description of the desacralization of the king nicely captures the resulting separation between state and civil authority (between the "sovereign's person" and "the man in the street"): "On the one hand, the king was no longer anything more that a private person whose physical body, afflicted or radiant, had lost all symbolic value. On the other hand, the man in the street had radically separated his own fate from that represented by the state of the sovereign's person." See Roger Chartier, *The Cultural Origins of the French Revolution*, trans. Lydia G. Cochrane (Durham, N.C.: Duke University Press, 1991), 119.

11. Washington, letter to Thomas Jefferson, 6 July 1796, *Writings*, 952. In an earlier letter to Henry Lee, Washington targets the *Aurora* and *Gazette* as particularly troublesome examples of a more general trend: "The publications in Freneau's and Beeche's [*sic*] papers are outrages on common decency; and they progress in that style, in proportion as their pieces are treated with contempt, and are passed by in silence, by those at whom they are aimed. The tendency of them, however, is too obvious to be mistaken by men of cool and dispassionate minds, and, in my opinion, ought to alarm them; because it is difficult to prescribe bounds to the effect." Washington, letter to Henry Lee, 21 July 1793, *Writings*, 842.

12. On Jefferson's role in establishing Freneau's *National Gazette*, see Stanley Elkins and Eric McKitrick, *The Age of Federalism: The Early American Republic, 1788–1800* (New York: Oxford University Press, 1993), 209–56.

13. In an argument parallel to my own, Zizek concludes his essay on post-communist, Eastern European nation formation by calling not for less, but for more alienation: "what Eastern Europe needs most now is more alienation: the establishment of an 'alienated' state that would maintain its distance from civil society, that would be

'formal,' 'empty,' embodying no particular ethnic community's dream (and thus keeping the space open for all of them)" Slavoj Zizek, "Eastern Europe's Republics of Gilead," *New Left Review* 183 (September/October 1990): 52, 62.

14. For a theoretical history of the troubled relation between the mortal and immortal bodies of the king, see Ernst H. Kantorowitz, *The King's Two Bodies: A Study in Medieval Political Theology* (Princeton, N.J.: Princeton University Press, 1957). For an extension (and revision) of that account, see Claude Lefort, "The Image of the Body and Totalitarianism," in *The Political Forms of Modern Society: Bureaucracy, Democracy, Totalitarianism* (Cambridge: MIT Press, 1986), 292–306.

15. Michael Warner, *The Letters of the Republic: Publication and the Public Sphere in Eighteenth-Century America* (Cambridge: Harvard University Press, 1990), 173. See also Lauren Berlant, *The Anatomy of Nationalist Fantasy: Hawthorne, Utopia, and Everyday Life* (Chicago: University of Chicago Press, 1991); Larzar Ziff, *Writing in the New Nation: Prose, Print, and Politics in the United States* (New Haven, Conn.: Yale University Press, 1991); Lawrence Buell, "American Literary Emergence as a Post-colonial Phenomenon," *ALH* 4, no. 3 (Fall 1992): 411–42. For recent historical and theoretical accounts of the distinction between nationality and nationalism, see Eric Hobesbawm, *Nations and Nationalism Since 1780: Programme, Myth, Reality* (Cambridge: University of Cambridge Press, 1990); Benedict Anderson, *Imagined Communities: Reflections on the Origin and Spread of Nationalism* (New York: Verso, 1983); and Homi K. Bhabha, "DissemiNation: Time, Narrative and the Margins of the Modern Nation," *the location of culture* (New York: Routledge, 1994).

16. J. G. A. Pocock, *The Machiavellian Moment: Florentine Political Thought and the Atlantic Republican Tradition* (Princeton, N.J.: Princeton University Press, 1975). In a parallel argument, Pocock suggests that republicanism opposes the development of an imperialism legitimated through liberal theories of representation. "Law," Pocock writes, "is of the empire rather than the republic": "We are discovering (1) that liberty defined by law invests the citizen with rights but no part in *imperium*; (2) that law discriminates between the *libertas* which it guarantees to the citizen and the *imperium* or *auctorias* of the prince or magistrate who administers the law; (3) that the law defines the citizen in terms of the *ius ad rem* and *ius in re* which he [*sic*] acquires through his role in the possession, conveyance, and administration of things." See J. G. A. Pocock, "Virtues, rights, and manners" in *Virtue, Commerce, and History* (Cambridge: Cambridge University Press, 1985), 40, 44.

17. This republican opposition to liberalism plays out the canonical distinction within political philosophy between positive and negative liberty. The clearest articulation of this distinction appears in Isaiah Berlin, "Two Concepts of Liberty" in *Four Essays on Liberty* (Oxford: Oxford University Press, 1969). For critical attempts to rethink Berlin's championing of negative liberty, see Chantal Mouffe, "American Liberalism and its Critics: Rawls, Taylor, Sandel and Walzer" in *Praxis International* 8, no. 2 (July 1988): 193–205, and Quentin Skinner, "The Idea of Negative Liberty: Philosophic and Historical Perspectives" in *Philosophy in History: Essays on the Historiography of Philosophy*, eds. Richard Rorty, J. B. Schneewind, Quentin Skinner (Cambridge: Cambridge University Press, 1984). For a general introduction to the topic, see Norberto Bobbio, *Liberalism and Democracy*, trans. Martin Ryle and Kate Soper (New York: Verso, 1990).

18. "If a democratic republic subdues a nation in order to govern them as subjects," Montesquieu argues, "it exposes its own liberty. Contrary is it to the nature of things that a democratic republic should conquer towns which cannot enter into the sphere of democracy. It is necessary that the conquered people should be capable of enjoying the privileges of sovereignty as it was settled in the very beginning among the Romans. The conquest ought to be limited to the number of citizens fixed for the democracy." Baron de Montesquieu, *The Spirit of the Laws*, trans. Thomas Nugent (New York: Macmillan, 1949), 138.

19. "The Address and Reasons of the Dissent of the Minority of the Convention of the State of Pennsylvania to their Constituents," in *The Antifederalists*, ed. Cecelia M. Kenyon (Boston: Northeastern University Press, 1985), 39. For Montesquieu on the possibility of a confederation of specifically commercial republics, see *The Spirit of the Laws*, 46, 120.

20. Alexander Hamilton, John Jay, James Madison, *The Federalist Papers*, ed. Roy Fairfield (Baltimore, Md.: Johns Hopkins University Press, 1961), 20. On the historical novelty of Madison's redefinition of republicanism as representative government, see J. G. A. Pocock, "States, Republics, and Empires: The American Founding in Early Modern Perspective" in *Conceptual Change and the Constitution*, eds. Terence Ball and J. G. A. Pocock (Lawrence, Kans.: University of Kansas Press, 1988). Seven years later, a "Federal Republican" extends Madison's argument in a letter to the editor of the *New York Journal* concerning the Democratic Society of the City of New York: "It is idle to cavil about the words *Democratic* and *Republican*; it is sufficient that the governments of America are *Representative*." Madison and the "Federal Republican" here provide the theoretical polemic behind the social-political transformations that later historians narrate as teleological and necessary. Foner, ed., *The Democratic-Republican Societies*, 159.

21. For an example of the anthologization of the "Farewell Address" as an "early nationalist" document, see Richard D. Heffner, ed., *A Documentary History of the United States* (New York: New American Library, 1985). Elkins and McKitrick's brief reading of the "Address" in *The Age of Federalism* is an exception to this rule since it does link the question of "foreign relations" to the question of "domestic sedition." Elkins and McKitrick, *The Age of Federalism*, 489–97.

22. "The integration of idealistic assumptions constitutes the distinguishing feature of the Farewell Address. Thus it could have an appeal in the following century of rising democracy when foreign policy demanded legitimation by clearly felt and recognized values and needed to be conducted in accordance with the will of the people." Felix Gilbert, *To the Farewell Address: Ideas of Early American Foreign Policy* (Princeton, N.J.: Princeton University Press, 1961), 136.

23. Ibid., 133, 139.

24. Echoing the third, fourth, and fifth of Washington's nine instructions to Hamilton, the "Address" counsels that "[t]he great rule of conduct for us, in regard to foreign nations, is in extending our commercial relations, to have with them as little *political* connection as possible" (15–16). While Washington's instructions hold out the possibility of political or, at least, just international relations between nations, the final version of the "Address" discredits that possibility while redefining the nation, in terms of foreign policy, as a purely commercial entity. Due to this contrast, the

"Address" splits, for Gilbert, between Washington's democratic "idealism" and Hamilton's political (i.e., economic) "realism." See Binney, *An Inquiry*, 179.

25. Gilbert, *To the Farewell Address*, 137ff.

26. Quoted in Eugene P. Link, *The Democratic-Republican Societies, 1790–1800* (New York: Columbia University Press, 1942), 136.

27. Quoted in Elkin and McKitrick, *The Age of Federalism*, 362.

28. Washington, Letter to Henry Lee, 26 August 1794, *Writings*, 876.

29. For a narrative history of the events leading to the Alien and Sedition Acts, see James Morton Smith, *Freedom's Fetters: The Alien and Sedition Laws and American Civil Liberties* (Ithaca, N.Y.: Cornell University Press, 1956).

30. Thomas Jefferson, Letter to Philip Mazzei, 24 April 1796, in *Federalists, Republicans and Foreign Entanglements, 1789–1815*, ed. Robert McColley (Englewood Cliffs, N.J.: Prentice Hall, 1969), 82.

31. Emerson's essay also signals a shift in the site of national identity formation from state politics to national culture: "Leave government to clerks and desks. This revolution is to be wrought by the gradual domestication of the idea of Culture." I will return to this second, arguably more significant shift, in my conclusion to this chapter. See Ralph Waldo Emerson, "The American Scholar," in *Selections from Ralph Waldo Emerson*, ed. Stephen E. Whicher (Boston: Houghton Mifflin, 1957), 79, 76.

32. The same desire for national harmony appears when Washington, in the first of his instructions to Hamilton, wishes that "party disputes among all the friends and lovers of their country may subside." See Binney, *An Inquiry*, 177.

33. Quoted by Philip S. Foner in "The Democratic-Republican Societies: An Introduction," in *The Democratic and Republican Societies*, 37.

34. Foner, *The Democratic-Republican Societies*, 227.

35. George Washington, Letters to Alexander Hamilton, 29 July 1795, and Gouverneur Morris, 22 December 1795, *Writings*, 914–16, 924–29.

36. Washington's characterizations of the Democratic and Republican Societies along these lines appear in both his personal letters and public speeches. See, in particular, *The Writings of George Washington*, ed. Jared Sparks, vol. 10 (New York: Harper & Brothers, 1847), 425–55, and *Annals of Congress*, 3rd Congress, 1794, 1787–93.

37. Bhabha, "DissemiNation," 139–70.

38. Ibid., 146.

39. I use the terms "Lockean" and "Rousseauist" intentionally. I am less interested here in an historical contrast between Locke and Rousseau than I am in using them to mark two theoretically plausible and historically influential understandings of social contract theory: as an apology for the historically dominant regime to which the people once consented, and as an ahistorical fiction with which to critique that regime on the basis of consent. For a reading of Locke which places him in a Rousseauist tradition, see J. G. A. Pocock, "The varieties of Whiggism from Exclusion to Reform: A history of ideology and discourse," in *Virtue, Commerce, and History*, 215–310.

40. Etienne Balibar, "Citizen Subject," in *Who Comes After the Subject*, ed. Eduardo Cadava, Peter Conner, Jean-Luc Nancy (New York: Routledge, 1991), 51. I stress this point because Balibar's distinction between "association" and "subjection"

seems to me more useful than Bhabha's analogous distinction between the "perfor-mative" subject of the nation and the "pedagogical" object of nationalism. The latter contrast strikes me as untenable, though it does parallel the contrast between partic-ipation and representation central to my reading of the "Address." Where Bhabha focuses on two discrete forms of public address, I want to emphasize the structural underpinning of those forms by differentiating between the nation-state and the (trans)national public sphere. Throughout *the location of culture*, Bhabha maintains a distance from this structural argument. In "DissemiNation," for instance, he re-fuses to align the nation with the public sphere: "Neither can cultural homogeneity or the nation's horizontal space be authoritatively represented within the familiar territory of the *public sphere*." Given the current institutional, economic and cultural boundaries of the public sphere, this argument seems to me understandable, as does his claim that "performative" ruptures within nationalist narratives are inevitable. But at the risk of aligning Bhabha's position with the most insidious of the "Ad-dress"'s counter-subversive strategies, I would also suggest that this portrayal of "performative" ruptures as inevitable echoes the "Address"'s assurance that there will "always be enough of that spirit [of party, faction] for every salutory purpose" (11). Bhabha clearly intends his argument to enable critical opposition to the nation-alist strategies of the nation-state, while the "Address" intends its argument to disable such opposition. Yet both lead away from consideration of the institutional and cul-tural bases of such opposition. Both ignore, in other words, the structures of civil society (economic and domestic) that enable and disable, encourage and discourage democratic participation within anti-nationalist public spheres. Having suggested this much, let me add that a democratic conception of the nation needs not only to emphasize, as Bhabha does, the inevitability of "performative" ruptures, but also to encourage, along with Balibar, an egalitarian proliferation of "associational" public spaces for "performative" reconstructions of nationality. Bhabha, "DissemiNation," 140, 154.

41. Madison succinctly articulated the Republican position while arguing against the Alien and Sedition Acts in Congress: "If we advert to the nature of Republican Government, we shall find that the censorial power is in the people over the Govern-ment and not in the Government over the People." Quoted in Foner, "The Demo-cratic-Republican Societies: An Introduction," 32.

42. Richard Hofstadter, *The Idea of a Party System: The Rise of Legitimate Oppo-sition in the United States, 1780–1840* (Berkeley, Calif.: University of California Press, 1969), 74–121.

43. The Alien and Sedition Acts radicalize this paranoid structure by encoding virtually any politically significant public debate as subversive, while simultaneously locating the "good people of the United States" outside of that debate:

[I]f any person shall write, print, utter or publish, or shall cause or procure to be written, printed, uttered or published, or shall knowingly and willingly assist or aid in writing, printing, uttering or publishing any false, scandalous and malicious writing or writings against the government of the United States, or the President of the United States, with intent to defame the said government, or either house of the said Congress, or the said President, or to bring them, or either of them, into contempt or disrepute; or to excite against them, or either or any of them, the hatred of the good people of the United States, or to stir up sedition within the United States . . . such person . . . shall be punished by a fine not exceeding two thousand dollars, and by imprisonment not exceeding two years.

Quoted in James Morton Smith, *Freedom's Fetters*, 441–42.

44. Washington, Letter to Henry Lee, 26 August 1794, *Writings*, 876.

45. Benjamin Rush, "Of the Mode of Education Proper in a Republic," in *The Selected Writings of Benjamin Rush*, ed. Dagobert D. Runes (New York: The Philosophical Library, 1947), 92.

46. Michel Foucault, *Discipline and Punishment: The Birth of the Prison*, trans. Alan Sheridan (New York: Vintage, 1977); Ronald Takaki, *Iron Cages: Race and Culture in 19th-Century America* (New York: Oxford University Press, 1979); Thomas L. Dumm, *Democracy and Punishment: Disciplinary Origins of the United States* (Madison, Wis.: The University of Wisconsin Press, 1987). While both Takaki and Dumm focus specifically on the United States, Foucault's argument in *Discipline and Punishment* is, of course, the best known of the three. For my purposes, the importance of this argument lies less in its totalizing and dystopian vision of contemporary post-Enlightenment societies as "disciplinary," than it does in Foucault's emphasis on the co-existence of multiple enlightenments: "The Roman reference that accompanies this formation certainly bears with it this double index: citizens and legionaries, law and manoeuvres. While the jurists and philosophers were seeking in the pact a primal model for the construction or reconstruction of the social body, the soldiers and with them the technicians of discipline were elaborating procedures for the individual and collective coercion of bodies" (169). Without this double reference to both normative and ideological aspects of the democratic revolutions, Foucault's own analysis would devolve into the reactive, pure critique characteristic of current pragmatist and historicist readings of Foucault in the United States. For an interview in which Foucault is pressed on these questions, see Michel Foucault, "Politics and Ethics: An Interview," in *The Foucault Reader*, ed. Paul Rabinow (New York: Pantheon, 1984).

47. Jürgen Habermas, *The Structural Transformation of the Public Sphere: An Inquiry Into a Category of Bourgeois Society*, trans. Thomas Burger (Cambridge: MIT Press, 1989), 19.

48. Washington, Letter to Alexander Hamilton, 25 August 1796, *Writings*, 955.

49. Claude Lefort, "The Image of the Body and Totalitarianism," in *The Political Forms of Modern Society: Bureaucracy, Democracy, Totalitarianism*, ed. John B. Thompson (Cambridge, MIT Press, 1986), 303, 299.

50. I stress *vicarious* because this experience of national embodiment itself relies on an abstraction from other "local" and "transnational" forms of corporeality. Lauren Berlant emphasizes this point in her essay "National Brands/National Body: *Imitation of Life*": "[W]e can see a real attraction of abstract citizenship in the way the citizen conventionally acquires a new body by participation in the political public sphere. The American subject is privileged to suppress the fact of his historical situation in the abstract 'person': but then, in return, the nation provides a kind of prophylaxis for the person, as it promises to protect his privileges and his local body in return for loyalty to the state." In the "Address," "Washington" names the national body offered to the citizen by the state. Lauren Berlant, "National Brands/National

Body: *Imitation of Life*," in *The Phantom Public Sphere*, ed. Bruce Robbins (Minneapolis: University of Minnesota Press, 1993), 176. Michael Warner makes a similar argument in his essay, "The Mass Public and the Mass Subject," in *Habermas and the Public Sphere*, ed. Craig Calhoun (Cambridge: MIT Press, 1992), 377–401.

51. Washington, Letter to Henry Knox, 20 September 1795, *Writings*, 916.

52. Jay Fliegelman, *Declaring Independence: Jefferson, Natural Language, and the Culture of Performance* (Stanford, Calif.: Stanford University Press, 1993), 121.

53. Washington, Letter to Henry Lee, 21 July 1793, *Writings*, 842.

54. The context of Derrida's neologism is significant since it links the destabilization of national ontology to the mediating institutions of modern republicanism:

> [T]his frontier between the public and the private is constantly being displaced, remaining less assured than ever, as the limit that would permit one to identify the political. And if this important frontier is being displaced, it is because the medium in which it is instituted, namely, the medium of the media themselves (news, the press, tele-communications, techno-tele-discursivity, techno-tele-iconicity, that which in general assures and determines the *spacing* of public space, the very possibility of the *res publica* and the phenomenality of the political), this element itself is neither living nor dead, present nor absent: it spectralizes. It does not belong to ontology, to the discourse of the Being of beings, or the essence of life or death. It requires, then, what we call, to save time and space rather than just to make up a word, *hauntology*. (Jacques Derrida, *Specters of Marx*, trans. Peggy Kamuf [New York: Routledge, 1994], 50–51).

Though Derrida portrays *Specters of Marx* as a new attempt to clarify the relations among deconstruction, justice, and democracy, such connections are evident in his earlier writings as well. In a reading of the Declaration of Independence from 1976, for example, Derrida glosses Jefferson's historical anxiety as author as attesting to his awareness of a gap between history and symbol—a gap that opens up between Jefferson as founding author and the not-yet-sovereign people whom he, as both founding author and one of the people, must represent himself as representing. Only after authorizing the Declaration, Jacques Derrida observes, will the now sovereign people in turn authorize the narrative through which both Jefferson and the Declaration become, retroactively, representative. What is at stake, prior to any question of Jefferson's authorship as representative of the people, is the democratic coup that establishes the people as sovereign and capable of authorizing representations. The endpoint of Jefferson's anxiety thus lies in his would-be invocation of the "laws of nature and nature's God"—an invocation that both attests to the absolute quality of Jefferson's anxiety as political representative of the "people," and to the resolution of that political anxiety through its displacement to a natural-theological register (with its attendant anxieties, of course). "God is the name," Derrida writes, "the best one, for this last instance and this ultimate signature. Not only the best one in a determined context (such and such a nation, such and such a religion, etc.), but the name of the best name in general." Jacques Derrida, "Declarations of Independence," in *New Political Science: A Journal of Politics and Culture* 15 (Summer 1986): 12. For a less schematic exploration of this rhetorical and political logic, see his "The Laws of Reflection: Nelson Mandela, in Admiration," in *For Nelson Mandela*, eds. Jacques Derrida and Mustapha Tlili (New York: Seaver, 1987), 13–43.

55. *Debates in Congress*, 22nd Congress, 1st session, Feb. 13, 1832, vol. 8, pt. 2: 1794.

56. Ibid., 1798.

57. George Washington, "Last Will and Testament," *Writings*, 1035. *Debates in Congress*, 1795. The problems raised by the protests of Washington's family are never addressed directly, though a (successful) resolution the following day to remove Martha Washington's remains along with those of George seems sensitive to the issue. Representative Bates of Maine explained this addition as resulting from his objections during the previous debate to the "idea of separating the dust of Washington from that of his beloved consort." Ibid., 1811.

58. Lefort, "The Image of the Body and Totalitarianism," 300.

59. *Debates in Congress*, 1783.

60. Ibid., 1786.

61. Ibid., 1788.

62. Ibid., 1801.

63. Ibid.

64. Ibid., 1806–07.

65. Ibid., 1806.

66. Ibid., 1805.

67. Washington, Letter to Alexander Hamilton, 1 September 1796, *Writings*, 960.

68. I emphasize that Washington *seems* to imagine this possibility because his grouping of "Belle Letters" with "Arts" and "Sciences" (as well as his institutional alignment of literary and political apparatuses) marks the distance between the broad understanding of "literature" as coextensive with publication typical of republicanism, and the narrower modern understanding of "literature" characteristic of both Emerson and the Young Americans. On the Young Americans and other forms of literary nationalism in the antebellum period, see Priscilla Wald, *Constituting Americans: Cultural Anxiety and Narrative Form* (Durham, N.C.: Duke University Press, 1995), 106–71. On the category of the "literary" within republicanism, see Michael Warner, *The Letters of the Republic*, 34–72.

69. Chartier, *The Cultural Origins of the French Revolution*, 37.

70. Washington, Letter to Edmund Pendleton, 22 January 1795, *Writings*, 904.

Chapter 4
Corresponding Sentiments and Republican Letters

1. Immanuel Kant, "What is Enlightenment," in *On History*, trans. Lewis White Beck, Robert E. Anchor, Emil Fackenheim (New York: Macmillan, 1984), 3.

2. Susanna Rowson, *Charlotte Temple*, ed. Cathy Davidson (New York: Oxford University Press, 1986), 31.

3. Abigail Adams and John Adams, *The Book of Abigail and John: Selected Letters of the Adams Family: 1762–1784*, eds. L. H. Butterfield, Marc Friedlaender, and Mary-Jo Kline (Cambridge: Harvard University Press, 1975), 153.

4. Ibid., 121.

5. Ibid., 153.

6. Ibid., 139.

7. Ibid., 114.

8. On the relation between the press and the post, see Richard B. Kielbowicz, "The Press, Post Office, and Flow of News in the Early Republic," *Journal of the Early Republic* 3 (Fall 1983): 255–80.

9. Butterfield, Friedlaender, and Kline, introduction to Adams and Adams, *Selected Letters*, 7.

10. Adams and Adams, *Selected Letters*, 143.

11. For the canonical statement of consensus historiography, see Louis Hartz, *The Liberal Tradition in America: An Interpretation of American Political Thought Since the Revolution* (New York: Harcourt, Brace & Co., 1955). For sympathetic and critical responses to consensus history, see, respectively, Richard Hofstadter, *The Progressive Historians: Turner, Beard, Parrington* (Chicago: University of Chicago Press, 1968), 437–66; and Michael Denning, "Marxism and American Studies," *American Quarterly*, no. 38 (1986): 356–80. On the 1950s neo-liberals, see Thomas Schaub, *American Fiction in the Cold War* (Madison, Wis.: University of Wisconsin Press, 1991), 3–87.

12. Jürgen Habermas, *The Structural Transformation of the Public Sphere: An Inquiry into a Category of Bourgeois Society*, trans. Thomas Burger (Cambridge: MIT Press, 1989), 16–17.

13. In his early dispute with Andrew Bradford, a more established Philadelphia printer who also kept the post office, Franklin objects to both the general assumption that Bradford's news was better than his own, as well as to Bradford's unwillingness to allow him to employ postal riders in order to circulate his papers. "As he [Bradford] kept the Post Office, it was imagined he had better Opportunities of obtaining News, his paper had a better Distributor of Advertisements than mine, and therefore had many more, which was a profitable thing to him and a disadvantage to me. For tho' I did indeed receive and send Papers by the Post, yet the public Opinion was otherwise; for what I did send was by Bribing the Riders who took them privately: Bradford being unkind enough to forbid it." Benjamin Franklin, *Autobiography*, ed. J. A. Leo Lemay and P. M. Zall (New York: W. W. Norton, 1986), 55.

14. Cited in Kielbowicz, "The Press, Post Office, and Flow of News in the Early Republic," 258.

15. Habermas, *The Structural Transformation*, 43.

16. Ibid., 48–49.

17. Much ink has been spilled in arguments that emphasize either of these two extremes. In *The Structural Transformation*, for example, Habermas commits the second half of the book to a narrative of decline. Like the Frankfurt School studies out of which it evolves, *The Structural Transformation* charts a shift from publication to propaganda, from expressive to managed public opinion. In contrast, I argue in my second chapter that the utopian possibility of a public sphere open to structural democratization has co-existed alongside the dystopian possibility of a public sphere structured anti-democratically since the late eighteenth century. For the clearest restatement of Habermas's position, see his "Further Reflections on the Public Sphere" and "Concluding Remarks," in *Habermas and the Public Sphere*, ed. Craig Calhoun (Cambridge: MIT Press, 1992), 421–79.

18. Mary Favret, *Romantic Correspondence: Women, Politics and the Fiction of Letters* (Cambridge: Cambridge University Press, 1993), 17. Favret's insight parallels Habermas's reconstruction of the eighteenth-century literary public sphere:

"Subjectivity, as the innermost core of the private, was always already oriented to an audience (*Publicum*). The opposite of the intimateness whose vehicle was the written word was indiscretion and not publicity as such." Habermas, *The Structural Transformation*, 49.

19. Adams and Adams, *Selected Letters*, 125, 131.

20. Ibid., 123.

21. John Adams to James Sullivan, in *The Feminist Papers: From Adams to de Beauvoir*, ed. Alice Rossi (Boston: Northeastern University Press, 1988), 13–15. For a reading of Adams's letters concerning women's citizenship in the republic, see Joan R. Gundersen, "Independence, Citizenship, and the American Revolution" in *Signs* 13 (Autumn 1987): 63–64.

22. Adams and Adams, *Selected Letters*, 136.

23. On the ideologies of republican motherhood and domestic feminism, see Nancy Cott, *The Bonds of Womanhood: "Woman's" Sphere in New England, 1780–1835* (New Haven, Conn.: Yale University Press, 1977); Linda Kerber, *Women of the Republic: Intellect and Ideology in Revolutionary America* (New York: W. W. Norton, 1980); Mary Beth Norton, *Liberty's Daughters: The Revolutionary Experience of American Women, 1750–1800* (Boston: Little, Brown, 1980); Jan Lewis, "The Republican Wife: Virtue and Seduction in the Early Republic," *William and Mary Quarterly* 44 (1987): 689–721; Rosemarie Zagarri, "Morals, Manner, and the Republican Mother," *American Quarterly* 44, no. 2 (1992): 192–215.

24. On the legal history of "coverture," see Kerber, *Women of the Republic*, 137–55.

25. Habermas, *The Structural Transformation*, 56.

26. Mary Wollstonecraft, *Maria; or The Wrongs of Woman*, ed. Moira Ferguson (New York: W. W. Norton, 1975), 101.

27. Hannah Foster, *The Coquette; or, the History of Eliza Wharton*, ed. Cathy Davidson (New York: Oxford University Press, 1986), 38. All further references to *The Coquette* will appear in the text set off in parentheses.

28. The details of the following account of historical basis of *The Coquette* are taken from Cathy Davidson, *Revolution and the Word: The Rise of the Novel in the United States* (New York: Oxford University Press, 1988), 140–50. A similar account is provided in Frank Shuffelton, "Mrs. Foster's *Coquette* and the Decline of the Brotherly Watch," in *Studies in Eighteenth-Century Culture* 16 (1986), 211–24.

29. Quoted in Davidson, *Revolution and the Word*, 141.

30. Ibid., 141.

31. Ibid.

32. Ibid., 142–3.

33. Michael Warner, *The Letters of the Republic: Publication and the Public Sphere in Eighteenth-Century America* (Cambridge: Harvard University Press, 1990), 175.

34. Ibid., 174. For a similar account, see J. G. A. Pocock, "Virtue, rights, and manners: A model for historians of political thought" in *Virtue, Commerce, and History* (Cambridge: Cambridge University Press, 1985).

35. Ibid., 176. For a complementary argument concerning the shift from a republican model of literature that is communicative and participatory to a liberal model that is consumerist and proprietary, see Grantland S. Rice, *The Transformation of*

Authorship in America (Chicago: University of Chicago Press, 1997). Despite Rice's (odd) suggestion that Warner's (and Habermas's) reading of republicanism is too "optimistic," the contours of his analysis echo those of Warner's *The Letters of the Republic*.

36. Jürgen Habermas, *The Structural Transformation*, 50.

37. Ibid., 51.

38. Judith Butler, "The Force of Fantasy: Feminism, Mapplethorpe, and Discursive Excess," *differences: A Journal of Feminist Cultural Studies* 2, no. 2 (1990): 105.

39. In *Declaring Independence*, Jay Fliegelman similarly criticizes Warner for ignoring "the degree to which eighteenth-century print culture, unable to stand apart from the politics of sincerity and authenticity, rejected the notion of 'power embodied in special persons' only to redefine those special persons—not by office, but by sensibility." The difference between this analysis and my own is that Fliegelman sees an unresolvable antinomy between the scientific "authority of impersonality" and the affective "authority of sincerity" as structuring eighteenth-century republican culture, whereas I (not unlike Warner) am interested in the structures of "impersonality" that mediate and authorize different expressions of affect. Jay Fliegelman, *Declaring Independence: Jefferson, Natural Language and the Culture of Performance* (Stanford, Calif.: Stanford University Press, 1993), 128–29.

40. Jean-Baptiste de Boyer, *Therese Philosophe: Or, Memoires About the Affair Between Father Dirrag and Mademoiselle Eradice*, in Robert Darnton, *The Forbidden Best-Sellers of Pre-Revolutionary France* (New York: W. W. Norton, 1996), 296.

41. Ibid., 295–96.

42. Ibid., 296–97.

43. Ibid., 287. For a fuller exploration of this contradiction, see Robert Darton's reading in *The Forbidden Best-Sellers of Pre-Revolutionary France*, 85–114.

44. Jane Tompkins, *Sensational Designs* (New York: Oxford University Press, 1985).

45. At times, characters do distinguish between good and bad books. In a letter to Eliza, for example, Lucy Freeman/Sumner says that she has sent a few books, noting that "[t]hey are of the lighter kind of reading; yet perfectly chaste" (112). The point, however, is that Foster nowhere polemicizes against the novel as a genre.

46. Davidson: "The generic shift from sermon to novel in the Whitman/Wharton narrative entails a concomitant transformation of focus and philosophy. Set within a specific context of limiting marriage laws and restrictive social mores, the novel is less a story of the wages of sin than a study of the wages of marriage." Davidson, *Revolution and the Word*, 143. William Hill Brown's "moralistic" use of Whitman's story in his earlier novel *The Powers of Sympathy* should trouble Davidson's reading. Brown falls on the right side of Davidson's dualism between news and novel, but on the wrong side of that between men and women.

47. Ibid., 144.

48. Nina Baym, *Woman's Fiction: A Guide to Novels by and about Women in America, 1820–1870* (Ithaca, N.Y.: Cornell University Press, 1978), 51.

49. Davidson, *Revolution and the Word*, 148, 144.

50. de Boyer, *Therese Philosophe*, 250.

51. On this shift in the institution and ideology of marriage, see Michael Grossberg, *Governing the Hearth: Law and Family in Nineteenth-Century America* (Chapel

Hill, N.C.: University of North Carolina Press, 1985); and Nancy Cott, "Giving Character to Our Whole Civil Polity: Marriage and the Public Order in the Late Nineteenth Century," *U.S. History and Woman's History*, eds. Linda K. Kerber, Alice Kessler Harris, Kathryn Kish Skler (Chapel Hill, N.C.: University of North Carolina Press, 1995), 107–21.

52. Davidson, *Revolution and the Word*, 143, 123.

53. Baym, *Woman's Fiction*, 51.

54. Davidson, *Revolution and the Word*, 135.

55. Ibid., 142.

56. Though Davidson begins her chapter on early seduction narratives by noting that the "female reader" is no more "a monolith than is 'the female reader' today," her argument nevertheless hinges on the hermeneutic stability of that category: "Both were 'women,' a social construct as much as a biological entity." Ibid., 112.

57. Butler, "The Force of Fantasy," 106.

58. Ibid., 106–7. Butler's understanding of fantasy relies on Jean Laplanche and Jean-Bertrand Pontalis' reconstruction of a Freudian theory of fantasy in "Fantasy and the Origins of Sexuality," in *Formations of Fantasy* (New York: Methuen, 1986), 5–34.

59. Laqueur, *Making Sex: Body and Gender from the Greeks to Freud* (Cambridge: Harvard University Press, 1990); Londa Schiebinger, *The Mind Has No Sex?: Women in the Origins of Modern Science* (Cambridge: Harvard University Press, 1989).

60. Thomas Laqueur, *Making Sex*, 5–6. In *The Social Origins of Private Life*, Stephanie Coontz draws a similar conclusion not only in relation to gender, but also race and class: "Although specific explanations of inequality differed for women, Blacks, and later the poor, a common approach informed them all: rejection of the social necessity to *impose inequality* and insistence on the *natural* bases of *differences* in role and position." Stephanie Coontz, *The Social Origins on Private Life: A History of American Families, 1600–1900* (New York: Verso, 1988), 134. See also, Nina Baym, "Between Enlightenment and Victorian: Toward a Narrative of American Women Writers Writing History," *Critical Inquiry* 18, no. 1 (1991). For an analysis of transformations in gender ideology in late-eighteenth- and early-nineteenth-century France, see Joan Landes, *Women and the Public Sphere in the Age of the French Revolution* (Ithaca, N.Y.: Cornell University Press, 1988). On the historical debate between egalitarian and essentialist feminisms, see Denise Riley, "*Am I that Name?*": *Feminism and the Category of "Women" in History* (Minneapolis: University of Minnesota Press, 1988).

61. Quoted in Schiebinger, *The Mind Has No Sex?*, 189.

62. Benjamin Rush, *Lectures on the Mind*, eds. Eric T. Carlson, Jeffrey L. Wollock, Patricia S. Noel (Philadelphia: American Philosophic Society, 1981), 698.

63. Nancy Armstrong, *Desire and Domestic Fiction: A Political History of the Novel* (New York: Oxford University Press, 1987), 21; Robyn Weigman, *American Anatomies: Theorizing Race and Gender* (Durham, N.C.: Duke University Press, 1995), 179–202. While Habermas focuses on early novels' epistolary form, Armstrong focuses on their gendered content, arguing that they participate in the reduction of a political and potentially democratic model of the social contract to a depoliticized model of heterosexual complementarity.

64. For a critique of this type of essentialist feminism, see Diana Fuss, *Essentially Speaking: Feminism, Nature and Difference* (New York: Routledge, 1989).

65. For a reading of the novel along these lines, see Kristie Hamilton, "An Assault on the Will: Republican Virtue and the City in Hannah Webster Foster's *The Coquette*," *Early American Literature* 24, no. 2 (1989): 135–51.

66. Rowson, *Charlotte Temple*, 5. For an analysis of the threat embodied by these ambiguously feminine characters in British writings of the 1790s, see Claudia Johnson, *Equivocal Beings: Politics, Gender, and Sentimentality in the 1790s* (Chicago: University of Chicago Press, 1995).

67. Benjamin Rush, "Thoughts on Female Education, Accomodated to the Present State of Society, Manners, and Government in the United States of America," in *Essays on Education in the Early Republic*, ed. Frederick Rudolph (Cambridge, Mass.: Belknap, 1965), 27, 31.

68. Benjamin Rush, *Lectures on the Mind*, 697.

69. Ibid., 696–97.

70. G. J. Barker-Benfield, *The Culture of Sensibility: Sex and Society in Eighteenth-Century Britian* (Chicago: University of Chicago Press, 1992). Barker-Benfield's reconstruction of the "sentimentalizing process" alludes directly to Norbert Elias's study of the history of manners, *The Civilizing Process* (New York: Pantheon, 1978).

71. Immanuel Kant, *Critique of Judgment*, trans. J. H. Bernard (New York: Hafner, 1951), 38.

72. Ibid., 46–47.

73. Ibid., 136. By merging social and aesthetic forms of judgment, the awkward phrase "socio-aesthetic" glosses over the central distinction between abstraction and embodiment that pervades Kant's writings. I will return to a discussion of the radical implications of this distinction in my next chapter.

74. Ibid., 136.

75. Rush, *Lectures on the Mind*, 696. Later sentimental novels regularly draw on a similar language in order to police other forms of desire and identification as well. In Lydia Maria Child's *Hobomok*, for example, the heroine (Mary Conant) both gives an "involuntary shriek of terror" when Hobomok appears in the "circle" intended for her future husband, and later "shudders" at the idea of marrying "some stray Narraganset, or wandering Tarateen." As in *The Coquette*, this response naturalizes an ideological prohibition (racial intermarriage, in this case) by encoding it as an immediate reaction of Mary's body, while also making that natural(ized) response the mark of Mary's (refined) difference from other (cruder) women like her friend Sally Oldham who jokingly suggests the possibility of intermarriage to her. Lydia Maria Child, *Hobomok: A Tale of Early Times* (New Brunswick, N.J.: Rutgers University Press, 1992), 13, 19.

76. Barker-Benfield, *The Culture of Sensibility*, 206. For a present-day version of this argument, see Pierre Bourdieu, *Distinction: A Social Critique of the Judgment of Taste* (Cambridge: Harvard University Press, 1984).

77. Barker-Benfield, *The Culture of Sensibility*, 215–86. For similar analyses, see Karen Haltunnen, *Confidence Men and Painted Women: A Study of Middle-Class Culture in America, 1830–1860* (New Haven, Conn.: Yale University Press, 1982), 124–52, and Eva Cherniavsky, *That Pale Mother Rising: Sentimental Discourses and*

the Imitations of Motherhood in 19th-Century America (Bloomington, Ind.: Indiana University Press, 1995), 25–40. On the political history of eighteenth-century funeral practices, see Ann Fairfax Withington, *Toward a More Perfect Union: Virtue and the Formation of American Republics* (New York: Oxford University Press, 1991), 92–184.

78. Habermas, *The Structural Transformation*, 45. For similar accounts, see, Schiebinger, *The Mind Has No Sex?*, 10–36, and Landes, *Women and the Public Sphere*, 15–65.

79. Barker-Benfield, *The Culture of Sensibility*, 1–36, 287–395.

80. Paula Baker, "The Domestication of American Politics, 1780–1920," *The American Historical Review*, 89, no. 3 (1984): 620–47. Throughout the novel, Eliza and her sororal confidantes elaborate plans for public reform and, specifically, for the reform of women's position within the republic. As I have already suggested, the most obvious of these plans involves the elimination of self-avowed seducers like Sanford who, Lucy and Mrs. Richman agree, "ought to be banished from all virtuous society" (20, 132). "I look upon the vicious habits, and abandoned character of Major Sanford," Lucy writes, "to have more pernicious effects on society, than the perpetrations of the robber or assassin" (63). While Eliza disagrees with "banishment" as the means Lucy and Mrs. Richman suggest to achieve this end, she does agree with the end itself. In her final meeting with Sanford, for example, she insists that she wishes "not to be [his] accuser, but to be [his] reformer" (163) and, in this sense, even Eliza's rejection of Boyer can be seen as indicating her commitment to the project that nineteenth-century reformers would refer to as "moral suasion." Though she eventually views that rejection as a mistake, Eliza initially bases it upon her objection to "those contracted notions which confine virtue to a cell" (13). Politically more virtuous than the members of the morally "virtuous society" Mrs. Richman and Lucy inhabit, Eliza maintains a commitment to the public reform of Sanford, while her correspondents advocate her acceptance of Boyer and retreat into what Mrs. Richman refers to as the "safety" of the domestic sphere.

81. This distinction is also highlighted in the narrative context of Eliza's response. The letter itself focuses on Julia Granby's arrival as, in short, a manager of Eliza's actions and emotions, while Eliza's response to Lucy is immediately preceded by her assertion that she ought to follow her own "taste" in the company she keeps (in this case, Sanford's new wife).

82. Though it is unlikely, in other words, that Eliza envisions the managerial skills of "women" like the circus performers as solving the class and gender problems raised by the circus performers in the first place, nothing in the letter precludes this possibility. This contradiction is heightened elsewhere by Foster's use of a theatrical metaphor in organizing Eliza's story. "The drama is now closed!" writes Julia Granby in her final letter, "A tragical one indeed it has proved!" (161). Rather than dismissing theatrical representation altogether, Foster suggests that sympathetic "female managers" like Lucy, Julia, and herself ought to manage those representations. For a reading of *The Coquette* that emphasizes its failure to construct a "sorority of affection and care," see Frank Shuffelton, "Mrs. Foster's *Coquette* and the Decline of the Brotherly Watch," *Studies in Eighteenth-Century Culture* 16 (1986): 211–24.

83. Joan Scott, *Only Paradoxes to Offer: French Feminists and the Rights of Man* (Cambridge: Harvard University Press, 1996), 27, 52.

84. John Winthrop, "A Modell of Christian Charity," in *The Puritans in America: A Narrative Anthology*, eds. Alan Heimert and Andrew Delbanco (Cambridge: Harvard University Press, 1985), 83.

85. Harriet Beecher Stowe, *Uncle Tom's Cabin* (New York: Penguin, 1986), 624. While Eliza's conclusions differ, she consistently portrays her dilemma in similar terms. "My reason and judgment," she writes to Lucy, "entirely coincide with your opinion; but my fancy claims some share of the decision; and I cannot yet tell which will preponderate" (28). In *Toward a More Perfect Union*, Ann Withington refers to these two forms of authority (opinion and feeling) as "aesetic" and "aesthetic morality." Where the first is characteristic of Mrs. Wharton, the second encompasses both Eliza and her correspondents. Withington, *Toward a More Perfect Union*, 48–50.

86. For a gendered analysis of those differences, see Ruth Bloch's discussion of "virtue," in "The Gendered Meanings of Virtue in Revolutionary America," *Signs* 13, no. 1 (1987): 37–58.

87. In "The Assault on the Will," Hamilton similarly focuses on the epistolary form of Foster's novel as destabilizing its otherwise conservative ideology. Hamilton, "The Assault on the Will," 149. For a complementary reading of Rowson's *Charlotte Temple*, see Blythe Forcey, "*Charlotte Temple* and the End of Epistolarity," *American Literature* 63, no. 2 (1991).

88. Butler, "The Force of Fantasy," 119–20. This emphasis on the performative basis of gender (and any other) identity obviously echoes Butler's arguments in both *Gender Trouble* and *Bodies That Matter*. The advantage of this account is that the legal and political controversies surrounding Mapplethorpe force Butler to specify the legal and institutional contexts within which identities are performed.

89. Michel Foucault, *Herculine Barbin: Being the Recently Discovered Memoires of a Nineteenth-Century Hermaphrodite*, trans. Richard McDougall (New York: Pantheon, 1980), vii.

90. Hannah Foster, *The Boarding School; or, Lessons of a Preceptress to her Pupils* (Boston: I. Thomas and E. T. Andrews, 1798), 31–32.

91. Ibid., 33.

92. On the structure of epistolary discourse in the late eighteenth century, see "The Familiar Letter in the Eighteenth Century: Some Generalizations" in *The Familiar Letter in the Eighteenth Century*, eds. Howard Anderson, Philip B. Daghlin, Irvin Ehrenpries (Lawrence, Kans.: University of Kansas Press, 1966), 269–82. See also, Jerome Christensen, *Practicing Enlightenment: Hume and the Formation of a Literary Career* (Madison, Wis.: University of Wisconsin Press, 1987), 120–200.

93. Stowe, *Uncle Tom's Cabin*, 223.

94. Elizabeth Grosz, *Volatile Bodies: Toward a Corporeal Feminism* (Bloomington, Ind.: Indiana University Press, 1994), 23.

95. Wollstonecraft, *Maria; or The Wrongs of Woman*, 232.

96. Ibid., 148.

97. Ibid., 146.

98. Ibid., 103, 149.

99. Ibid., 149.

100. On divorce laws, see Kerber, *Women of the Republic*, 139–84. While Wollstonecraft's paternalistic judge reproduces the ideological underpinnings of this separation of virtue and affect when he asks "What virtuous woman thought of her

feelings," Maria critiques the effects of that separation in both the legal and the literary fields. "When novelists and moralists," she writes, "praise as a virtue, a woman's coldness of constitution, and want of passion . . . I am disgusted." Where Lucy's disgust trains readers to focus their attention away from the circus performers' indecorous bodies, Maria's disgust produces an antithetical effect. It serves as a reminder of the embodied and exclusive nature of such refined judgments of taste.

101. Michel Foucault, *The History of Sexuality*, trans., Robert Hurley (New York: Vintage, 1990), 100–102.

102. Harriet Jacobs, *Incidents in the Life of a Slave Girl* (Cambridge: Harvard University Press, 1987), 54. On Fanny Fern's mobilization of the category "woman" in *Ruth Hall*, see Lauren Berlant, *The Female Woman: Fanny Fern and the Form of Sentiment*, American Literary History 3, no. 3 (1991): 429–54.

103. Stowe, *Uncle Tom's Cabin*, 495.

104. Shirley Samuels, introduction to *The Culture of Sentiment: Race, Gender, and Sentimentality in Nineteenth-Century America*, ed. Shirley Samuels (New York: Oxford University Press, 1992), 4.

Chapter 5
Masochism and Male Sentimentalism

1. Abigail Adams and John Adams, *The Book of Abigail and John: Selected Letters of the Adams Family, 1762–1784* (Cambridge: Harvard University Press, 1975), 123.

2. Leopold von Sacher-Masoch, *Venus in Furs*, in *Masochism*, trans. Jean McNeil (New York: Zone, 1989), 271.

3. Gilles Deleuze, *Coldness and Cruelty*, in *Masochism*, 92. On the contractual basis of masochism, see Walter Benn Michaels, *The Gold Standard and the Logic of Naturalism* (Berkeley, Calif.: University of California Press, 1987), 113–36.

4. Kaja Silverman, *Male Subjectivity on the Margins* (New York: Routledge, 1992), 206. My reading of Sacher-Masoch is admittedly teleological and, as such, ignores a more subversive reading that would stress the tenuousness of the connection between the concluding moral and the tale itself. As will become clear, my more serious objection to analyses of male masochism like Silverman's is that their psychoanalytic (Freudian/Lacanian) grounding dictates that the "social order" be divided into male and female. Within such an analysis, any other social antagonisms (race, class, ethnicity, to name three) vanish, as well as any possibility of a move away from the heterosexist ideology of gender difference. Male masochism may be an example of "male subjectivity at the margins," but it is also evidence of how, as a text, the ideology of gender difference inscribes its own margins. On the complicity between "dominant" and "submissive heterosexual men" in American Renaissance writings, see Christopher Newfield, "The Politics of Male Suffering: Masochism and Hegemony in the American Renaissance," *differences: A Journal of Feminist Cultural Studies* 1, no. 3 (1989): 55–87.

5. von Sacher-Masoch, *Venus in Furs*, 217.

6. Hawthorne's well-known damning appears in a letter to William Ticknor on January 19, 1855. See Nathaniel Hawthorne, *Centenary Edition of the Works of Nathaniel Hawthorne*, vol. 17 (Columbus, Ohio: Ohio State University Press, 1987), 304. Howells's less-known submission appears in "The Man of Letters as a Man of

Business": "The man of letters must make up his mind that in the United States the fate of the book is in the hands of the women. . . . If they do not always know what is good, they do know what pleases them, and it is useless to quarrel with their decisions, for there is no court of appeal from them. To go from them to the men would be going from a higher to a lower court." William Dean Howells, "The Man of Letters and the Man of Business," in *Criticism and Fiction and Other Essays* (New York: New York University Press, 1959), 305–6.

7. Leslie Fiedler, *Love and Death in the American Novel* (New York: Dell, 1960), 8, 31.

8. Ann Douglas, *The Feminization of American Culture* (New York: Anchor, 1988), 124. Read with this in mind, the Douglas-Tompkins debate over the political impact of women's sentimental writings is a debate between two readings of the masochistic potential inscribed within the ideology of republican motherhood. For Douglas, that masochistic potential is never realized; for Tompkins, it is realized though the "sentimental power" of those texts. Jane Tompkins, *Sensational Designs: The Cultural Work of American Fiction, 1789–1860* (Oxford: Oxford University Press, 1985), 122–85. On the Douglas-Tompkins debate, see Laura Wexler, "Tender Violence: Literary Eavesdropping, Domestic Fiction, and Educational Reform," in *The Culture of Sentiment: Race, Gender and Sentimentality in Nineteenth-Century American Culture* (New York: Oxford University Press, 1992), 9–38.

9. Ibid., 42.

10. Richard von Krafft-Ebbing, *Psychopathia Sexualis*, trans. Franklin S. Klaf (London: Staples, 1965), 111.

11. William Dunlap, *The Life of Charles Brockden Brown* (Philadelphia: James P. Parke, 1815), 2:100.

12. Bill Christophersen, *The Apparition in the Glass: Charles Brockden Brown's American Gothic* (Athens, Ga.: University of Georgia Press, 1993), 149.

13. Fiedler, *Love and Death in the American Novel*, 89.

14. Norman S. Grabo, *The Coincidental Art of Charles Brockden Brown* (Chapel Hill, N.C.: University of North Carolina Press, 1983), 129.

15. Paul Witherington's earlier, positive appraisal of Brown's late novels seems to me a less significant exception. In contrast to other critics' contempt for *Clara Howard* and *Jane Talbot*, Witherington's New Critical sensibilities allow him to applaud the formal coherence of Brown's "other novels." But his analysis merely repeats the critical commonplace that the novels "show the victories of social normalcy over individuality and of order over eccentricity and indecisiveness." Paul Witherington, "Brockden Brown's Other Novels: *Clara Howard* and *Jane Talbot*," *Nineteenth-Century Fiction* 29 (December 1975): 258. Fritz Fleischmann's synthetic account of Brown's career reaches a similar conclusion. Though Brown never abandoned either his "pursuit of fiction" or his "feminist impulse," his late novels, Fleischmann suggests, are marked by his growing awareness of the "impossibility of making a living as a writer of fiction . . . an unremunerative career as a novelist was no way to satisfy the demands of a family." Fritz Fleischmann, "Charles Brockden Brown: Feminism in Fiction," in *American Novelists Revisited: Essays in Feminist Criticism*, ed. Fritz Fleischmann (Boston: G. K. Hall, 1982), 36.

16. Sidney Krause, "*Clara Howard* and *Jane Talbot*: Godwin on Trial," in *Critical Essays on Charles Brockden Brown*, ed. Bernard Rosenthal (Boston: G. K. Hall, 1981), 187.

17. Ibid., 199.

18. Ibid., 189, 199.

19. I stress *theoretically* gendered and ungendered because both virtue and reason—key terms of republican and democratic political theory—are *historically* gendered as masculine. At the same time, the historical association of virtue and reason with masculinity can be established only by disavowing the ideal of ungendered democratic citizenship which informs the republic of letters. On the political history of this disavowal, see Mark Kahn, *On the Man Question: Gender and Civic Virtue in America* (Philadelphia: Temple University Press, 1991).

20. Brown's naming of his protagonist Hartley alludes to MacKenzie's Harley, as well as his own Huntly. *The Man of Feeling* along with Lawrence Sterne's *A Sentimental Journey* provide the two best-known examples of the eighteenth-century "man of feeling." Read straight, they demonstrate the non-contradiction between sentiment and masculinity in the period, at least for middle-class men; read parodically, they still resist the nineteenth-century equation of sentiment and femininity. Even as parodies, they undercut the figure of the sentimental male not by accusing him of gender cross-identification, but by exposing the illicit, unrefined, and erotic sensibility that lies beneath his claims to refinement and moral discernment. A significant turning point in this cultural tradition appears in William Godwin's *Fleetwood: or, The New Man of Feeling*, published four years after *Clara Howard* in 1805. For the best reading of the eighteenth-century male sentimentalist, see G. J. Barker-Benfield, *The Culture of Sensibility: Sex and Society in Eighteenth-Century Britain* (Chicago: University of Chicago Press, 1992), 104–53.

21. Quoted in Jay Fleigelman, *Declaring Independence: Jefferson, Natural Language and the Culture of Performance* (Stanford, Calif.: Stanford University Press, 1993), 61.

22. Grabo, *The Coincidental Art of Charles Brockden Brown*, 132.

23. Charles Brockden Brown, *Clara Howard; In a Series of Letters* (Kent, Ohio: Kent State University Press, 1986), 43. All further references to *Clara Howard* will appear as page numbers in parentheses in the text.

24. Fleischmann, "Charles Brockden Brown: Feminism in Fiction," 32.

25. Margaret Fuller, *Papers on Art and Literature*, in *Critical Essays on Charles Brockden Brown*, 63. Lillie Demming Loshe, *The Early American Novel* (New York: Frederick Unger, 1958), 48.

26. Henry James, *The Bostonians* (New York: Vintage, 1991), 418.

27. Krause convincingly argues that the problems of moral decision making that Brown explores in both *Clara Howard* and *Jane Talbot* are directly influenced by Godwin. Indeed, one of the principle characters in the later novel speaks directly of Godwin's *Political Justice* as a "fascinating book," but one that deploys "the art of the grand deceiver; the fatal art of carrying the worst poison under the name and appearance of wholesome food." Charles Brockden Brown, *Jane Talbot: A Novel* (Kent, Ohio: Kent State University Press, 1986), 228. I have no interest in establishing a similarly direct connection between Brown and Kant (though Brown is clearly aware of German Enlightenment and Romantic culture, as evinced in the title of *Wieland*, his attacks on the "Bavarian Illuminati," etc.). Rather, what I am interested in is their shared exploration of the republican principles of self-abstraction, principles that structure the writings of far more authors than Godwin, Brown, and Kant. For a reading of Brown's *Arthur Mervyn* along these lines, see Michael Warner, *The Let-*

ters of the Republic: Publication and the Public Sphere in the Eighteenth-Century America (Cambridge: Harvard University Press, 1990), 151–76.

28. Immanuel Kant, *The Critique of Practical Reason*, trans. Lewis White Beck (New York: Macmillan, 1985), 77.

29. Ibid., 82.

30. Ibid., 126.

31. Ibid., 81.

32. Ibid., 88.

33. Ibid., 156–57.

34. Michael Warner, "The Mass Public and the Mass Subject," in *Habermas and the Public Sphere*, ed. Craig Calhoun (Cambridge: MIT Press, 1992), 382, 383.

35. Kant, 151–52.

36. Ernst Bloch, *Natural Law and Human Dignity*, trans. Dennis J. Schmidt (Cambridge: MIT Press, 1987), 103.

37. Ibid., 105.

38. Gilles Deleuze, *Coldness and Cruelty*, 63. On Sacher-Masoch's relation to Bachofen, see Deleuze, 47–55.

39. Sigmund Freud, "The Economic Problem of Masochism," *General Psychological Theory* (New York: Collier, 1963), 198.

40. Nina Baym, "Between Enlightenment and Victorian: Toward a Narrative of American Women Writers Writing History," *Critical Inquiry* 18, no. 1 (Autumn 1991): 38.

41. Ibid., 41.

42. Joan Scott, *"Only Paradoxes to Offer": French Feminists and the Rights of Man* (Cambridge: Harvard University Press, 1996), 4.

43. Martha Minow, *Making All the Difference: Inclusion, Exclusion, and the American Law* (Ithaca, N.Y.: Cornell University Press, 1990).

44. Judith Sargent Murray, *The Gleaner* (Schenectady, N.Y.: Union College Press, 1992), 805.

45. Judith Sargent Murray, *The Story of Margaretta*, in *Selected Writings of Judith Sargent Murray*, ed. Sharon M. Harris (New York: Oxford University Press, 1995), 215, 216.

46. Murray, *The Gleaner*, 805.

47. Charles Brockden Brown, *Alcuin: A Dialogue* (Kent, Ohio: Kent State University Press, 1987), 19.

48. Ibid., 17.

49. Thomas Laqueur, *Making Sex: Body and Gender from the Greeks to Freud* (Cambridge: Harvard University Press, 1990), 156–57. See also Gilbert Herdt, ed., *Third Sex, Third Gender: Beyond Sexual Dimorphism in Culture and History* (New York: Zone, 1994).

50. Brown, *Alcuin*, 18.

51. Ibid., 32.

52. Ibid., 44.

53. Ibid., 39.

54. Ibid., 43. Nor does this example prove his point, since there is no reason that a mother (or sister or brother or friend) could not provide the son with the razor as well. What the passage does suggest is Brown's intention of invoking the prohibition

against "sensual" relations between men (or women) only in order to suggest the irrationality of that prohibition as well.

55. Ibid., 40–42, 43–46, 46–49.

56. Ibid., 47.

57. Ibid., 66.

58. Murray, *The Story of Margaretta*, 205.

59. Brown, *Alcuin*, 66.

60. Michael Grossberg, *Governing the Hearth: Law and the Family in Nineteenth-Century America* (Chapel Hill, N.C.: University of North Carolina Press, 1985); Nancy Cott, "Giving Character to Our Whole Civil Polity: Marriage and the Public Order in the Late Nineteenth Century," *U.S. History as Woman's History*, eds. Linda K. Kerber, Alice Kessler Harris, Kathryn Kish Skler (Chapel Hill, University of North Carolina Press, 1995), 107–21.

61. The novelty of this assumption is notable. As late as 1928, Noah Webster's *Dictionary* defined "sex" and "sexual" in terms that are associated today with gender: "Sex: The distinction between male and female"; "Sexual: Pertaining to sex . . . as *sexual* characteristics; *sexual* intercourse, connection or commerce." "Sensualize," in contrast, refers to what we call "sexuality": "Sensualize: to make sensual; to subject to the love of sensual pleasure; to debase by carnal gratifications; as *sensualized* by pleasure." The subsequent equation of the two terms marks one of the points of origin of the modern reduction of sensuality to (hetero)sexuality. Noah Webster, *American Dictionary of the English Language* (San Francisco: Foundation for American Christian Education, 1987).

62. Brown, *Alcuin*, 32.

63. "The region is far indeed, but a twinkling is sufficient for the longest of journeys." Ibid., 44.

64. Mary Wollstonecraft, *Mary: A Fiction*, in *A Mary Wollstonecraft Reader* (New York: Mentor, 1983), 126. This reading of *Alcuin* appears most notably in Cathy Davidson, "The Manner and Matter of Charles Brockden Brown's *Alcuin*," in *Critical Essays on Charles Brockden Brown*, 71–86, and in Fritz Fleischmann, "Charles Brockden Brown: Feminism in Fiction," in *American Novelists Revisited: Essays in Feminist Criticism*, ed. Fritz Fleischmann (Boston: G. K. Hall, 1982), 6–14.

65. Brown, *Alcuin*, 53.

66. "For the time being," Sacher-Masoch concludes, "there is only one alternative; to be the hammer or the anvil." This conclusion figures gender equality as both desirable *and* unrealistic through the axiomatic assertion, here, of sexual antagonism and, elsewhere, of sexual complementarity.

67. Mary Wollstonecraft, *Vindication of the Rights of Woman* (New York: Penguin, 1982), 84.

68. Niklas Luhmann, *Love as Passion: The Codification of Intimacy*, trans. Jeremy Gaines and Doris L. Jones (Oxford, England: Polity, 1986), 132.

69. Luhmann's incisive analysis fails to account for the logic of sexual difference that structures the history of romantic love and, in doing so, reinscribes that logic as nonpolitical. *Love as Passion* could be referred to more accurately as *Love as Heterosexual Passion*. Critics of *Clara Howard* repeat this oversight when they equate Clara's resistance to Edward's "passion" with a resistance to all forms of sensuality. On the relations among sex, gender, and sexuality in this context, see Michael

Warner, "Homo-Narcissism; or, Heterosexuality," *Engendering Men*, eds. Joseph A. Boone and Michael Cadden (New York: Routledge, 1990), 190–206. For a collection of more general critiques (including critiques of Luhman), see Michael Warner, ed., *Queer Politics and Social Theory* (Minneapolis: University of Minnesota Press, 1993).

70. The term "hetero-critical" appears in Carla Kaplan's "Reading Feminist Readings: Recuperative Reading and the Silent Heroine of Feminist Criticism," in *Listening to Silences: New Essays in Feminist Criticism*, ed. Elaine Hedges and Shelley Fisher Fishkin (New York: Oxford University Press, 1994), 183.

71. Mary Ryan, *The Empire of the Mother: American Writing about Domesticity, 1830–1860* (New York: Harrington Park, 1982), 129–30.

72. Margaret Fuller, "The Great Lawsuit," in *The Feminist Papers*, ed. Alice S. Rossi (Boston: Northeastern University Press, 1973), 179.

73. Ibid., 182. On the tension between feminism and abolitionism, see Karen Sanchez-Eppler, "Bodily Bonds: The Intersecting Rhetorics of Feminism and Abolition," in *The Culture of Sentiment: Race, Gender and Sentimentality in Nineteenth-Century America*, ed. Shirley Samuels (New York: Oxford University Press, 1992) 92–114.

74. Nina Baym, "Melodramas of Beset Manhood: How Theories of American Fiction Exclude Women Authors" in *The New Feminist Criticism*, ed. Elaine Showalter (New York: Pantheon, 1985), 77.

75. Jane Tompkins, *Sensational Designs*, 122–85, and Gillian Brown, *Domestic Individualism: Imagining the Self in Nineteenth-Century America* (Berkeley, Calif.: University of California Press, 1990), 135–69.

76. This passage appears in Samuels's 1992 introduction to the collection of essays *The Culture of Sentiment*. While Samuels emphasizes an expansive definition of sentimentalism as a "project about the nation's bodies and the national body," and while the essays themselves are concerned with logics of embodiment other than gender, the vast majority of those essays focus on women authors. See Shirley Samuels, introduction to *The Culture of Sentiment*, 6, 3, and Nina Baym, *Woman's Fiction: A Guide to Novels by and about Women in America, 1820–1870* (Ithaca, N.Y.: Cornell University Press, 1978).

77. Baym, *Woman's Fiction*.

78. Pursuing this line of argumentation, Berlant writes that the complaint's "sentimental abstraction of the values 'woman' from the realm of material relations meant that intersections among classes, races and different ethnic groups also appear to dissolve in their translation into sentimental semiosis." This "dissolve" of racial, class, and ethnic identifications into a scene of gender identification also structures the male complaint. Lauren Berlant, "The Female Woman: Fanny Fern and the Form of Sentiment," in *The Culture of Sentiment*, 268, 269. See also, Berlant, "The Female Complaint," *Social Text*, no. 19/20 (Fall 1988): 237–59.

79. Judith Butler, *Gender Trouble: Feminism and the Subversion of Identity* (New York: Routledge, 1990).

80. I am referring specifically to chapter 52 of *Ruth Hall* in which Fern satirizes Mr. Skiddy's desire to escape from his wife's dominance by going West, and to chapter 17 of *Huck Finn* in which Twain satirizes Emmeline Grangerford's sentimental poetry. Fanny Fern, *Ruth Hall and Other Writings* (New Brunswick, N.J.: Rutgers

University Press, 1986) 103–109; Mark Twain, *Adventures of Huckleberry Finn* (New York: W. W. Norton, 1977), 79–86.

81. Monique Wittig, in "The Straight Mind," in *The Straight Mind and Other Essays* (Boston: Beacon, 1992), 31. On Wittig's retrieval of Enlightenment categories for feminist theory, see Linda Zerilli, "The Trojan Horse of Universalism: Language as 'War Machine' in the Writings of Monique Wittig," in *The Phantom Public Sphere*, ed. Bruce Robbins (Minneapolis: University of Minnesota Press, 1993), 142–73.

82. For examples of such arguments that focus specifically on a re-evaluation of the category of sentimentalism, see James Creech, *Closet Writing/Gay Reading: The Case of Melville's Pierre* (Chicago: University of Chicago Press, 1993), 44–61; Julie Ellison, "The Gender of Transparency: Masculinity and the Conduct of Life," *American Literary History*, 4, no. 4 (Winter 1992); 584–606; Glenn Hendler, "Tom Sawyer's Masculinity," *Arizona Quarterly* 49, no. 4 (Winter, 1993): 33–59; D. A. Miller, *The Novel and the Police* (Berkeley, Calif.: University of California Press, 1988), 192–220; Eve Sedgwick, *Epistemology of the Closet* (Berkeley, Calif.: University of California Press, 1990), 131–81. Along this path, Alcuin's guide again proves instructive. Far from dismissing the political significance of the body, his form of rationalism allows him to see through and beyond the self-evidence of sexual difference: "The influence on my character which flows from my age, from the number and quality of my associates, from the nature of my dwelling place, as sultry or cold, fertile or barren, level or diversified, the art that I cultivate, the extent or frequency of my excursions cannot be of small moment. In comparison with this, the qualities which are to be ascribed to my sex are unworthy of being mentioned." Brown, *Alcuin*, 45–46.

Chapter 6
Obscene Publics

1. Jean-Baptiste de Boyer, *Therese Philosophe: Or, Memoires About the Affair Between Father Dirrag and Mademoiselle Eradice*, in Robert Darton, *The Forbidden Best-Sellers of Pre-Revolutionary France* (New York: W. W. Norton, 1996), 296.

2. Harriet Jacobs, *Incidents in the Life of a Slave Girl*, ed. Jean Fagan Yellin (Cambridge: Harvard University Press, 1987), 52. (All further references to *Incidents* will appear in parentheses in the text.)

3. Valerie Smith, "'Loopholes of Retreat': Architecture and Ideology in Harriet Jacobs's *Incidents in the Life of a Slave Girl*," in *Reading Black, Reading Feminist: A Critical Anthology* (New York: Penguin, 1990), 212–26; Michelle Burnham, "Loopholes of Resistance: Harriet Jacobs's Slave Narrative and the Critique of Agency in Foucault," *Arizona Quarterly* 49, no. 2 (Summer 1993): 53–73. For similar readings, see Lindon Barrett, "African-American Slave Narratives: Literacy, the Body, Authority." *American Literary History* 7, no. 3 (Fall 1995): 415–42, and Harryette Mullen, "Runaway Tongues: Resistant Orality in *Uncle Tom's Cabin, Our Nig, Incidents in the Life of a Slave Girl*, and *Beloved*," in *The Culture of Sentiment: Race, Gender and Sentimentality in Nineteenth-Century American Culture*, ed. Shirley Samuels (New York: Oxford University Press, 1992), 244–64.

4. See, for example, Jacobs's descriptions of Southern Christianity (74–75), her Aunt Nancy's funeral (146–47), and even the Flint's silver candlelabra (11).

5. For critical accounts of this generic shift, see Jean Fagan Yellin, introduction to *Incidents*, xiii–xxxiv, and Hazel Carby, *Reconstructing Womanhood: The Emergence of the Afro-American Woman Novelist* (New York: Oxford University Press, 1987), 40–61.

6. Lauren Berlant, "The Queen Goes to Washington City: Harriet Jacobs, Frances Harper, Anita Hill," *American Literature* 65, no. 3 (Sept. 1993): 553, 564.

7. For critical accounts of Jacobs's strategic use of silence, see Carla Kaplan, "Narrative Contracts and Emancipatory Readers: *Incidents in the Life of a Slave Girl*," *Yale Journal of Criticism* 6, no. 1 (1993): 93–119; Joanna Braxton and Sharon Zuber, "Silences in Harriet 'Linda Brent' Jacobs's *Incidents in the Life of a Slave Girl*," in *Listening to Silences: New Essays in Feminist Criticism*, ed. Elaine Hedges and Shelley Fisher Fishkin (New York: Oxford University Press, 1994), 146–55; and Eva Cherniavsky, *That Pale Mother Rising: Sentimental Discourses and the Imitation of Motherhood in 19th-Century America* (Bloomington, Ind.: Indiana University Press, 1996), 92–111.

8. Like other nineteenth-century sentimentalists, Jacobs writes through the social and political contradictions that Mary Kelley condenses in the phrase "literary domesticity." The fact the Jacobs lacks a secure domestic space only heightens those contradictions since she must construct, within *Incidents*, a simulacrum of the privacy that her publication then betrays. See Mary Kelley, *Public Stage/Private Woman: Literary Domesticity in Nineteenth-Century America* (New York: Oxford University Press, 1984). For a quick history of domestic anti-slavery fiction, see Mary Ryan, *The Empire of the Mother: American Writings about Domesticity: 1830–1860* (New York: Harrington Park, 1982), 115–41.

9. David Reynolds, *Beneath the American Renaissance: The Subversive Imagination in the Age of Emerson and Melville* (Cambridge: Harvard University Press, 1989), 214.

10. Ibid., 211–24.

11. *Revelations of a Slave Smuggler* (Northbrook, Ill.: Metro Books, 1972), viii.

12. Kaplan, "Narrative Contracts and Emancipatory Readers," 115.

13. Walter Kendrick, *The Secret Museum: Pornography in Modern Culture* (New York: Penguin, 1987), 31. Here I am differing from Kendrick who insists that the term "pornography" names "an argument, not a thing." Kendrick emphasizes the "argumentative" character of all descriptions of pornography in order to underline the arbitrariness of any absolute distinction between publicizable and obscene representations. While I accept Kendrick's general point (as well as his distinction between pornography and obscenity), I want to highlight the centrality of the (continuously shifting) boundary between public and private spheres within any democratic polity.

14. On this point, see Darton, *The Forbidden Best-Sellers of Pre-Revolutionary France*, 85–114.

15. Lynn Hunt, ed., *The Invention of Pornography: Obscenity and the Origins of Modernity, 1500–1800* (New York: Zone, 1993), 15; Beverley Brown, "Troubled Vision: Legal Understandings of Obscenity," *new formations*, no. 10 (Spring 1993): 29–44; Walter Kendrick, *The Secret Museum*.

16. Kendrick, *The Secret Museum*, 126. For an account of the historical interface between moral and market economies, see Charles Sellers, *The Market Revolution:*

Jacksonian America, 1815–1846 (New York: Oxford University Press, 1991), esp. 237–68, 364–95.

17. Donald Downs, *The New Politics of Pornography* (Chicago: University of Chicago Press, 1989), 9. See also, Cindy Patton, *Fatal Advice: How Safe-Sex Education Went Wrong* (Durham, N.C.: Duke University Press, 1996), 139–55. On the centrality of privacy within democratic political theory, see Jean L. Cohen, "Democracy, Difference, and the Right of Privacy," in *Democracy and Difference: Contesting the Boundaries of the Political*, ed. Selya Benhabib (Princeton, N.J.: Princeton University Press, 1996), 187–217.

18. *Commonwealth v. Sharpless* in *Sergeant & Rawle's Reports* (Philadelphia: Kay & Brothers, 1872), 2:91–92. (All further references to *Sharpless* will appear in parentheses in the text.)

19. Peter Stallybras and Allon White, *The Politics and Poetics of Transgression* (Ithaca, N.Y.: Cornell University Press, 1986), 100–118.

20. Isaiah Berlin, "Two Concepts of Liberty," in *Four Essays on Liberty* (Oxford: Oxford University Press, 1969). See also, Nancy Rosenblum, *Another Liberalism: Romanticism and the Reconstruction of Liberal Thought* (Cambridge: Harvard University Press, 1987), 59–82. On this distinction between positive and negative liberty within the context of republicanism, see Luc Ferry and Alain Renaut, *From the Rights of Man to the Republican Idea*, trans. Franklin Philip (Chicago: University of Chicago Press, 1992), esp. 110–28.

21. Jürgen Habermas, *The Structural Transformation of the Public Sphere: A Category of Bourgeois Society*, trans. Thomas Burger (Cambridge: MIT Press, 1989), 134.

22. Lynn Hunt, "Pornography and the French Revolution," in *The Invention of Pornography*, 305, 330.

23. Randolph Trumbach, "Erotic Fantasy and Male Libertinism in Enlightenment England," in *The Invention of Pornography*, 253.

24. John Cleland, *Memoirs of Fanny Hill* (New York: Penguin, 1965), 15. For a modern version of this type of argument, see Laura Kipnis, "(Male) Desire and (Female) Disgust: Reading *Hustler*," in *Cultural Studies*, ed. Lawrence Grossberg, Cary Nelson, Paula Treichler (New York: Routledge, 1992), 373–91.

25. Hunt, "Pornography and the French Revolution," 302, 335. The final line of Hunt's essay suggests a less totalizing interpretation: "Pornography would continue to have political and social meanings, as it still has political and social meanings, but these would now be less intentional and much more subtle, even as the genre became more widely visible" (339). Despite this qualification, Hunt's understanding of morality as apolitical renders those meanings largely invisible. The (non)political origins of obscenity coincide with the historical origins of modernity only if one equates the latter with the rise of liberalism.

26. The exception that proves the rule is a novel published in 1795 which merges sentimentalism and pornography by "reducing the explicit sexual descriptions to a minimum and embedding them in a narrative." Lynn Hunt, "Pornography and the French Revolution," 338. The best historical account of the early eighteenth-century origins of sentimentalism is G. J. Barker-Benfield's *The Culture of Sensibility: Sex and Society in Eighteenth-Century Britain* (Chicago: University of Chicago Press, 1992). Jonathan Elmer provides a similar context, and draws parallel conclusions concerning the generic interdependence of sensationalism and sentimentalism in *Reading at*

the Social Limit: Affect, Mass Culture and Edgar Allan Poe (Stanford, Calif.: Stanford University Press, 1995), 93–125.

27. Marquis de Sade, "Reflections on the Novel," in *The 120 Days of Sodom and Other Writings*, trans. Richard Seaver (New York: Grove, 1966), 106.

28. In *Leaves of Grass* (1855), Whitman both parodies and transforms sentimental anti-obscenity discourse: "Through me forbidden voices, / Voices of sexes and lusts. . . . Voices veiled, and I remove the veil, / Voices indecent by me clarified and transfigured. / I do not press my finger across my mouth, / I keep as delicate around the bowels as around the head and heart, / Copulation is no more rank to me than death is." Walt Whitman, *Leaves of Grass* (New York: Vintage, 1992), 50–51. For a reading of Whitman's contradictory investment in contemporary (sexual) reform movements, see Michael Moon, *Disseminating Whitman: Revision and Corporality in Leaves of Grass* (Cambridge: Harvard University Press, 1991). Originally titled "Last Supper at Uncle Tom's Cabin Featuring 52 Handsome Nudes," the final act of Jones's performance concludes with all of the dancers (including those from the local community) naked on stage. *"The Promised Land,"* Jones writes, "with its hordes of naked flesh coming wave after wave into the footlights, pubic patches, pert breasts, sagging breasts, wrinkled knees, blissful eyes, furtive expressions of shame, is a visual manifestation of my profound sense of belonging. This was my portrait of us. All of us. And this is who I am too. One of us. It was my battle to disavow any identity as a dying outcast and to affirm our commonality. In it, some one thousand people from thirty cities stood naked, took a bow, and said, 'We are not afraid.'" Bill T. Jones, *Last Night on Earth* (New York: Pantheon, 1995), 223. On sentimentality in Jones's performance, see Jacqueline Shea Murphy, "Unrest and Uncle Tom: Bill T. Jones/Arnie Zane Dance Company's *Last Supper at Uncle Tom's Cabin/The Promised Land,"* in *Bodies of the Text: Dance as Theory, Literature as Dance*, eds. Ellen W. Goellner and Jacqueline Shea Murphy (New Brunswick, N.J.: Rutgers University Press, 1994), 81–106.

29. In 1836, the Mississippi legislature enacted a resolution literalizing this exclusion of slavery from public debate through an analogy with domesticity: "We hold discussions upon the subject of slavery as equally impertinent with discussions of our relations, wives, and children." By encoding both slavery and domesticity as "private" concerns, this resolution sets the stage for Jacobs's later merging of the slave narrative and the sentimental novel. Quoted in Stephanie Coontz, *The Social Origins of Private Life: A History of American Families, 1600–1900* (New York: Verso, 1988), 200. Despite Northern Whig objections, petitions concerning slavery were also tabled by the U.S. House of Representatives in 1836. See Sellers, *The Market Revolution*, 396–427.

30. Eve Kosofsky Sedgwick, "Privilege of Unknowing: Diderot's *The Nun,"* in *Tendencies* (Durham, N.C.: Duke University Press, 1993), 23–51.

31. As Eva Cherniavsky points out, the later dialogue between Jacobs and her daughter in which the latter allows the content of her mother's "confession" to remain unspoken further locates Jacobs (and her daughter) as sentimental subjects (188–89). While Cherniavsky accurately reads the "unspoken" within this exchange as a denial of any paternal legacy on the part of Jacobs's daughter ("a refusal of object status that is not, however, an accession to discursive subjectivity"), I would argue that the "unspoken" intertwines the (patriarchal) history of the slavery with the de-

nial to slave women of the sexual privacy central to both liberal subjectivity and sentimental ideology. "I loved the dear girl better," Jacobs concludes, "for the delicacy she had manifested towards her unfortunate mother" (189). In this context, Child's editorial advice to eliminate a final chapter on John Brown and to group the various incidents of slaveholding cruelty within a single chapter takes on added significance (244). The graphic descriptions of slaveholders' physical violence in the latter chapter spiral inevitably toward a description of sexual corruption in which a slaveholder's daughter chooses "one of the meanest slaves" on her father's plantation to be the "father of his first grandchild" (52). "No pen," Jacobs writes, "can give an adequate description of the all-pervading corruption produced by slavery" (51). "Sketches of Neighboring Slaveholders" adheres to sentimental conventions by locating a nondescription of sexuality at the center of the narrative, while the new concluding chapter follows the same conventions by ending with Jacobs's reflections on her grandmother's legacy. See Cherniavsky, *That Pale Mother Rising*, 104–5.

32. Michel Foucault, *The History of Sexuality*, trans. Robert Hurley (New York: Vintage, 1990), 103.

33. Downs, *The New Politics of Pornogaphy*, 26.

34. Clor's essay is entitled "Obscenity and Public Morality" and was published, appropriately enough, a year after the "summer of love," in 1969. Quoted in Rosenblum, *Another Liberalism*, 78.

35. Charles Sellers's otherwise useful account of antebellum sexual reform movements in the context of the "market revolution" is marred by a similar ideology. Rather than seeing anti-onanist and temperance movements as equally focused on the discipline and management of the body and its political relations, Sellers portrays anti-onanism as "private" and temperance as "public": "While struggling for effort on the private battlegrounds of libido, self-making Northerners transformed themselves publicly by banding together to purge self and socety of alcohol." This naturalization of "libido" as both "human" and "private" leads to a (sentimental) narrative in which sexuality becomes a thing that is, in turn, either expressed freely *or* subject to external discipline. What this narrative misses is the more basic deployment through which "libido" is (among other things) isolated from civil and political relations, universalized as a source of human emancipation, and privatized so as to contain the effects of that emancipation. See Sellers, *The Market Revolution*, 259.

36. Jacobs's anxiety concerning potential (mis)readings of her narrative explains her need to distance herself from Luke by opposing his quoted dialect ("dey *gub* it to me") to her own narrative voice. As elsewhere in *Incidents*, language and literacy are markers of moral and educational differences. The poor whites who invade her grandmother's home after Nat Turner's insurrection are unable to read Jacobs's letters, but their dialect evinces their unreasoned excitement in discovering them: "We's got 'em! Dis 'ere yaller gal's got letters" (65). The exception to this association of illiteracy with ignorance appears in a passage where an uneducated slave woman reports the following story to Jacobs: "She said her husband told her that the black people had sent word to the queen of 'Merica, that they were all slaves; that she didn't believe it, and went to Washington city to see the president about it. They quarrelled; she drew her sword upon him, and swore that he should help her to make them all free." Like Zora Neale Hurston who uses the free indirect style to similar ends some seventy years later in *Their Eyes Were Watching God*, Jacobs's un-dis-

tanced sympathy with this "poor, ignorant woman" is indicated by the incorporation of her unquoted dialect into *Incidents*'s narrative (45). (I thank the graduate students in my English 812 at the University of Wisconsin, Madison—Spring 1995—for drawing this point to my attention.)

37. Appropriately then, Jacobs's claim to sexual purity becomes both her link to her Northern audience and a point of contention in her struggle with Flint. In the appendix to *Incidents*, Amy Post attests that the author's "deportment indicated remarkable delicacy of feeling and purity of thought"—an observation that is supported by the fact that "her sensitive spirit shrank from publicity" (203). In an argument with Flint, Jacobs echoes this ideology when she defends her relationship with an unnamed "young colored carpenter" in similar terms: "[H]e would not love me if he did not think me a virtuous woman" (39). Just as the "delicacy" of Jacobs's "virtuous" sensibility positions her firmly within sentimental norms of "womanliness," the violence of Flint's response ("He sprang upon me like a tiger, and gave me a stunning blow") indicates his distance from sentimental norms of "manliness" (39). In this context, Frederick Douglass's 1845 *Narrative* provides an instructive comparison to *Incidents*. When he narrates the sexualized beating of his Aunt Hester (a beating whose cause Douglass leaves to "conjecture," but which he clearly attributes to her master's jealous response to her "noble form" and "graceful proportions"), Douglass concludes by describing his own fear: "I was so terrified and horror-stricken at the sight, that I hid myself in a closet, and dared not venture out until long after the bloody transaction was over. I expected it would be my turn next." Two readings of this scene seem possible. Douglass may fear that he, like Luke, will be the next victim of his master's specifically sexual rage—an experience that will render his later claims to full masculine subjectivity even more problematic than they already are. Or Douglass may intentionally desexualize that rage so as to construct a gender-indifferent interpretation of the violence inflicted on both male and female slaves—an alliance that is rendered suspect both by *Incidents*'s generic commitment to the conventions of female sentimentalism, and by its generic critique of the male slave narrative in the chapter "The Slave Who Dared to Feel like a Man" (17–26). In either case, Douglass's *Narrative* shares with *Incidents* a set of rhetorical strategies for describing sexual and sexually violent relations ("[H]e took her into the kitchen, and stripped her from neck to waist, leaving her neck, shoulders, and back, entirely naked."), while also preserving a writing position that is uncontaminated by those descriptions ("Why master was so careful of her, may safely be left to conjecture.") Frederick Douglass, *Narrative of the Life of Frederick Douglass, An American Slave* (New York: Penguin, 1982), 51–52.

38. A similar strategy prevents Jacobs's grandmother from being sold to the highest bidder (11), and it also protects Jacobs from Flint's sexual coercion: "It was lucky for me that I did not live on a distant plantation, but in a town not so large that the inhabitants were ignorant of each other's affairs. Bad as are the laws and customs in a slaveholding community, the doctor, as a professional man, deemed it prudent to keep up some outward show of decency" (29).

39. Jacobs's two arguments echo contemporary moral reform rhetoric concerning prostitution, which wavered between portraying prostitutes as passive victims of seduction and as active strategists making the best of their impoverished position within a class-stratified society. Jacobs's awareness of such reform movements is

indicated, within *Incidents*, by her recommendation of domestic missionary work as a solution to Southern (and Northern) immorality: "I am glad that missionaries go out to the dark corners of the earth; but I ask them not to overlook the dark corners at home. Talk to American slaveholders as you talk to savages in Africa" (73). For histories of the sexual reform movements, see Christine Stansell, *City of Women: Sex and Class in New York, 1789–1860* (Chicago: University of Chicago Press, 1987), 171–92, and Lori Ginsberg, *Women and the Work of Benevolence: Morality, Politics, and Class in the 19th-Century United States* (New Haven, Conn.: Yale University Press, 1990).

40. Jacobs's class position marks another potentially significant difference between herself and her audience. While Jacobs's Preface highlights her less privileged social position ("Since I have been at the North, it has been necessary for me to work . . . and it has compelled me to write these pages at irregular intervals, whenever I could snatch an hour from my household duties" [1]), Child's introduction places a veil over it ("During the last seventeen years, she has lived the greater part of the time with a distinguished family in New York" [3]).

41. Karen Halttunen, *Confidence Men and Painted Women: A Study of Middle-Class Culture in America, 1830–1870* (New Haven, Conn.: Yale University Press, 1982). *Incidents* stages this dialectic repeatedly, but nowhere more forcefully than in its analysis of master-slave relations. Jacobs justifies her sexual strategies with the "eloquence" she learns from her politician-lover Sands: "There is something akin to freedom in having a lover who has no control over you, except that which he gains by kindness and attachment. A master may treat you as rudely as he pleases, and you dare not speak; moreover, the wrong does not seem so great with an unmarried man, as with one who has a wife to be made unhappy." But she also dismisses that eloquence as immoral "sophistry" (55). That Jacobs uses the same language in her penultimate paragraph as she describes her attachment of Mrs. Bruce—"Love, duty, gratitude, also bind me to her side" (201)—should alert the reader to Jacobs's awareness of the "sophistry" with which she glosses the inequalities in that relationship as well.

42. On the late-twentieth-century relations between liberalism, privacy, and public sexual culture, see Pat Califia, *Public Sex: The Culture of Radical Sex* (San Francisco: Cleis, 1994), Beverley Brown, "Troubled Vision" (see note 2 above); Lauren Berlant and Michael Warner, "Sex in Public," *Critical Inquiry* 24, no. 2 (Winter 1998): 547–66; and Cindy Patton, *Fatal Advice: How Safe-Sex Education Went Wrong*.

Chapter 7
Afterword

1. Walt Whitman, *Leaves of Grass* (New York: Vintage, 1992), 30.

2. Sigmund Freud, *Three Essays on the Theory of Sexuality*, trans. James Strachey (New York: Basic, 1975), 18–19.

3. Ibid., 49–50.

4. Herman Melville, *Billy Budd and Other Stories* (New York: Penguin, 1986), 367.

5. Hannah Arendt, *On Revolution* (New York: Penguin, 1963), 86.

6. Ann Douglas, *The Feminization of American Culture* (New York: Anchor, 1988), 326.

7. The modernity of Vere's closet thus lies not simply in its policing the boundary between public and private life, between "politics" and "compassion." Nearly two centuries earlier, Jonathan Edwards concluded his "Personal Narrative" by similarly staging an affective life that is both private and sentimental. His "sense," he reports, of "how sweet and blessed a thing it was, to walk in the way of duty" led him to "break forth in a kind of loud weeping": it "held me some time; so that I was forced to shut myself up, and fasten the doors." It would be a mistake, though, to read Edwards's religious affections as sexual since, in fact, the reverse is more accurate: Edwards's affective life—including any sexual aspects—is properly religious. In contrast, the modernity of Vere's closet, as well as the private affect it shelters, is that it locates sexuality as its obscene content and unnameable referent. See Jonathan Edwards, "Personal Narrative," in *Selected Writings of Jonathan Edwards*, ed. Harold P. Simonson (New York: Frederick Ungar, 1970), 44.

8. Quoted in David M. Halperin, *Saint Foucault: Towards a Gay Hagiography* (New York: Oxford University Press, 1995), 91.

9. Melville, *Billy Budd*, 362.

10. Ibid., 321–22, 353–66. While Billy may be, in Eve Sedgwick's words, a "sentimentalized *object*," Vere is a "sentimentalizing *subject*, an active wielder of the ruses of sentimentality for the satisfaction of needs that can be stably defined neither as public nor as private." Eve Sedgwick, *Epistemology of the Closet* (Berkeley, Calif.: University of California Press, 1990), 121.

11. Melville, *Billy Budd*, 375.

12. Ibid., 377.

13. Ibid., 376, 378.

14. Ibid., 297.

15. Ibid., 297–98.

16. Sedgwick, *Epistemology of the Closet*, 93.

17. Melville, *Billy Budd*, 291.

Index

abolition, 15, 110, 138–40, 148, 151

Adams, Abigail, 81–87, 96, 106, 112

Adams, John, 12, 37–38, 62, 81–87, 96, 112–13, 127–28

Adams, Sam, 18

The Adventures of Huckleberry Finn (Twain), 115, 132

affect, 3, 5, 22, 95, 111, 114, 157–58, 186n.39, 190–91n.100, 204n7. *See also* sensation; sentiment; sympathy

Agrarian Justice (Paine), 12, 45, 47

Alcuin (Brockden Brown), 125

Alien and Sedition Acts, 62, 68, 180–81nn. 41 and 43

American character, 55, 67–68,70–71, 73

American Dictionary of the English Language (Webster), 195n.61

American foreign policy, 60–64

American Revolution, 5–6, 34, 40, 82, 94, 158

The Anatomy of National Fantasy (Berlant), 76

Ancora. *See* public sphere

Anderson, Benedict, 59

anti-onanism, 15, 201n.35

Arato, Andrew, 11

Arendt, Hannah, 6, 11, 32–41, 47–49, 53–54, 169–70nn.31–32; on the body, 21, 34; on the body politic, 36–37; on citizenship, 33, 36–38; and liberalism, 32, 36–38; and *persona*, 36–39; on public-private binary, 48; on public sphere, 14, 21, 32–36, 40, 45, 47; on sentiment, 6, 21, 32, 35–36, 42, 156–58; on the social, 40, 174–75n.90

Armstrong, Nancy, 95, 97, 187n.63

Arthur Mervyn (Brockden Brown), 114

The Authority of Law (Raz), 167n.6

Bache, Benjamin, 58

Bachofen, Johann, 122–23

Bailyn, Bernard, 11

Baker, Paula, 102

Bakhtin, Mikhail, 166n.57

Balibar, Etienne, 65, 179–80n.40

Ballard, J. G., 3, 17–19

Barker-Benfield, G. J., 15–17, 98–100

Bavarian Illuminati, 62, 193n.27

Baym, Nina, 91–93, 95, 105, 123–24, 131

Benhabib, Seyla, 48

Bercovitch, Sacvan, 30, 167n.7

Berlant, Lauren, 16, 18, 76, 132, 138, 181n.50, 196n.78

Berlin, Isaiah, 146

Bhabha, Homi K., 64, 180n.40

Billy Budd (Melville), 23, 156–59

Binney, Horace, 56–57, 60

Bloch, Ernst, 31, 122–23

The Boarding School (Foster), 106

Bodies That Matter (Butler), 190n.88

body, 4, 166n.57; Arendt on, 21, 34; and authorship, 56–58; within the body politic, 3–4, 6–7, 13, 19, 49, 98, 155–59; and citizenship, 14–16, 69; and civil society, 15; disestablishment of, 15; and mind, 124–25; as national symbol, 5, 8–9, 55–59, 69–77, 85, 176n.10, 181n.50; patriotic, 59, 69–72; and privacy, 15, 34, 42, 91, 101, 106, 109, 137–38, 143, 147, 149, 153–54, 157; and publication, 17, 19, 23, 84, 90, 148; and sentimentalism, 3, 15–17, 19, 43, 49, 88, 91, 95, 98–103, 105–9, 111, 154; and sexuality, 18, 108, 123, 149, 153–59. *See also* embodiment; gender; liberalism; public sphere; republicanism

body politic, 3–13, 23, 34–37 57, 59; and egocrat, 74; gendering of, 132; liberal model of, 49, 156; republican model of, 4, 6, 156; and sexuality, 149; and the state, 53, 65. *See also* body

Boorstin, Daniel, 30

The Bostonians (James), 118

Boyer, Jean-Baptiste de, 137

Bradford, Andrew, 184n.13

Bright, Susie, 142

Brown, Beverley, 141

Brown, Charles Brockden, 22, 48, 114–21, 125, 192n.15, 193nn. 20 and 27

Brown, Gillian, 131

Brown, William Hill, 186n.46

Burke, Edmund, 4, 98

Butler, Judith, 17–18, 90, 94, 105, 132, 163n.27, 190n.88

Calhoun, Craig, 57

capitalism, 11–12, 40, 45–47, 50–51, 57, 66, 138, 141, 144–46

Charlotte Temple (Rowson), 73, 81, 87, 114

Chartier, Roger, 176n.10

Cherniavsky, Eva, 200–201n.31

Child, Lydia Maria, 138, 140, 150–51, 188n.75, 200–201n.31, 203n40

Christophersen, Bill, 114

citizenship, 3; Arendt on, 33, 36–38; and embodiment, 3, 13–16, 69–70, 127, 138, 181n.50; Habermas on, 40, 46; and law, 30; as mediated by sex and gender, 86–87, 101–2, 121, 193n.19; and pornography, 138; republican, 12–14, 107, 121–22, 127; and sensation, 148; and sentiment, 3, 22; and the state, 30, 68; versus subjection, 4, 21, 30–32, 45, 60, 62, 68–70, 109, 179–80n.40

civil society, 3, 19, 31; associations within, 65, 67, 84, 164n.35; and the body, 15; and law formation, 29; liberal model of, 29; and novel reading, 90; as pornographic, 148; and public sphere, 31, 40; and reason, 126; republican model of, 31; versus the state, 3–4, 10, 32, 40–41, 59, 65–67, 69, 87, 140, 154, 165n.56, 176n.10, 176–77n.13

Clara Howard (Brockden Brown), 22, 48, 114–21, 125, 127–33, 192n.15, 193n.27, 195–96n.69

Clarissa (Richardson), 87, 138

class, 10, 20, 35, 89, 96–97, 116–17, 189n.82, 203n.40

Cleland, John, 146–47

Clor, Harry, 149

Cohen, Jean, 11

Cold War, 27–32, 36

Commonwealth v. Sharpless, 142–46, 148, 151, 153–54

Comstock, Anthony, 142

The Concept of Law (Hart), 29

consensus historiography, 11, 30–31, 35, 46, 83

Constitution, 58, 60, 67, 83

Coontz, Stephanie, 187n.60

The Coquette (Foster), 22, 48, 73, 87–111, 114, 116, 126–27, 138, 145, 186n.45, 188n.75, 189n.80, 190–91n.100

corporeality. *See* body; embodiment

Cott, Nancy, 126

coverture, 86, 129

The Crisis of Democracy (Huntington), 27

Critique of Judgement (Kant), 98

Critique of Practical Reason (Kant), 41, 120–21

Critique of Pure Reason (Kant), 122

cultural studies, 21

Customs Act of 1842, 142

Davidson, Cathy, 88, 91–95, 105, 186n.46, 187n.56

The Day the Earth Stood Still, 27–31, 34, 37, 42, 50, 53, 166–67nn. 2 and 7, 172n.68, 174n.88

Debates in Congress, 55

Declaration of Independence, 82, 182n.54, 186n.39

"Declaration of Sentiments," 12

Defining the Political (Howard), 162–63n.26

Deleuze, Gilles, 113, 123

democracy, 19; Arendt on, 36; and capitalism, 66; democratization, 11, 40, 90, 184n.17; and embodiment, 7, 127–28; Habermas on, 44; Lefort on, 9, 16–17, 20; and obscenity, 141–48; and power, 169n.25; and publicity, 83–86; Tocqueville on, 84–85. *See also* republicanism

Democracy in America (de Tocqueville), 6, 164n.35

Democratic and Republican Societies, 57, 61, 63, 68, 70, 178n.20

Derrida, Jacques, 49, 72, 182n.54

Dietz, Mary, 163n.27

Discipline and Punishment (Foucault), 181n.46

"DissemiNation" (Bhabha), 180n.40

domesticity, 91, 101–103, 128, 130, 139, 152, 198n.8, 200n.29. *See also* intimate sphere; marriage; privacy

Douglas, Ann, 4, 15, 23, 113, 130, 156–58, 192n.8

Douglass, Frederick, 202n.37

Downs, Donald, 149

Dumm, Thomas, 68, 181n.46

Edgar Huntly (Brockden Brown), 114, 131

education: in Jacobs, 201–2n.36; republican, 119–21; versus seduction, 71–73; by the state, 64–69, 76; of women, 81–82, 87, 89, 97, 98

Edwards, Jonathan, 204n.7

The Eighteenth Brumaire of Louis Napoleon (Marx), 7

Eley, Geoff, 173–74n.80

Elias, Norbert, 98
Elmer, Jonathan, 15, 97
embodiment: and citizenship, 3, 13–16, 69–
    70, 127, 138; different forms of, 8, 14–15,
    122; and maternity, 122–23; racial logics of,
    95, 131; versus rationality, 123–25; versus
    self-abstraction, 14, 121–22, 125, 127–30;
    and sentiment, 3. *See also* body
Emerson, Ralph Waldo, 62, 76, 179n.31
Emile (Rousseau), 22
Engels, Friedrich, 7
Enlightenment, 3, 101, 115, 123, 127, 141
equality, 20, 35–36, 59; of genders, 20, 44–48,
    113, 125, 128, 187n.60, 195n.66
essentialism: in feminist criticism, 94–95, 105,
    163n.27; anti-essentialism, 10

The Fall of Public Man (Sennett), 169n.31
fantasy, 92–94, 108
"Farewell Address" (Washington), 21, 48, 55–
    73, 85, 178–79nn. 22 and 24, 181n.50
Favret, Mary, 85, 184–85n.18
Federalism, 56, 61–63, 65, 104
The Federalist Papers, 31, 53, 60, 66–67
female readers, 88–89, 113; as critical con-
    struct, 86, 91, 93–95, 187n.56; Jacobs's re-
    lation to, 138–39, 148–49, 153, 203n.40
feminism, 10, 12, 21, 22; and abolition, 15;
    and citizenship, 133; and domesticity, 86,
    93; and history, 14; in literary criticism, 91–
    95, 138; on mind-body opposition, 123–24,
    132; production of sexual difference by,
    124, 163n.27; on public sphere, 47–48, 98
femininity, 97, 103, 157; and sentiment, 22,
    113–16, 118, 132, 193n.20. *See also* gender;
    "woman"
The Feminization of American Culture
    (Douglas), 113
Fern, Fanny, 110, 132
Fiedler, Leslie, 113–14
Fielding, Henry, 42, 147
Fleetwood (Godwin), 193n.20
Fleischmann, Fritz, 117, 192n.15
Fliegelman, Jay, 13, 71, 186n.39
"foreign," category of, versus "domestic," 61–
    64, 66, 72
Foster, Hannah, 22, 48, 73, 87–111, 186n.45
Foucault, Michel, 17–18, 49, 68, 105, 110,
    149, 154, 157, 181n.46
Franklin, Benjamin, 30, 57, 83, 184n.13
Fraser, Nancy, 48, 174n.81
Freedom. *See* liberty

French-American Treaty of Alliance, 61
French Revolution, 4–6, 34, 47, 62–63, 77, 94,
    158
Freneau, Philip, 56, 58, 73, 176n.11
Freud, Sigmund, 123, 155–57
Fuller, Margaret, 118, 131

gender, 19, 22, 193n.19; and class, 97,
    189n.82; and embodiment, 15–16, 94–95,
    97–102, 108, 124, 127, 129, 131; and sen-
    timentalism, 87, 89, 95, 98–104, 107, 112–
    116; and sex, 94–104, 108, 115, 125–27,
    163n.27, 195n.61. *See also* equality; femi-
    ninity; masculinity; "woman"
Gender Trouble (Butler), 163n.27, 190n.88
Genet, Edmond Charles (Citizen), 61–63
Gerry, Elbridge, 81, 84
Gilbert, Felix, 60–61, 178–79n.24
The Gleaner (Murray), 124–25
Godwin, William, 114–15, 193nn. 20 and 27
Gouges, Olympe de, 98, 103–4
Grabo, Norman, 114
Gramsci, Antonio, 8, 48, 162n.26
"The Great Lawsuit" (Fuller), 131
Grossberg, Michael, 126
Grosz, Elizabeth, 108–9

Habermas, Jürgen, 14, 21, 39–49, 52–54, 66,
    76, 170n.42, 172n.59, 172n.62, 173n.71,
    184n.17; and citizenship, 40, 46; and gen-
    der, 47–48, 86; and the novel, 42–43, 90,
    171n.56, 187n.63; on "principle of pub-
    licness," 171n.49; and public opinion, 39,
    41, 146; and public-private binary, 41, 48,
    101, 175n.92; and public sphere, 11, 32,
    39–47; and republican sphere of letters,
    83–84; and the social, 39–40
Halttunen, Karen, 153
Hamilton, Alexander, 45–46, 48, 56–57, 61,
    63, 65–66, 73, 172n.68, 178–79n.24,
    179n.32
Hancock, John, 18, 70
Haraway, Donna, 175n.92
Harrington, James, 31
Hart, H.L.A., 29–31, 34, 42, 167n.6
Hartz, Louis, 30, 167n.7
Havel, Václav, 165n.56
Hawthorne, Nathaniel, 76, 113
Hayek, F. A., 167n.6
heart, as sentimental category, 16–17, 19, 36,
    42, 67, 72, 104, 111, 118, 129–30, 147, 155,
    171n.52

Hegel, Georg Wilhelm Friedrich, 17, 39, 41–42, 53, 171n.50

Hegemony and Socialist Strategy (Leclau and Mouffe), 10

Henry, Patrick, 67

heterosexuality, 86, 116, 127, 129, 132, 187n.63, 191n.4, 195n.61

An Historical and Moral View of the Origin and Progress of the French Revolution and the Effect It Has Produced in Europe (Wollstonecraft), 4

The History of Sexuality (Foucault), 110, 157

Hobbes, Thomas, 29, 31

Hobomok (Child), 188n.75

Hofstadter, Richard, 30, 67

homosexuality, 156–59

Horowitz, Morton, 45–46

Howard, Dick, 162–63n.26

Howells, William Dean, 113, 191–92n.6

The Human Condition (Arendt), 33–35

Hunt, Lynn, 141, 146–47, 199n.25

Huntington, Samuel, 27, 36–37, 169n.25

identification: and affect, 22; as fancy, 90; by novel readers, 90–94, 96, 102, 105, 109, 111; political, 59–60, 68, 70–71, 111; versus projection, 99; and publication, 91–94, 107, 153; and sentiment, 70, 102

immanence, 9, 162n.20

The Importance of Being Earnest (Wilde), 42–43

Incidents in the Life of a Slave Girl (Jacobs), 12, 23, 48, 110, 137–40, 145, 148–54

individual, 11, 13, 36, 43, 90. *See also* subject

An Inquiry into the Formation of Washington's Farewell Address (Binney), 56

interest, 11–13; moral, 120–22; private, 39, 66, 164n.35

intimate sphere, 33–34, 41–43, 45, 52, 172n.62, 174–75n.90, 184–85n.18, 187n.60. *See also* domesticity; privacy

Invasion of the Body Snatchers, 29

The Invention of Pornography (Hunt), 147

Jacobs, Harriet, 12, 23, 48, 110–11, 137–40, 145, 148–54, 198n.8, 200–201nn. 29 and 31, 202–3nn.37–41

Jane Talbot (Brockden Brown), 114, 192n.15, 193n.27

Jay, John, 57, 66

Jay Treaty, 63

Jefferson, Thomas, 37–38, 45, 56–58, 62, 65–66, 70, 103, 182n.54

Johnson, Claudia, 165n.56

Jones, Bill T., 147–48, 200n.28

Kant, Immanuel, 41–42, 44, 81, 98, 120–24, 171nn. 50 and 52, 193n.27

Kaplan, Carla, 140

Kelley, Mary, 198n.8

Kendrick, Walter, 140–42, 198n.13

Kerber, Linda, 45–46

Knox, Henry, 70

Kraft-Ebbing, Richard von, 114

Krause, Sidney, 114–15, 193n.27

labor movements, 12, 21

Laclau, Ernesto, 10, 12, 162–63n.26, 164n.35

Lacoue-Labarthe, Phillipe, 162n.20

The Lady Eve, 132

La Metrie, Julian, 15

Landes, Joan, 47, 173–74n.80

Laqueur, Thomas, 15–16, 94, 125

"Last Supper at Uncle Tom's Cabin/The Promised Land" (Jones), 148

law: Arendt on, 35–38; moral, 41, 119–22, 128; and obscenity, 140–47, 153; rational, 41–42; rule of, 29, 42, 50–53, 158; and sensation, 158; versus society, 144; and the state, 29–31, 37, 50–51, 53, 58–60, 140–41, 143, 145–46, 153; and violence, 29–31. *See also* liberalism; privacy

Leaves of Grass (Whitman), 147, 200n.28

Lectures on the Mind (Rush), 94–95

Lee, Henry, 68, 71, 176n.11

Lefort, Claude, 8–12, 16–17, 20, 31, 69–70, 74, 162n.20, 164n.35

letters, 77, 81–87; in novels, 84, 100–11, 118–19, 121; popularity of, 84; and public debate, 84; as sentimental publication, 83, 105–6, 111

The Letters of the Republic (Warner), 13, 59, 76

liberty, 6, 9, 46, 66, 159, 164n.35; Arendt's view of, 36–38, 45, 169–70n.32; and the body, 18–19, 49, 107, 157–58; negative, 39, 59, 146, 177n.17

liberalism, 6–7, 19–20, 167n.7; and the body, 14–15, 23, 76, 109, 137–38, 149, 151–54; critique of, 48–54, 169n.31; and democracy, 9, 48; Habermas on, 39–44; and identification, 90, 153; and law, 29–31, 37, 42, 50, 53, 58–59, 140, 146–47, 158, 183,

174n.88, 177n.16; and letters, 83–85; Marx
  on, 7; and nationalism, 72; and obscenity,
  145–49, 152–54; and public-private binary,
  138–40, 143, 145–46, 149, 152; versus republicanism, 12, 14, 20–21, 31, 33, 48, 59–
  60, 64, 67, 73, 83, 85, 129, 146, 156, 158,
  165n.50, 172n.68, 177n.16; and sexuality,
  22, 129, 146, 149–54; and the state, 44, 49,
  51–54, 140–41, 143, 145–46, 153; versus totalitarianism, 31–32. See also privacy; public sphere; sentimentalism
Locke, John, 15, 30–31, 34, 65, 179n.39
Looby, Christopher, 13
Loshe, Lillie Demming, 118
love: versus passion, 128; and republicanism,
  120, 129
Love and Death in the American Novel (Fiedler), 113
Love and Passion (Luhman), 128, 195–96n.69
Lowe, Donald, 19
Luhman, Nicholas, 49, 128, 195–96n.69

Machiavelli, Niccolò, 31
The Machiavellian Moment (Pocock), 12,
  163n.35
Mackenzie, Henry, 115, 193n.20
Madison, James, 55–57, 60, 180n.41
"A Manifesto for Cyborgs" (Haraway),
  175n.92
The Man of Feeling (MacKenzie), 193n.20
"The Man of Letters as a Man of Business"
  (Howells), 191–92n.6
Marbury v. Madison, 83
Maria, or the Rights of Women (Wollstone-
  craft), 87, 98, 109–10, 161n.8, 190–91n.100
marriage, 92, 101–3, 106, 113, 126, 129. See
  also domesticity; intimate sphere; privacy
Marx, Karl, 7–8, 10, 16, 19, 34, 46, 66,
  173n.71
masculinity, 113–17, 132, 193nn. 19 and 20,
  202n.37
masochism, 22, 112–33, 191n.4, 192n.8
materialism, 3; and the body, 18, 22, 101; versus idealism, 7
maternity, 122–23, 130, 166n.57. See also republican motherhood
Mazzei, Philip, 62
Meese, Edwin, 142
Melville, Herman, 23, 156–59
Memoirs of a Woman of Pleasure (Cleland),
  146
Mill, John Stuart, 39

Minow, Martha, 124
"A Modell of Christian Charity" (Winthrop),
  104
modernity, 12–13, 32–34, 49, 89, 110,
  175n.92
Monroe, James, 63
Montesquieu, Charles-Louis de Secondat, 60,
  178n18
morality, 41, 120, 122, 139, 141, 143–49, 151,
  170n.42, 199n.25, 201–2n.36, 202–3n.39
Morris, Gouverneur, 63
Mouffe, Chantal, 10, 12, 162–63n.26, 164n.35
Murray, Judith Sargent; 124, 126

Nancy, Jean-Luc, 162n.20
Narrative of the Life of Frederick Douglass
  (Douglass), 202n.37
"National Brands/National Body: Imitation of
  Life" (Berlant), 181n.50
nationalism: corporate, 68–77; and liberalism,
  72
nationality, 57; versus nationalism, 56, 59–60,
  64
National Security State, 53, 68
"Natty Bumpo," 115
The New Politics of Pornography (Downs),
  149
novel, 42; and class, 89, 97; condemnations of
  42, 88–91, 186n.45; and development of
  public sphere, 42, 171n.56; epistolary, 84,
  105–6, 116, 187n.63; and fancy, 90, 103–4;
  and fantasy, 93–94, 108; and gender, 89;
  and identification, 90–94, 96, 102, 105, 109,
  111; versus reality, 88–90, 93, 186n.46; and
  sensation, 90, 99; sentimental, 42, 87–133,
  119, 138, 152, 188n.75; women readers of,
  88–89, 119

obscenity, 23, 138–54, 156, 159, 199n.25,
  200n.28. See also pornography
"On the Jewish Question" (Marx), 7
On Liberty (Mill), 39
On Revolution (Arendt), 6, 32–39
Ormond (Brockden Brown), 114

Paine, Thomas, 12, 45–48, 66, 73, 148, 172–
  73nn. 63 and 68
Pamela (Richardson), 42–43, 87, 95
Pateman, Carole, 173–74n.80
patriotism, 63, 66–67, 69
"people," as category, 9, 13, 64, 67, 77
The People versus Larry Flint, 50

personality: and the political, 82–84, 86–87; and publicity, 42, 85, 87, 90; republican, 71; sentimental, 130. *See also* privacy

"Personal Narrative" (Edwards), 204n7

Philadelphia, 50

The Philosophy of Right (Hegel), 39

Pocock, J.G.A., 12, 31–32, 37, 46, 59–60, 76, 163n.35, 177n.16

Political Justice (Godwin), 193n.27

politics: divergent meanings of, 8, 162n.24, 169n.25; and literature, 3, 19; of obscenity, 146–47; and personality, 82–84, 86–87; and sentimentalism, 90–91, 95, 97, 101, 105, 115; versus the social, 6–9, 36, 40, 147, 162n.20; and violence, 40. *See also* public sphere

pornography, 90–91, 105, 138–39, 141, 146–49, 198n.13; and law, 140–47. *See also* obscenity

Post, Amy, 202n.37

power, 9, 14 18–20, 32, 60, 67, 128, 169n.25; and sexual difference, 132; of the state, 11, 40; state versus civil forms of, 35, 39, 84, 146, 164n.35

The Powers of Sympathy (Brown), 186n.46

press, 58, 77, 83, 84, 167n.6

privacy, 19, 137–54; Arendt on, 33–36; and embodiment, 15, 34, 42, 91, 101, 106, 109, 137–38, 143, 147, 149, 153–54, 157; and law, 36–38, 50, 122, 140–41, 143–44, 146, 153; and obscenity, 138–42, 144–54; and pornography, 91, 138–39, 147–48; as privation, 137, 139; as privilege, 137–39, 146, 148, 153–54; publication of, 42–43, 83–84, 91, 138–54, 198n.8; and republicanism, 83, 89, 101, 142–44, 148; and sexuality, 138–39, 149–53, 156–57. *See also* domesticity; intimate sphere; public-private binary; state

"Proclamation of Neutrality" (Washington), 63

Project for a Glossary of the Twentieth Century (Ballard), 3

publication, 23, 184n.17; and authenticity, 153, 186n.39; and identification, 91–94, 107, 153; versus ideology, 105; and letters, 83–85; of private relations, 42–43, 83–84, 91, 138–154, 198n.8; as regulated by the market, 141; and republicanism, 17, 84–85, 89; and sensation, 90; and sentimentality, 43–44, 147, 149, 152–56; and sexuality, 23,

138–140, 144, 149, 151–52, 108; technologies of, 17

public debate, 40, 43, 48, 58–59, 64, 69, 71–72, 77, 84, 90, 142–46, 152, 167n.6, 172n.59, 200n.29. *See also* public opinion

public opinion, 39–41, 67–72, 162n.24; formation of, 48, 58, 60, 64, 67, 71–72, 77; versus personal opinion, 85. *See also* public debate

public-private binary, 4, 7, 14; Arendt on, 33–37, 48; and gender, 86, 130; Habermas on, 41, 48, 101, 175n.92; and letters, 84; and liberalism, 31, 83; and obscenity, 138–48, 151–54; and republicanism, 83, 89, 142, 147; and the sentimental body, 22, 109; in sentimental culture, 42, 130, 153, 204n7; as separate spheres ideology, 86–87, 115; and sexuality, 138, 141. *See also* intimate sphere; privacy; public sphere

public sphere, 3; Arendt on, 6, 21, 32–39, 169–70n.32; and bodies, 4, 8, 19, 21, 36, 39, 42, 43, 77, 84, 87, 101, 106, 114, 124, 138, 147, 153, 156; and gender, 45–48, 84, 86–87, 101, 106, 114, 124; Habermas on, 11, 21, 32, 39–47, 146, 170n.42; institutions of, 8, 11, 21, 40, 71; and letters, 84; liberal model of, 8, 11, 31, 44, 46, 84–87, 106, 111, 114, 140, 146, 153, 156; limits to, 61, 72, 74, 140, 152, 156; literary, 4, 41, 43–44, 46, 84, 86–87, 101, 106, 111, 114, 124, 147, 151; and obscenity, 138, 140–42, 144–45, 148, 153; political, 4, 87; and publicity, 19, 38, 85, 138, 167n.6; republican model of, 8, 22, 31–38, 48, 57–61, 83–84, 86–87, 89, 101, 111, 143–47; as site of mediation, 40; and the state, 11, 32, 37, 39–40, 60–61, 77, 86, 140–41, 143–46, 153–54; transnational, 61–62, 72, 77, 180n.40. *See also* public-private binary; sentimentalism

queer theory, 133

Rabelais and His World (Bakhtin), 166n.57

race, 15–16, 95, 131, 138–39, 196nn. 76 and 78

"Rallying Song of the Tea Party," 18

rationality, 123–26; versus embodiment, 123–25; and feminism, 124; gendering of, 115, 123, 125, 193n.19; and republicanism, 41; versus sentiment, 7, 36, 115, 118, 120, 127, 129–30

Raz, Joseph, 167n.6
reason. *See* rationality
Reflections on the Revolution in France (Burke), 98
reform, 21; antebellum, 15, 22, 43, 103, 140, 189n.80, 201n.35, 202–3n.39; and class, 97; new social movements, 10, 43, 46, 165n.56
Report on the Governability of Democracies (Huntington et al.), 36
Report on Manufactures (Hamilton), 45
representation: of nation, 57–59, 73, 77; feminist demands for, 86; obscene, 141; and participation, 84; versus participation, 77, 82; of the people, 60, 69, 182n.54; of sovereignty, 57–59
republicanism, 4–17, 19–23, 31–49, 172n.63; classical, 32–41, 90; cosmopolitanism of, 61–63, 75–77; and democracy, 12–14, 40–41, 46, 48, 69, 93, 178n18; and embodiment, 4, 7, 14–16, 23, 58, 76–77, 95, 98, 101–102, 109, 124–25, 147, 159; and letters, 83–85; versus liberalism, 12, 14, 20–21, 31, 33, 59–60, 64, 67, 73, 83, 85, 129, 146, 156, 158, 165n.50, 172n.68, 177nn 16, 17; and love, 120, 129; and maternity, 123; and nationality, 60, 65–66; and novels, 89; and privacy, 83, 89, 101, 142–44, 148; and publication, 17, 84–85, 89; and sentimentalism, 44, 89, 101–102, 109, 147, 150, 153; and sovereignty, 57–61, 63; and women, 82, 85–87, 91, 96, 102, 109, 125. *See also* citizenship; public sphere; self-abstraction
republican motherhood, 86, 192n.8. *See also* republican womanhood
"Republican Synthesis," 13, 32
republican womanhood, 14, 86–87, 91, 96, 102, 109
Revelations of a Slave Trader, 139
Revere, Paul, 18
Reynolds, David, 139
Richardson, Samuel, 42, 44, 87, 147, 171n.56
The Rights of Man (Paine), 73
The Rise of the Novel (Watt), 171n.56
Robocop, 27, 50–54, 174–75nn. 88 and 90
Rogers, Daniel, 20
Rousseau, Jean-Jacques, 15, 22, 31, 57, 65, 67, 114, 122, 124, 179n.39
Rowson, Susan, 73, 81
Rush, Benjamin, 68, 94–95, 97–99
Russian Revolution, 36–38

Ruth Hall (Fern), 132
Ryan, Mary, 47–48, 130

Sacher-Masoch, Leopold von 112–13, 122–23, 191n.4, 195n.66
Sade, Marquis de, 146–48
Samuels, Shirley, 15, 111, 131, 196n.76
Sanchez-Eppler, Karen, 15
Scarry, Elaine, 17–18
Schiebinger, Londa, 94
Schudson, Michael, 173–74n.80
Scott, Joan, 103, 124
Sedgwick, Eve, 149, 158, 204n.10
Sedley, Sir Charles, 143
self-abstraction, 13–14, 120–29, 193n.27
Sellers, Charles, 201n.35
Sennett, Richard, 169n.31
sensation, 3, 19, 43, 157; and citizenship, 148; and gender norms, 99, 107, 127; and law, 110, 158; and letters, 108; and literary public sphere, 106; versus norm, 109; and publication, 90–91; and sentimentalism, 3, 49, 100, 107, 109–10; 156–57; and sex, 110; sexual versus nonsexual, 156; and taste, 99, 102. *See also* affect
sensuality, 7, 112, 119–21, 127, 195n.61, 195–96n.69
sentiment, 3–4, 19, 21–22; as basis for public debate, 76–77; and citizenship, 3, 22; and embodiment, 3; and French Revolution, 32, 35–36; and gender, 89–116, 193n.20; and letters, 77, 83–84, 111; and novel as political representation, 70–73; versus rationality or reason, 7, 36, 115, 118, 200, 127, 129–30; reading, 89–90, 108, 119; versus sentimentality, 100, 109. *See also* affect; sentimentalism; sympathy
sentimentalism, 3–4, 8, 14–16, 19; anti-sentimentalism, 23, 113–14, 131, 157–58; and class, 97; female, 22, 87–111, 114–15, 131–33; as feminist literary genre, 91, 95, 105, 131; and gender, 87, 89, 95, 98–104, 107, 112–16, 130–31; and identification, 22, 70, 90–94; and liberalism, 140, 147, 151- 54, 156, 158; male, 22, 112–33, 193n.20; management of sensation by, 16–17, 100, 107–9, 145, 151–52, 154, 156–57, 188n.75; and obscenity, 138–40, 152, 156; and politics, 3, 90–91, 95, 97, 101, 105, 115; and pornography, 90–91, 147; and publication, 43–44, 147, 149, 152–56; and public sphere, 8, 21,

sentimentalism (*cont.*)
  42–43, 77, 83–84, 87, 101, 106, 111, 114,
  138, 140, 147, 151, 153, 156; and republicanism, 44, 89, 101–2, 109, 147, 150, 153;
  and sexuality, 138, 140, 149–58. *See also*
  body; sentiment; sympathy
A Sentimental Journey (Sterne), 193n.20
sex, 16, 19, 22; and gender, 94–104; 108, 115,
  125–27, 163n.27, 195n.61; and reason,
  125
sexual dimorphism, 94–95, 102, 110, 121–22,
  125, 131
sexuality, 18–19, 22–23, 108, 138–40, 149–59,
  195n.61, 195–96n.69, 200–201n.31,
  201n.35. *See also* sensuality
Shallope, Robert, 13
Shamela (Fielding), 42–43
Silverman, Kaja, 113, 191n.4
slave narratives, 138–39, 151
slavery, 15, 35–36, 95, 110, 137–39, 148–53,
  200n.29, 200–201n.31, 202–3n.39, 203n.41
Smith, Adam, 15
social, 19; Arendt on, 33–36, 38, 40; corporeality of 69–70; Habermas on, 39–41, 43–45;
  and law, 144; versus the political, 6–9, 36,
  40, 147, 162n.20; and sentiment, 89, 110
social contract, 65, 140, 173–74n.80, 179n.39
The Social Contract (Rousseau), 57
socialism, 6, 7, 9–10, 30
The Social Origins of Private Life (Coontz),
  187n.60
society, 13, 39
Song of Myself (Whitman), 17, 155, 157
sovereignty: Arendt's view of, 40; location of,
  60, 75; popular, 31, 35, 59–61, 67, 69,
  178n.18; representation of, 10, 57–59
Specters of Marx (Derrida), 182n.54
The Spirit of the Laws (Montesquieu), 60
Stallybrass, Peter, 143
Stansell, Christine, 46
state, 3, 9, 11, 19, 37; apparatus of, 21, 58, 60;
  and morality, 143–45, 153; and obscenity,
  140–41, 143, 145–46, 153–54; and privacy,
  20, 140, 143, 145–46, 148, 153–54, 157; and
  publication, 105, 141, 148, 153; and public
  sphere, 11, 32, 37, 39–40, 60–61, 77, 86,
  140–41, 143–46, 153–54; representation
  by, 60, 65, 68, 69; representation of, 57, 59;
  tutelary function of, 64–69, 76. *See also*
  civil society; law; liberalism;
Sterne, Lawrence, 193n.20
Stewart, John, 61

The Story of Margaretta (Murray), 124, 126
Stowe, Harriet Beecher, 104, 108
*The Structural Transformation of the Public
  Sphere* (Habermas), 32, 39–49, 52–54, 83,
  184n.17
subject, and law, 30, 57, 67. *See also* citizenship; individual
subjectivity, 42, 52–53, 84, 101, 171n.56,
  184–85n.18
Sullivan, James, 85
sympathy, 35, 66, 121, 158, 161n.8

Takaki, Ronald, 68, 181n.46
taste, 98–99, 102
Taussig, Michael, 53
temperance, 15, 201n.35
Therese Philosophe (de Boyer), 90–92, 108,
  137, 141
"Thoughts upon Female Education" (Rush),
  97–98
Three Essays on the Theory of Sexuality
  (Freud), 155–57
Tocqueville, Alexis de, 6, 30, 68, 84, 164n.35,
  169n.31
Todd, Janet, 15
Tompkins, Jane, 4, 15, 91, 131, 192n.8
totalitarianism, 30, 32
Toward a More Perfect Union (Withington),
  190n.85
true womanhood, 150
Trumbach, Randolph, 146
Twain, Mark, 132

Uncle Tom's Cabin (Stowe), 104, 107, 200n.28

Van Sant, Ann, 15
Venus in Furs (von Sacher Masoch), 112–13,
  127
Verhoeven, Paul, 50
A Vindication of the Rights of Women (Wollstonecraft), 45, 128
violence, 29–31, 40, 150, 200–201n.31,
  202n.37
virtue, 12, 40, 45, 73, 75, 83, 89–90, 104, 110,
  118, 171n.52, 172n.68, 189n.80, 193n.19,
  202n.37

Warner, Michael, 13–15, 22, 59–60, 76, 89–
  90, 122, 186n.39
Washington, George, 21, 48, 55–77, 85, 127,
  176n.11, 178–79n.24, 179n.32, 181n.50,
  183nn. 57 and 68

Watertown Belle, 81–82, 86, 96
Watt, Ian, 171n.56
Webster, Noah, 195n.61
"What is Enlightenment?" (Kant), 81
White, Allon, 143
Whitman, Elizabeth, 88–91, 95–96, 104, 107, 113
Whitman, Walt, 17, 147, 155, 157, 200n.28
Wiegman, Robyn, 15–16, 95
Wieland (Brockden Brown), 114, 193n.27
Wilde, Oscar, 42
Wilentz, Sean, 46
Winthrop, John, 104
Wise, Robert, 27, 29
Witherington, Paul, 192n.15

Withington, Ann, 190n.85
Wittig, Monique, 132
Wollstonecraft, Mary, 4–5, 8, 10, 13, 16–17, 20, 45, 48, 87, 98, 109, 127–28, 148, 161n.8, 190–91n.100
Wood, Gordon, 11–12
Woodhull, Victoria, 142
"woman," as category, 22, 94–99, 110, 125, 128, 187n.56, 189n.82, 196n.78
Woman's Fiction (Baym), 131

XYZ Affair, 62

Ziff, Larzar, 13
Zizek, Slavoj, 58, 176–77n.13

About the author

Bruce Burgett is Associate Professor of English
at the University of Wisconsin, Madison.